The Barbizon

PAULINA BREN

The Barbizon

The New York Hotel That Set Women Free

✕

PAULINA BREN

First published in Great Britain in 2021 by Two Roads
An Imprint of John Murray Press
An Hachette UK company

1

Copyright © Paulina Bren 2021

A CIP catalogue record for this title is available from the British Library

Hardback ISBN 978 1 529 39302 6
Trade Paperback ISBN 978 1 529 39303 3
eBook ISBN 978 1 529 39305 7

Printed and bound in Great Britain by Clays Ltd, Elcograf S.p.A.

John Murray policy is to use papers that are natural, renewable and
recyclable products and made from wood grown in sustainable
forests. The logging and manufacturing processes are expected to
conform to the environmental regulations of the country of origin.

Two Roads
Carmelite House
50 Victoria Embankment
London EC4Y 0DZ

www.tworoadsbooks.com

For Zoltán and Zsofi

CONTENTS

INTRODUCTION

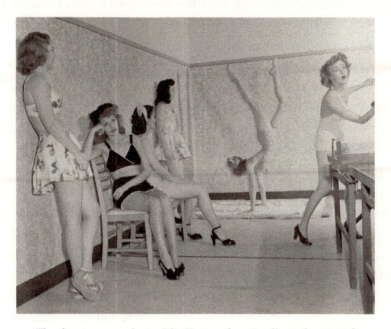

The glamorous movie star Rita Hayworth pretending to be petered out from a day of practicing for her role as a model in the 1943 movie *Cover Girl*. Here she is posing for *Life* magazine in the Barbizon's gymnasium with real working models.

Who was the woman who stayed at New York's famous Barbizon Hotel? She could be from anywhere—just as likely from small-town America as from across the George Washington Bridge—but more often than not she arrived in a yellow Checker cab because she didn't yet know how to use the New York subway. She had the address on a piece of paper in her hand, and she carefully read it aloud to the taxi driver: "The Barbizon Hotel, 140 East Sixty-Third Street." But in all likelihood the taxi driver knew where she was going even before she spoke. Perhaps he noticed how she timidly waved down his cab, or how she tightly held on to the handle of her brown suitcase, or how she wore her best clothes, this out-of-town girl newly arrived in Manhattan.

The piece of paper was most probably crumpled by now, or certainly worse for wear, having traveled with her by train, by bus, or even by plane if she was lucky or well-off, or if, like Sylvia Plath and Joan Didion, she was a *Mademoiselle* magazine contest winner. The rush of excitement when this young woman walked through the front doors of the Barbizon would be impossible to replicate later in life because of what it meant in that moment: she had made her escape from her hometown and all the expectations (or none) that came with it. She had left that all behind, resolutely, often after months of pleading, saving, scrimping, plotting. She was here now, in New York, ready to remake herself, to start an entirely new life. She had taken her fate into her own hands.

Throughout the years, magazine advertisements for the Barbizon Hotel exclaimed: "OH! It's great to be in NEW YORK . . . especially when you live at the Barbizon for Women." The tagline was always the same, reassuring in its tenacity: *New York's Most Exclusive Hotel Residence for Young Women*. But magazine pieces also warned of the wolves, those men who roamed New York's streets on the lookout for pretty, naive young things, and the Barbizon promised both protection and sanctuary. Yet that wasn't the only reason America's young women wanted to stay there. Everyone knew the hotel was packed full with aspiring actresses, models, singers, artists, and writers, and some had already gone from aspiring to famous. When Rita Hayworth posed for *Life* magazine in the hotel's gymnasium, looking both sexy and impertinent, she was signaling these possibilities.

But first, this new arrival had to get past Mrs. Mae Sibley, the assistant manager and front-desk hawk, who would look her over and ask for references. She had to be presentable (preferably attractive) and with letters attesting to her good and moral character. Mrs. Sibley would quietly mark her as an A, B, or C. A's were under the age of twenty-eight, B's were between twenty-eight and thirty-eight, and C's, well, they were over the hill. More often than not, the girl from out of town with a Sunday school hat and a nervous smile was an A. This initial hurdle was the easy one, however. Once Mrs. Sibley had approved of her, and handed her a key, a room number, and a list of the do's and don'ts, the new Barbizon resident would take the elevator up to the floor with her room, her new home, where no men were allowed, ever, and contemplate what to do next. The room was a step up for some and a step down for others. But for all the young women at the Barbizon, the narrow bed, dresser, armchair, floor lamp, and small desk in a tiny room with a floral bedspread and matching curtains, represented some sort of liberation. At least at the beginning.

+

The Barbizon tells the story of New York's most famous women's hotel from its construction in 1927 to its eventual conversion into multimillion-dollar condominiums in 2007. It is at once a history of the singular women who passed through its doors, a history of Manhattan through the twentieth century, and a forgotten story of women's ambition. The hotel was built in the Roaring Twenties for the flocks of women suddenly coming to New York to work in the dazzling new skyscrapers. They did not want to stay in uncomfortable boarding houses; they wanted what men already had—exclusive "club residences," residential hotels with weekly rates, daily maid service, and a dining room instead of the burden of a kitchen.

Other women's hotels sprang up in the 1920s too, but it was the Barbizon that grabbed hold of America's imagination. It would outlast most of the others, in part because it was associated with young women, and later, in the 1950s, with beautiful, desirable young women. The hotel was strictly women only, with men allowed no farther than the lobby, on weekend nights called "Lovers' Lane," as couples hovered in the shadows, embracing behind the foliage of strategically placed potted plants. The reclusive writer J. D. Salinger, while no wolf, hung around the Barbizon coffee shop and pretended to be a Canadian hockey player. Other men became unusually tired and needed to rest up at the very moment when they crossed Lexington Avenue at Sixty-Third Street, and the Barbizon lobby seemed a perfect place for respite. Malachy McCourt, brother of the author of *Angela's Ashes*, as well as a handful of other men claimed to have made it up the stairs to the carefully policed bedroom floors; while others tried and failed, dressing up as plumbers and on-call gynecologists, much to the amusement (and wrath) of Mrs. Sibley.

The Barbizon's residents read like a who's who: *Titanic* survivor Molly Brown; actresses Grace Kelly, Tippi Hedren, Liza Minnelli, Ali MacGraw, Candice Bergen, Phylicia Rashad, Jaclyn Smith, and Cybill Shepherd; writers Sylvia Plath, Joan Didion, Diane Johnson, Gael Greene, Ann Beattie, Mona Simpson, and Meg Wolitzer; designer Betsey Johnson; journalists Peggy Noonan and Lynn Sherr; and many more. But before they were household names, they were among the young women arriving at the Barbizon with a suitcase, reference letters, and hope. Some of them had their dreams come true, while many did not. Some returned to their hometowns, while others holed up in their Barbizon rooms and wondered what had gone wrong. Each of them expected her stay to be temporary, a soft landing until she had established herself, given voice to her ambition, her aspirations. But many found themselves still there, year after year. These holdouts would become known to the younger residents as "the Women," harbingers of what was to come if they did not move on and move out.

In the 1970s, as Manhattan temporarily turned from glitzy to derelict, the Women gathered nightly in the lobby to comment on the younger set, offering them unsolicited advice on the length of their skirts and the wildness of their hair. They had even more to say when, in the 1980s, no longer able to support the original vision of a women-only sanctuary, management opened the hotel to men. But despite their threats to leave, the Women remained. When Manhattan remade itself into a hot property market, and the Barbizon underwent its own last reimagining from hotel to luxury condominium building, the Women got their own refurbished floor, where the remaining few still live, in what is now called Barbizon/63. They have their mailboxes alongside another current resident, British actor and comedian Ricky Gervais.

The Barbizon Hotel for Women, when it opened its doors in 1928, never needed to say it was intended for white, middle- and upper-class young women: the address on the Upper East Side said it, the advertisements depicting a typical resident said it, the required reference letters of a certain kind said it. But in 1956, a student at Temple University, a talented artist and dancer by the name of Barbara Chase, appeared at the Barbizon. She was most likely the first African American to ever stay at the hotel. Her time there was without incident, although she was shielded not only by her good looks and accomplished résumé but also by *Mademoiselle* magazine. The magazine's editor-in-chief, Betsy Talbot Blackwell, a force in New York's publishing world, had brought her to New York for the month of June as one of the winners of the magazine's prestigious guest editor program. No one was sure if the Barbizon management would let Barbara Chase in. But they did, even if they failed to mention the swimming pool in the basement. Back in the *Mademoiselle* offices on Madison Avenue, Betsy Talbot Blackwell would usher Barbara out of the room when Southern clients showed up to meet with that year's young guest editors.

The Barbizon and *Mademoiselle* magazine were in many ways symbiotic, catering to the same kind of women, being at the forefront of change, often radically so, only to find themselves eventually overtaken by shifting interests and priorities among the very women to whom they catered. It is therefore impossible to tell the story of the Barbizon without also stepping along the corridors of the *Mademoiselle* offices. In 1944, Betsy Talbot Blackwell had made the decision that the winners of the guest editor program—brought to Manhattan for June to shadow the magazine's editors by day and to indulge in fancy dinners, sparkling galas, and sophisticated cocktail parties by night—must stay at the Barbizon. The contest attracted the crème de la crème of young college women, and opened the Barbizon doors to the likes of Joan Didion, Meg Wolitzer, and Betsey Johnson. But it was Sylvia Plath, *Mademoiselle*'s most famous guest editor, who would also bring the greatest notoriety to the hotel. Ten years after her stay there, and shortly before her final, successful suicide attempt, she would disguise the Barbizon as "the Amazon," spilling out its secrets in her famous novel, *The Bell Jar*.

The brainy guest editors, *Mademoiselle*'s contest winners, shared the hotel with students from the iconic Katharine Gibbs Secretarial School, who resided across three floors of the hotel, with their own "house mothers" and curfews and teas. These young women in their white gloves and perfectly perched hats, regulation attire for a Gibbs girl, were synonymous with the new opportunities for the small-town girl who could not act, sing, or dance her way to New York but who sure could type her way out of her hometown and into the glitz and glamour of Madison Avenue. But it was the presence of models, first working for the Powers Agency and then many escaping to the new Ford agency, run by two daring women out of a shoddy brownstone, that solidified the Barbizon's reputation as a "dollhouse." Yet behind the walls in which these serial-dating, kitten-heeled glamour women resided, there was also disappointment. Writer Gael Greene returned to the Barbizon two years after her initial stay there as a guest editor alongside Joan Didion, this time to document everyone who wasn't considered a "doll": she called the overlooked residents the "Lone Women." Some were lonely enough to commit suicide: often on Sunday mornings, because as one of the Women noted, Saturday night was date night . . . or not. And Sunday was sorrow. The Barbizon management, Mrs. Sibley and manager Hugh J. Connor, made sure the suicides were hushed, seldom appearing in the papers. They knew that appearances mattered above all else and it was better to advertise the Barbizon's most glamorous resident, Grace Kelly, than it was to advertise the forlorn.

✢

By the time the Barbizon opened its doors to men, the very premise upon which it had been built—that women's ambitions, however large or small, could best be supported in single-sex residences with daily maid service and no chance of being pushed back into the kitchen because there wasn't one—seemed outdated. So why do I wish a place like this had existed when I came to New York after graduating from college? And why do women-only spaces, supportive of women's ambition, keep springing up? Women did not come to the Barbizon to network, but that's what they did anyway. They helped each other find work, they talked over problems with one another, they applauded each other's successes and gave solace to those with disappointment and heartbreak. They felt empowered just by being at the Barbizon. Actress Ali MacGraw, a resident in the summer of 1958, recalls cradling her morning coffee in its paper blue-and-white Greek coffee cup, feeling like she was "going somewhere" just by being there.

The Barbizon Hotel for Women, built in the midst of the Roaring Twenties, opened its doors in 1928 to women pursuing independent lives in Manhattan.

The Barbizon tells a story that, until now, has been heard only in snippets. When I first set out to write about this unique hotel and the remarkable women who passed through its doors, I did not realize others before me had wanted to tell the story of the Barbizon, and then given up. Like them, at first I too hit a wall in my research: there were just too few sources about the hotel. At the New-York Historical Society Archive, where I expected to find a stack of documents, I was handed only a thin folder marked "Barbizon" with nothing more than a few newspaper articles. There are also too few sources about the kind of women who stayed at the Barbizon; the "women in between," one might say; those who were neither upper-class, letter-writing society women nor union-organizing, working-class women. Of course these archival and historiographical gaps I encountered tell us something: they tell us how the memory of women's lives is easily forgotten and how the silence can make us believe that women were not fully participating in everyday life throughout the twentieth century.

But they were, very much so, in creative ways and with ambitious plans. I learned this as I slowly began to unravel the Barbizon's hidden stories—as a historian, an interviewer, an internet sleuth. I located its former residents, now lively, funny, and sharp-minded ladies in their eighties and nineties. I found scrapbooks, letters, photographs. I even discovered an archive in Wyoming. Together they reveal the history of single women of a certain set, of what it meant for them to finally have a room of their own and the air to breathe, without the burden of family and family expectations, in New York, the City of Dreams. The Barbizon Hotel was about the remaking of oneself, and nothing like it had existed before or has since.

CHAPTER ONE

BUILDING THE BARBIZON

The Unsinkable Molly Brown vs. the Flappers

The Unsinkable Molly Brown in her prime, already a suffragette and activist, but before she would become the *Titanic*'s most famous survivor and one of the Barbizon's early residents.

T he New Woman arrived in the closing decade of the nineteenth century. She was a woman intent on being more than just a daughter, wife, and mother. She wanted to explore beyond the four walls of her home; she wanted independence; she wanted liberation from everything that weighed her down. She could be seen pedaling down the street in her bloomers and billowing shirtsleeves on the way to *somewhere*.

The writer Henry James popularized the term "New Woman" when he used it to describe affluent American female expatriates in Europe living their lives independently of the restrictions back home. But the term gained traction: being a New Woman meant taking control of one's life.

First there was the Gibson girl, a sort of little sister of the New Woman; upper-middle-class, with flowing hair, voluptuous in all the right places, but cinched in at the waist with a swan-bill corset that had her leaning in, as if she were perpetually in motion, intent on moving forward. Then came World War I, the women's vote, the Roaring Twenties, and the Gibson girl gave way to a wilder version of herself, the flapper. This little sister dumped the corset, drank, smoked, flirted, and worse. She was all giggles and verve and too much exposed ankle. But the flapper made it clear to anyone willing to listen—or not—that the New Woman had been democratized. To defy traditional expectations was no longer the purview only of those who could afford it. Women, all women, were venturing out into the world now. The war and women's suffrage had poked holes in earlier arguments for why women needed to stay home. The time had come for the world to adjust. It was in this spirit that the Barbizon Club-Residence for Women was built in 1927.

The Unsinkable Molly Brown, made famous for surviving the *Titanic*, was among the Barbizon's first residents. The woman who had mustered up the courage to row-row-row, when the men did not, sat at her small desk in her Barbizon room, pen in hand. It was 1931, and Molly Brown (whose real name was Margaret Tobin Brown) was now a sixty-three-year-old former beauty, overweight, a little rough around the edges, her eccentric and flamboyant fashion sense looking gently comical. But Molly Brown could not care less; she still carried the confidence of a first-generation New Woman, and she knew that no matter what anyone said, she had planted her flag firmly in this new century.

She paused her letter to her friend in Denver and looked out the window of the Barbizon at the bleak February sky. It reminded her of the sky the night the *Titanic* began to list to the side, far faster than she would have thought possible. That was back in 1912, two years before the First World War, another era altogether now it seemed, when Molly Brown had joined her friends, the famous Astors, on a trip through Egypt and North Africa. Her daughter, a student at the Sorbonne in Paris, met her in Cairo, and together they posed in heavy Edwardian dresses for the must-have souvenir photograph sitting on top of two camels, with the Sphinx and the pyramids looming behind them. Molly returned with her daughter to Paris, but when news arrived that her grandson had fallen ill back home, she quickly booked a cabin on the same ship as the Astors. It was called the *Titanic*.

It was only the sixth night on board. She had had a nice dinner and was lying comfortably in her first-class cabin, reading, when she heard a crash. She was knocked out of bed, but being a seasoned traveler, she thought little of it even as she noticed the engines had stopped. It was not until James McGough, a Gimbels department store buyer from Philadelphia, ghoulishly appeared at her window, waving his arms and shouting, "Get your life preserver!" that she layered on clothes and headed out. Despite his alarm, up on deck Molly confronted a wide-eyed reluctance to board the lifeboats. She tried to cajole her fellow female first-class passengers onto them until she herself was unceremoniously tossed down into one by the *Titanic*'s crew. As the lifeboat pulled away, she heard gunshots; it was officers shooting at people on the lower decks who were desperate to jump into the boats reserved for the rich and now launching into the water half-empty.

In the dark, as lifeboat six bobbed in the water, Molly watched in horror. Those around her were crying out for loved ones still on board as water engulfed the *Titanic* until it was entirely gone, vanished, swallowed up whole. Screams rang out even as everything else had gone silent. It was night, the sea was pitch-black, and the utter incompetence of the two gentlemen on lifeboat six made their hopelessness all the more vivid. Molly Brown, disgusted, took over. She directed the rowing and the will to live, peeling off layers of clothing to give to those who had been less quick-witted. Around dawn, the lifeboat was picked up by the *Carpathia*, and by the time she and her fellow survivors had pulled into New York Harbor some days later, Molly, ever the activist, had established the Survivor's Committee, become its chairwoman, and raised $10,000 for its destitute. She wired her Denver attorney: "Water was fine and swimming good. Neptune was exceedingly kind to me and I am now high and dry." Neptune had been less kind to her friend John Jacob Astor IV; the richest man on board the *Titanic* was among the dead.

It was almost twenty years later when the Unsinkable Molly Brown took a room at the Barbizon, and the world looked very different despite that same night sky. World War I had been the catalyst for so much change, but for Molly personally, her separation from her husband, J. J. Brown, had been just as significant. They had parted ways: he a womanizer and she an activist. She was a feminist, a child-protection advocate, and a unionizer before it was fashionable to be any of those things. J.J. was a rags-to-riches gold-mining millionaire of Irish descent, and together he and Molly had stepped out of their shared poverty into great wealth, finding a place in Denver's high society. After their separation, and then J.J.'s death in 1922, which left the family with no will and instead five years of disputation, both Denver's society circles and Molly's children turned their backs on her. But this merely stoked her earlier dreams for a life on the stage. Enamored of the legendary French actress Sarah Bernhardt, Molly Brown moved to Paris to study acting, performing in *The Merchant of Venice* and *Antony and Cleopatra*. She had both wit and spirit, the kind that could be appreciated there, even in a woman of sixty, and she was soon dubbed the "uncrowned queen of smart Paris."

However exaggerated the Molly Brown mythology became, her gumption was real. She once wrote of herself: "I am a daughter of adventure. This means I never experience a dull moment and must be prepared for any eventuality. I never know when I may go up in an airplane and come down with a crash, or go motoring and climb a pole, or go off for a walk in the twilight and return all mussed up in an ambulance. That's my arc, as the astrologers would say. It's a good one, too, for a person who would rather make a snap-out than a fade-out of life." Molly Brown was no flapper, far from it, even as her adventurism might have made her one had she been younger. But she was not younger, and she harbored an antipathy toward the flappers, these young women of the Jazz Age who seemed to define themselves by one single hard-won victory that Molly Brown and her generation had worked hard to achieve: sexual liberation. Even so, it was here, at the Barbizon Club-Residence for Women, where Molly Brown decided to stay when she returned to New York from Paris—sharing space with the young women of whom she publicly disapproved but whose core spirit she might well have understood.

She chose to stay here because, like them, she wanted to test out different versions of herself, and the Barbizon was the place to do that.

A 1927 street view of the Barbizon, just as its construction was nearing completion.

Molly was delighted with her accommodations. She sent the Barbizon brochure to her Denver friend, marked up and defaced to explain her new life in New York. *There is even a radio in every room!*, she wrote. Here, circled in thick black ink, was the northwest turret with a bricked-in terrace, looking down onto the corner of Lexington Avenue and Sixty-Third Street. Inside was her suite, one of the best rooms to be had, but even so it was modest, much like the hotel's regular rooms, which featured a narrow single bed, small desk, a chest of drawers, and a pint-size armchair. One could open and close the door while lying in bed, and you barely had to get up to put something away in the dresser. Humble as it might be, she wrote to her friend that she used her room as her "workshop," "piled high to the ceiling with things."

She circled another Gothic window even farther up, on the nineteenth floor, in the Barbizon's Rapunzel-like tower filled with studios for its budding artists: in this soundproofed room with soaring ceilings Molly sang her arias, practicing for hours. The recital room, she noted, was where the resident artists and artists-to-be gave their concerts. The hotel's Italianate lobby and mezzanine were where she played cards with friends. The oak-paneled library accommodated her book club meetings. (She most likely participated in meetings of the Pegasus Group, a literary cooperative that gathered at the Barbizon "to encourage the expression of mental achievements by offering authors an opportunity to present their works before the public and to discuss them in an atmosphere of sane, fair and constructive criticism.") Men—all men other than registered doctors, plumbers, and electricians—were strictly barred from anywhere but the lobby and the eighteenth-floor parlor, to which a gentleman caller could receive a pass if accompanied by his date.

The front entrance of the club-hotel was on Sixty-Third Street, while the ground-floor shops, eight in all, were on the Lexington Avenue side of the corner building, and included a dry cleaner, hairdresser, pharmacy, hosiery store, millinery shop, and a Doubleday bookshop—everything a certain class of woman might need. All the stores had entrances from inside the hotel, off a small corridor, so Molly Brown did not have to venture out onto the street if she was not up to it. The Barbizon had opened only three years earlier, when New York was in the midst of a transformation. A building boom had been in full swing, a purposeful out with the old and in with the new. Public opinion declared that over the years Manhattan had expanded haphazardly, senselessly, illogically, but all that could still be brought to heel. The buildings that belonged to past centuries would be razed to the ground in favor of a new, ambitious, mechanized twentieth century; tenements and low-lying buildings were to give way to well-planned towers that sprang up into the sky in art deco silhouettes.

The architecture of the early twentieth century was as new as the New Woman who had broken free of old constraints. Critics of nineteenth-century New York condemned the "brown mantle spread out" across Manhattan, creating a sea of "monotonous brownstones" in its wake. Today's prized brownstones, quaint and historical, were then seen as a blight on the city. City planners pointed out that while they could no longer bring back the cheeriness and color blasts of the "old Dutch days of New Amsterdam" with its "red tile roofs, rug-patterned brick facades and gayly painted woodwork," they could conjure up a new century and its signature look: the skyscraper.

In the midst of this building boom, in 1926 Temple Rodeph Sholom sold its space on Sixty-Third Street and Lexington Avenue in Manhattan for $800,000. One of the oldest Jewish congregations in the United States, soon to be replaced by the premier women-only residential hotel, was moving to the Upper West Side. Temple Sholom had stood at this spot for fifty-five years, following its Jewish immigrant congregation uptown as they moved out of their Lower East Side tenements into new homes in Midtown Manhattan and the Upper East Side. Now again it was following its congregants out of this area that was rapidly building up, especially with the 1918 extension of the Lexington Avenue Line subway from Grand Central at 42nd Street up to 125th Street. The temple ended its half-century-long residency on New York's Upper East Side with its eldest worshippers onstage to commemorate this moment of change. Mrs. Nathan Bookman, ninety-seven, and Isador Foos, ninety-one, had been members since their confirmations at age thirteen; enthroned onstage, looking down at the congregation of upstanding New Yorkers, their parents and grandparents once Lower East Side German Jewish immigrants, they said goodbye to the nineteenth century. The Barbizon was about to say hello to the twentieth.

Just as Temple Sholom had been built on Sixty-Third and Lexington to accommodate a growing need, so now its planned replacement was responding to an entirely new one. World War I had liberated women, set them on the path to political enfranchisement in 1920 with the passing of the Nineteenth Amendment, and, just as important, made workingwomen visible and more acceptable. A record number of women were now applying to college, and while marriage continued to be the end goal, clerical work combined the glamour of flapper life—with its urban, consumerist excesses (Shopping at Bloomingdale's! Dinner at Delmonico's!)—with an acceptable form of training for married life. Clerical work had been a career stepping-stone for young men, but now, as thousands of women headed for the offices inside the sparkling new skyscrapers going up each year across Manhattan, the job of secretary ceased to be a career path with the promise of promotion: it was instead recast as a chance for young women to exercise the skills of "office wife" while also earning a salary and living a brief independent life before marriage. The new secretaries of this new world were to be for their bosses "as much like the vanished wife of his father's generation as could be arranged," declared *Fortune* magazine. They would type their boss's letters, balance his checkbook, take his daughter to the dentist, and offer him ego-boosting pep talks when necessary.

But the New Woman received something in exchange: the publicly sanctioned right to live independently, to express herself sexually (up to a point), to indulge as a consumer, to experience all the thrills of urban life, and to enter public space on her own terms. And to do that, she needed a place to live. The old-fashioned women's boarding houses—an earlier option for a single woman living and working in New York—were of a past era, now looked down on with scorn, associated, as the *New York Times* declared, with "horsehair sofas" and the "recurrent smell of beef stew." They were also associated with the working class, whereas the new breed of upper- and middle-class workingwomen wanted something better. Neither did they want house rules or patronizing philanthropy (the well-intentioned but demeaning engine behind so many old-fashioned boarding houses for widows, workers, and female outcasts) to be part of their living experience. And the address mattered—a lot.

But even if they had been able to look past the substandard rooms, the itchy horsehair, and the chewy beef, there were nowhere near enough of these boarding houses to accommodate the great numbers of young women pouring into the city. Residential hotels built high into the sky would have to be the answer instead.

Hotel residential living—for families and for bachelors—had been in vogue since the late 1800s. "In town it is no longer quite in taste to build marble palaces, however much money one may have," wrote one social commentator at the time. "Instead, one lives in a hotel." Residential hotel accommodations ranged from palatial suites for the perversely wealthy of the Gilded Age to practical rooms for the single and striving. Much fuss and attention were paid to the coziness of these hotel homes. The more modest residential hotels featured custom-made furniture that was intentionally smaller than the standard, making it easier to fit into small spaces and making the hotel rooms appear larger. The twin bed lost its footboard, and the headboard was lowered to create the illusion of space. Furniture corners were rounded for the same reason. At the opulent end of the residential hotel category, rooms were furnished with expensive reproductions of eighteenth-century pieces and fireplaces were commonplace. As the Waldorf Astoria was going up, dummy rooms and hallways were constructed in a warehouse off-site so that everything down to the wall color and faucets, let alone carpets, curtains, and cabinets, could be carefully interrogated. Interiors adviser for the Waldorf Astoria, Mrs. Charles Sabis, in charge of the installations, studied the sample rooms and then accepted or rejected them; as soon as decisions were made, one dummy room was torn down and another went up. For some suites, Mrs. Sabis chose English woodwork salvaged from a Yorkshire manor house, while pondering the eternal question of whether a "lacquered screen or Ming jar [was] just right for a room with a Queen Anne air?" Importantly, these high-end residential hotel rooms had to differ from one another; these were no cookie-cutter chain hotels.

The rapid rise of residential hotels was in large part because of a real estate loophole: the Tenement House Act of 1901 exempted New York City's height and fireproofing restrictions on buildings with kitchen-less apartments. However pecuniary the reason, the effect was inevitably glamorous because who would not want to live in a full-service hotel? And even if you didn't live in one, you could at least imagine it every Saturday morning at "the pictures," watching the most recent of the wildly popular Thin Man movies starring William Powell gliding between speakeasies and residential hotels—joyously, drunkenly traversing the city, a cocktail in hand. In 1903, New York hotelier Simeon Ford had made a pithy declaration of difference: "We have fine hotels for fine people, good hotels for good people, plain hotels for plain people, and some bum hotels for bums." So it was only a matter of time before a new category of hotels emerged: *women hotels for women*.

The Barbizon would be the most glamorous, but it would not be the first. The first was the Martha Washington, built on a different set of premises but laying the groundwork for the Barbizon. Opening in 1903, the Martha Washington was a squat twelve stories that stretched one city block along Madison Avenue from Twenty-Ninth to Thirtieth Street. Far ahead of its time, it addressed a need for accommodations for self-supporting white-collar women when New York hotel rules stipulated that no single female traveler could be offered a room after 6:00 p.m. unless she was hauling a heavy travel trunk to prove she was no prostitute. The situation could be so embarrassing that two upper-class women "confessed to having spent the night in Broad Street Station, Philadelphia, rather than run the risk of being turned away from a hotel." Even before World War I, there were women like these arriving in New York, alone, to work. Those better off and creative in spirit had found solutions here and there, including a community of women artists who had converted back alley stables into spruced-up accommodations with studio spaces in which to work. Other professional women rented tenement apartments and fixed them up inside so they were unrecognizable from their squalid exteriors. But the revolutionary Martha Washington became a place for these sorts of women to stay as well as a sanctuary for suffragettes, among them Dr. Mary Walker, medical doctor and famous feminist, who liked to challenge restrictive dress codes long before flappers did. At her wedding she refused to use the word "obey" in her vows, retained her last name, and wore a short skirt with trousers underneath.

Despite the need for such a place, the 1903 opening of the Martha Washington was met with all-around puzzlement at best, condemnation at worst. "Observation automobiles" full of gawkers would drive by slowly as if watching a freak show. Management itself seemed unsure of how to proceed: at first it deemed men necessary for the hotel's heavy lifting—those requisite trunks!—but a year later the male personnel were replaced by women, now believed to be more reliable. The *New York Herald* jeered at the gender switch: the bellhop "looks demure enough in her black gown, with plain white collar and cuffs." Moreover, no one seemed able to wrap their heads around the idea of so many women under one roof without the protection of men. An early brochure for the Martha Washington acknowledged the recurring doubts about how "it would be feasible to house so large a number of women as four hundred to five hundred under one roof."

At the same time, the hotel's residents were assured that the Martha Washington was out to make a profit and not based on any "paternalism or philanthropic idea," like the working-class boarding houses. The residential hotel, in other words, was intended as top-notch independent living (not charity), with an array of rooms and suites on offer, and with none of the restrictions previously associated with women's lodgings often sponsored by religious organizations, such as curfews or no-guests rules. Residents at the Martha Washington, whether in a single room or a spacious apartment, could enjoy reception rooms on each floor, a roof promenade, a dining room, modern steam heat, and mail chutes.

The kind of women who came to stay at the Martha Washington, while initially ridiculed, soon began to enter the mainstream: *Harper's Bazaar* magazine featured a series of articles in 1908 called "The Girl Who Came to the City" and the *Ladies' Home Journal* followed three years later with "Her Sister in the Country Who Wants to Come to the City to Make Her Way." In 1914, New York saw a second residential hotel for well-off career women, the aptly named Business Woman's Hotel, built just two blocks from the Martha Washington, and six blocks from the Altman's department store (just as the Barbizon would be built close to Bloomingdale's). Then came World War I, and the need for women's hotels seemed less pressing. But the end of the war initiated a building boom, and women's new independence meant new clientele, more profit.

The 1920s was *the* decade of women's residential hotels. The Allerton hotel on East Fifty-Seventh Street near Central Park opened in 1920. The Allerton was built by William H. Silk, who would soon develop the Barbizon. He and his partner, James S. Cushman, had constructed their first bachelor apartments in 1912 and moved on to a club-hotel for men in 1919. The Allerton House for Women was the obvious next step, tying in a growing taste for a certain kind of accommodation with the realities of post–World War I and women's new claims for independence outside of the protection of a male-headed household. Silk wanted to offer rooms to female "physicians, decorators, lecturers, politicians, writers, buyers, store executives." (That these residential hotel accommodations were marked as white and privileged never needed to be said out loud.) Silk envisioned a homelike environment, which would differentiate it from a standard hotel, with a sewing room, a ballroom, a "strictly up-to-the-minute laundry," and men-free lounging rooms. An Allerton guest was free to "be her own mistress." The hotel, built to accommodate five hundred women residents, was booked solid before it was even finished.

Such profit potential could hardly be ignored. Others followed, with the American Women's Association (AWA) hotel becoming the largest yet. Heralded by the *New York Times* as a "temple to the spirit of emancipated womanhood," Miss Smith, head of the AWA's board, berated anyone who dared to call it a hotel. It was to be no such thing, she said: it was a "movement." She was right. These women's club-hotels were the "physical manifestation" of a woman's right to live without the protection of her father, brother, uncle; to socialize as she pleased; to shop as she pleased; to work as she could. In the case of the AWA, the hotel's drawn-out funding drive and construction also brought in the city's wealthiest women to try their hands at a serious business venture. Led by Anne Morgan, of the famous Morgans, along with other women belonging to the city's social elite, they created a modern-day stock-selling campaign that they launched at the Plaza Hotel, handing out sales kits and calling cards to an army of stock sellers. They devised a full-scale advertising campaign based on a mascot they named "Miss Robinson Crusoe," the concept being that a single woman's loneliness in New York was akin to being stranded on a tropical island. "Miss Robinson Crusoe" had a pamphlet, a song, and Fifth Avenue display windows. The idea was that she would of course be saved by the AWA Clubhouse, where there would be others like her, of the same spirit and ambition; and where she would find community and luxury. The sales team regrouped two years later, now with $3.5 million collected with which to begin construction. Over champagne and canapés, Anne Morgan and her fellow socialites-turned-businesswomen handed out prizes of fur coats and salamander pins to the top stock sellers.

The AWA hotel found its site on West Fifty-Seventh Street, where professional women could be "as free as men." Women's independence at the AWA was declared in no uncertain terms: a full twenty-eight stories, with furnishings overseen by Mrs. William K. Vanderbilt, another member of the country's wealthiest clans, as well as a swimming pool with "nasturtium colored tiles" and a patio where "four fountains splash in melodious arpeggios." The "ultra-modern girl" could "order her coffee and cigarettes" in an array of themed rooms. The powder-blue tableware used in the muraled art deco dining room was the same as one would find in the wagon restaurants of the French trains because Mrs. Vanderbilt believed if it could withstand European rail tracks, it could survive the women of New York. She ordered crateloads. While a place to eat, drink, and smoke, the AWA hotel also offered 1,250 rooms with baths, making it the fifth-largest residential hotel in all of New York.

✦

But it was the Barbizon Hotel that truly captured America's imagination. It would become the go-to destination for young women from all over the country determined to give their New York dreams a shot. Whereas the Allerton and the AWA were built for professional career women, the Barbizon targeted a different kind of guest. She was the debutante who couldn't tell her parents she wanted to paint; she was the shopgirl from Oklahoma who dreamed of the Broadway stage; she was the eighteen-year-old who told her fiancé she would be right back, but first there was a typing course she needed to take.

The hotel would come to embody an entirely different persona from the others as a place of glamour, desire, and young female ambition.

William H. Silk, with the Allerton already on its way to completion, now aimed to combine femininity with this new independence, declaring that just as the modern woman's dress had shaken off the cumbersome frills of the Victorian age and embraced a "drastic" simplicity, so too her living quarters at the Barbizon needed to "reflect the larger life opened to the female sex," while keeping in mind that women "have by no means lost their feminine attributes." This is what Silk envisioned the Barbizon would be: twenty-three floors, 720 rooms; on the outside, it would offer the masculine, he declared, embodied in a building of the North Italian school, filled with everything that men demanded for training their intellect and their physique—swimming pool, gymnasium, roof gardens, lecture rooms, and library. But on the inside, in the Barbizon's interiors, the rooms hidden to men would be "highly feminine boudoirs," the colors "delicate and fresh," furnished in a modern French style. Like its predecessors, the Barbizon would be designed around a post-suffragette rethinking of domesticity along with the developers' bottom-dollar desire to maximize living space. The result was lines of private rooms off of long narrow corridors, intermingled with shared parlors, libraries, and laundry facilities.

Silk promised the Barbizon Club-Residence for Women, as it was first called, would open "on or about October 15"—1927—and indeed, print advertisements began to appear in September, announcing that applications for residence would begin on September 15. Among the features of the Barbizon was a radio in each room—which would so delight Molly Brown when she arrived. Rates started at $10 a week. Designed by the hotel specialists Murgatroyd & Ogden, the Barbizon, completed a few months past schedule, in February 1928, was impressive from both near and far, with four massive turrets at the corners of the towering building, like gradated steps moving up to its peak. The outside brickwork was chosen to convey color and light from salmon to light red, artistically arranged in diverse patterns, with a neutral limestone as the trim. A large solarium that functioned as a lounge, furnished tastefully, was located on the west side of the nineteenth floor, above which rooms were reserved for various college clubs. On the eighteenth floor, right below, was a loggia with expansive views. Once finished, *Architectural Forum* noted that while the Barbizon was for the most part Gothic in detail, it was a "Romanesque sort of Gothic." The large arched windows gave it a sense of the romantic and the sacred, and avoided the "mechanistic effect" in some of the new skyscrapers. Up in the clouds, roaming the roof gardens, peeking through its arcades, residents spied one dome window after another, built up on different angles, with setbacks and terra-cotta balconies. One could easily imagine a Gothic castle, arrows slung through the arched openings.

While simplicity, even a playful simplicity, was reserved for the outside, the lobby and mezzanine could be described as intricate and Italianate. Entering the Barbizon, a guest encountered an interior atrium designed in a luxurious modern style inspired by the Italian Renaissance and grand Italian country houses. Decorated in elaborate colors, textures, and patterns, the space offered a fully immersive experience with its painted ceilings and patterned floors, ornamented balustrades and stair railings, and upholstered classically styled furniture. Potted plants, a chandelier, and subtle lighting throughout the two-story-high space added to the ambience of arriving into the open-air courtyard of a grand Italian villa. Whether a mezzanine, located above the lobby, was intentionally chosen so the Barbizon's young ladies could peer down, looking out for their dates or, just as likely, checking out one another's dates and furtively rating them or desiring them, is hard to say. But the mezzanine was like an outsize Romeo and Juliet balcony that was wrapped up around the top of the lobby like a picture frame, with heavy stonework and an elaborate railing. From the northwest corner of the mezzanine, two steps led down into an oak-paneled library, while the dining room opened from the main floor of the lobby and was furnished in neoclassical "Adam style" to suggest intimacy rather than grandeur. *Architectural Forum* declared: "The Barbizon seems to give evidence of a new understanding of civilization, wholly convincing." Form and mission were now one.

From its inception the Barbizon was imagined as the rooming choice for the artistically inclined. The very name was intended to underscore this: the hotel was named after a nineteenth-century French art movement, the Barbizon School, centered around the village of Barbizon, southeast of Paris, surrounded by the Fontaine-bleau Forest. The inns along its narrow main street, the Grande Rue, were a haven for starving artists. Accommodating owners offered painters a full dinner, a dormitory bed, and a packed lunch to take into the woods, all for a minuscule sum. At New York's Barbizon Hotel, art students would live together in the Four Arts Wing, where one hundred rooms were reserved for them, as were the studios—the very ones in which Molly Brown found sanctuary—located in the tower, rising up from the eighteenth floor. The largest was fifty by seventeen feet, with soaring two-level ceilings to let the light pour in, while smaller studios for musicians were carefully soundproofed. But not everyone needed to be an artist; an eagerness to embrace all that New York could offer was enough.

If the Barbizon had found its niche as the place for young aspiring artists, actresses, musicians, and fashion models, then the interior provided all the necessary spaces in which these young women could express themselves—both as producers and consumers of art. In the first-floor lounge, with a stage and pipe organ, three hundred could comfortably enjoy a performance. The new post-suffrage femininity required that both the mind and the body be fed, and the Barbizon's library, lecture rooms, gym, and full-size swimming pool were up to the task. The early 1900s Gibson girl, freed up by her skirt and shirt separates, had enjoyed a good morning stretch or a bicycle ride, but the 1920s flapper was beginning to take on more rigorous exercise, and the basement of the Barbizon was a maze of workout options. With a strangely erotic choice of words, the *New York Times* exclaimed that "at all hours of the day the laughter of girls can be heard intermingling with the rhythmic thud of the balls in the squash courts and the splashing of water in the pool. Modern amazons in the making are learning to fence; swimmers of the future are being taught the crawl in the nether regions of the Barbizon."

+

Titanic survivor Molly Brown had had her skirmishes with the flappers who surrounded her now in New York. As a progressive-era suffragette, a New Woman in the least frivolous sense of the word, Molly Brown, like many of her generation, found the flappers insufferable. She saw herself as a true pioneer of women's rights whereas the flappers were merely putting on the finishing touches, gaudy ones no less. Before New York, when Molly Brown had escaped to Paris to study acting, she had been loud and clear about what she thought of this new breed of young women. When asked by a reporter, she said: "The American girl can't hold her liquor; she shows it right away and grows mushy or wants to fight . . . today, society girls drink industrial alcohol to warm up on before they arrive at a party."

But one society girl back home was having none of it and fired back, with a clear dig at the Molly Brown myth: "I think Mrs. Brown has enough to do to paddle her own canoe without trying to paddle for the younger set" because "as far as a woman's appearance goes, none looks her best after a few drinks. But there is no comparison between a younger woman and an older one. The younger one still looks fresh and pretty and seems to control herself better. But older women are disgusting." It's hard to imagine Molly did anything more than shrug; she had heard worse.

She might have had little patience for the flappers' shenanigans, but whether she liked it or not, they were everywhere, and not just in the rooms of the Barbizon. The flapper was on Main Street, USA, as much as she was on Broadway, New York. Harold Ross, the founder of a brand-new magazine called the *New Yorker*, was desperate to capitalize on her. With the magazine barely up and running but already teetering on bankruptcy, Harold Ross had to do something drastic to capture a steady audience. He had heard about a recent Vassar College graduate named Lois Long, who could be counted on to stir things up, and he hired her. Lois was twenty-three years old, a Connecticut girl and daughter of a minister—hardly the background for a rebel celebrity. Yet it was because of her background, rather than despite it, that Lois became the archetypal flapper of the 1920s. With her white-bread upbringing, she was the most typical of flappers because the flapper was not exclusively an urban sophisticate but, just as likely (if not more so), a teenage girl from Wichita, Kansas. But the eager young girl from Wichita needed to learn how to become a flapper, and this was where Lois "Lipstick" Long stepped in.

Initially writing anonymously, calling herself only "Lipstick," Lois bounded about Manhattan undisguised; she was tall, pretty, with dark brown bobbed hair, wearing the classic flapper dress that fell in one flat, vertical line from the chest down to just below the knees, and a red-lipsticked smile at all times. She was naughty, ready for fun, and—exactly as Molly Brown disapprovingly noted—not past getting drop-dead drunk (she advised her readers that it was only good manners to pay two dollars to the cabbie for throwing up in his car). Lois Long demonstrated that the 1920s had taken everything from the shadows and rebranded it as white, middle-class, American, decadent and fun: jazz came from the black ghetto, sexual experimentation from Greenwich Village, and rouge, powder, and eye shadow from the prostitute's toolbox. The flapper, the 1920s' best-known incarnation of the New Woman, was now at the center of it all.

+

At the stroke of midnight on January 16, 1920, the United States went dry. The purpose was to stop crime and bad behavior, but the very opposite happened. Manhattan, where the flamboyant mayor Jimmy Walker with a stout wife and a string of chorus girls for his mistresses did not believe drinking was a crime, was transformed into one big party. Speakeasies—the illegal, illicit, booze-soaked clubs of the Prohibition era—began to pop up all over the city, turning young, brash entrepreneurs into millionaires. One bootlegger, barely thirty years old, first chartered fleets of ships loaded with imported alcohol to break through the government cordon off Long Island. He became rich almost overnight but soon decided there had to be an easier way; he brought together experts, imported materials, and acquired the formula for a famous English gin. Next, he set up a pristine subterranean distillery beneath the surface of New York's streets and sold the "British gin" to speakeasies, whose bartenders declared they had never tasted a London gin as good as this. When London liquor manufacturers hired a detective to see why their illegal New York gin sales had dipped so dramatically, they soon figured out his scheme, but there wasn't a thing they could do: they couldn't very well call the police to complain their illegal sales of British gin to the United States were being undermined by the illegal manufacture of alcohol underneath New York's streets.

Women were also among Prohibition's new and clever entrepreneurs. One of the best known was Belle Livingstone, actress and showgirl, who claimed to have been abandoned as a baby in a backyard in Emporia, Kansas. She wanted to be an actress, but her foster father, publisher of Emporia's local newspaper, refused to let her onstage as a single woman.

"Fine," she said, and proposed to the first well-dressed man she saw. Strangely, he agreed, and though they parted ways immediately, stranger still, he left her the enormous sum of $150,000 at his death. She took the money and headed across the Atlantic, where, according to her memoirs, she was "the toast of Europe" for a good thirty years. Returning to America in 1927, just as the Barbizon was being built, and with Prohibition well under way, stout and stocky Belle, now in her fifties, saw an opportunity. She called her illegal saloons *salons*, as if they were the intellectual gathering places of Paris. And she played cat and mouse with federal agents, who often appeared at her salons in disguise and then dragged her to court, where reporters and the reading public eagerly hung on to her every word as she expressed her outrage in an outpouring of colorful language. One of her speakeasies was the Country Club, which both high society and the Broadway crowd frequented, paying a pricey five-dollar admission. But once in, customers could stroll through the grand room that resembled the Gardens of Versailles or head upstairs to play Ping-Pong or miniature golf. The only requirement was to keep on buying the dollar drinks.

Then there was Janet of France. Thoroughly French, she had made a living as a vaudeville and musical-comedy actor in New York until the work dried up and she had nothing more than twenty-nine dollars to her name. Contemplating her hopeless future, she took a stroll down West Fifty-Second, where she noticed an "ancient house squeezed in between garage buildings." It was for rent, and with a hundred borrowed dollars, she took it over and installed a simple wooden bar, cheap curtains, and a few tables and chairs. The first week, the only thing on the menu was onion soup along with bootleg Scotch, brandy, and rye. The booze was nothing special, but the onion soup was sublime. It received enough attention that she soon leased two more floors of the antiquated building. She added some cheap dinners to surround the crowning glory of the meal—the onion soup—and served up red wines à la France. Celebrities such as Marlene Dietrich, Douglas Fairbanks, and Lionel Barrymore were soon knocking on the door. Janet of France boasted that the Irish playwright George Bernard Shaw visited her and only her speakeasy—she always had an autograph book on hand to prove it.

Former chorus girl Texas Guinan was another star of New York's Prohibition scene. She was the one who coined the most famous phrase of the time—"Hello, sucker!" (The rest of her catchphrase, which she hollered at customers as they came in, went: "Come on in and leave your wallet on the bar.") She was already a well-known stage and film actress—or so she said—when the speakeasies lured her in with lucrative singing gigs. That's where she learned the trade. She opened her own eventually, the 300 Club, once visited by the Prince of Wales. Opening-night programming featured the marriage of a well-known American actress and her lover, a saucy Argentinian dancer.

While the Barbizon's residents did not open speakeasies, just like the *New Yorker*'s Lois "Lipstick" Long and other young women in New York in the 1920s, they frequented them. For the very first time in New York's history, women were being asked to pull up a stool at the bar. A muraled sign over the entrance door to Leon and Eddie on West Fifty-Second read, "Through These Portals, the Most Beautiful Girls in the World Pass OUT." New York's society girls especially were encouraged to take their place at the bar, drinking imported booze procured from rumrunners off the Long Island shores—although Lois preferred cognac after she learned it was the most difficult to fake and thus least likely to be contaminated. She left the booze brewed in New York's subterranean distilleries to others.

The swankiest speakeasy of all was Marlborough House at 15 East Sixty-First, just off Fifth Avenue. Among New York's Social Register, it was known simply as Moriarty's—after the brothers who started it. Anyone could enter the front door because it was too crass to ask who a person might be right there out on the street. So "in" meant only a vestibule, sealed in precious woods, where one then pushed a pearl button and presented their credentials. If they were let in, *really in*, they headed up the narrow stairs that opened onto a sumptuous room with walls scarlet up to chair level and silver the rest of the way to the ceiling. French wall benches ran the length of the walls, upholstered in silver leather, and mural storks of white with scarlet beaks streaked across the silver surface. Doors were enameled in scarlet too, and the lighting was dim to catch the silver flickers. But the showstopper was the cabaret room above, done up in royal blue, copper, and mirrors. The walls there were made entirely of mirrors so wherever one sat, one could see whoever else was there. For entertainment, Moriarty's chose novelty over big names to wow the jaded Social Register set: an Egyptian magician, a hot-torch singer, foreign dancers. The Moriarty brothers—Mort, Dan, and Jim—were saloon owners turned speakeasy aficionados, who were smart enough to know how to sidestep the gangsters and keep Marlborough House free of them. When Prohibition was finally repealed on December 5, 1933, Jim, the remaining brother, was on the Social Register himself, with a country estate and a stable of polo ponies.

Others already had the ponies but still could not resist the lure of the celebrity status of speakeasy operator. Roger Wolfe Kahn, son of financier and railroad magnate, Otto Kahn, opened one. Walter Chrysler Jr., son of the auto king, almost bought one before he was restrained by his family. The son of the drama critic for the *New York Herald* operated the Artists' Club in Greenwich Village, and hired as the hostess Yvonne Shelton, a trouser-wearing friend of a former New York mayor, while a plump Brooklyn-born Russian Jew, Bertha Levine, stage name Spivy, sang ditties that were far from subtle. New York's Broadway, filled in those days with "cafeterias, electric shoe-shining stands, nut shops, physical-culture demonstrations and five-cent dance halls," gave way to an "invisible paradise" of speakeasies in the Fifties that stretched from Fifth Avenue to Park Avenue. The best speakeasies began to rent out entire houses, leasing and remodeling the residences of industrial tycoons and old money. Once, a debutante fell apart after her fourth cocktail as it suddenly dawned on her that this was the very house in which she had spent much of her childhood.

Altogether there were hundreds of speakeasies all over Manhattan, catering to every class. At the Five O'Clock Club, Florenz "Flo" Ziegfeld would arrive with his bevy of beauties, and the orchestra would break into song. At the Napoleon Club, always popular, standing room at the bar was three to four persons deep, and included Believe-It-Or-Not Robert Ripley and Al Jolson, the "world's greatest entertainer," as he was known. Marlene Dietrich often visited the Embassy Club and Ethel Merman regularly sang there. At King's Terrace, Gladys Bentley, a Harlem Renaissance star, played to a packed house. Gladys was an African American woman who favored men's clothes, particularly a gleaming white tuxedo and top hat. When performing, she shockingly alternated between soprano and bass, between sentimental and risqué songs. Dark-skinned, masculine, corpulent, she was one of the few women on the scene who was openly, defiantly gay, flaunting her preferences as she growled popular contemporary songs whose sanitized words she switched out for her own obscene and often hilarious lyrics. It wasn't just the society set that was crazy for her: Langston Hughes called her "an amazing exhibition of musical energy." She'd been "discovered" by New York society at Harry Hansberry's Clam House in Harlem, the most overt of all of Harlem's homosexual speakeasy dives.

For the sake of appearances, before the evening's entertainment began, it was best to start with dinner at the speakeasy; gourmet meals of buttered lobster at bargain basement prices that did not even cover the cost of the ingredients but were subsidized by the illegal sale of alcohol. Delicacies were served up by French chefs who had jumped ship from New York's high-end restaurants because, with the onset of Prohibition, they had forfeited their bottle of wine a day, explicit in their salary contracts. With law-abiding restaurants no longer able to deliver on that promise, after a year European chefs had begun to abandon their posts, returning to France, Switzerland, and Italy. The speaks, as they were known, lured them back with the promise of free-flowing wine. At the Park Avenue speak, a modernist dream of black, green, rose, yellow, and silver that cost $85,000 to design, and that was even without the furnishings, Monsieur Lamaze served dinners in a room with vaulted green ceilings and two great circular, frameless mirrors opposite each other, so that the dark room seemed to stretch into infinity. The baby lamb on his menu came from a special farm in Ohio, and every morning the express train from Florida unloaded thirty pounds of pompano butter fish for his pompano bonne femme, served with mustard sauce—leftover pompanos were divided up among the staff. His lobster Lamaze was the talk of the town, and it wasn't past him to offer Burgundy snails or wild boar from the Vosges. There was no menu, only a clipboard of the day's groceries. A dollar for lunch, two and a half for dinner. It didn't even cover the train fare for the pompano.

Illegal booze, premarital sexual encounters, a body freed of Victorian restrictions in dress and manners and lifestyle were the definers of the 1920s as women began to come into their own in this decade. For those from an older generation, like Molly Brown, the changes were astonishing. Before World War I, a single woman at a bar with a drink was automatically labeled a "lady of the night." In 1904, a woman lit a cigarette while out on Fifth Avenue, and was summarily arrested—for being a woman smoking in public. But by the 1920s, such behavior was not only acceptable on the streets of Manhattan but mimicked across the country. Lois "Lipstick" Long played her part, touting the sort of madcap life that young women everywhere could begin to appropriate for themselves. It is what sixteen-year-old Lillian Clark Red from Canton, Ohio, did. Bored with high school, she grabbed a checkbook and took a train to Cincinnati. There she rented a room in a hotel on Walnut Street, outfitted herself splendidly from various stores, and then headed on over to a real estate agent, presenting herself as an heiress. She decided on a pretty bungalow overlooking the Ohio River, and wrote out a $25,000 check for its full purchase price. The house, of course, needed to be furnished, so she did that too, spending $6,000. The last touch was a car, and she found one she liked for $2,600. She was eventually found out and delivered back to her humdrum life. But Lillian Clark Red from Canton, Ohio, had followed the flapper's handbook and taken life to its extreme. She was not the "New Woman" as the suffragettes like Molly Brown had envisioned her, but she was thoroughly "modern."

Unsurprisingly then, censure for the modern woman, in all her variations, was widespread. Everyone had something to say about *her*. A Monsieur Cestre, professor at the Sorbonne in Paris, spent 1926 on a lecture tour of the United States, where, somewhat creepily, he "studied the American girl." "Loaned" to Vassar College—Lois "Lipstick" Long's alma mater—for two weeks he observed the Vassar girls with anthropological intensity and concluded that while everyone thought it was the French girl who was fast and easy, in fact it was "just the opposite. The French girl is very carefully reared, and it is not until she is married that she has any liberties to speak of. No, the American miss is much 'faster' than the Parisian mademoiselle." The *New York Times* sardonically noted that Professor Cestre "did not amplify his statement on the American girl in this regard." He hardly had to; he was clearly of the mind that women at bars were automatically suspect. But he was not entirely wrong if suspect meant sexually active. Of the women born before 1900, about 14 percent had had premarital sex, yet of the women who came of age in the 1910s and 1920s, between 36 and 39 percent did; and, statistically, they were also far more likely to have orgasms—even as they were most likely losing their virginity to the men who would become their husbands.

Criticism of *her* was not just about loose morals, however. There were other violations of cultural norms. New York's Rabbi Krass charged that the modern woman tended to "mimic man." With much greater originality, a Mrs. Ruth Maurer explained to a Chicago school of cosmeticians: "Many a modern woman has a face as hard as the crockery of a railroad lunch counter, and the reason is chewing gum. Human beings were not meant to be ruminating animals. . . ." In the long-held tradition of fat-shaming, numerous assertions claimed that the modern woman was uglier than her predecessors, and most definitely larger. When dress manufacturers were accused of failing to make clothes that fit contemporary women, they lashed out that the average hip size had recently increased by up to three inches. Women's feet were not free of scrutiny either. Between 1920 and 1926, precisely the heyday of the flapper, it was charged that the average shoe size had gone from four and a half to six and a half, and the ankle had become decidedly thicker because of the trend for wearing low-heeled oxfords.

Others defended this particular incarnation of the New Woman. In 1926, Lady Astor, a Virginia native and now first female member of the British Parliament, tried to make it back home incognito to the United States for a quiet family vacation. But already in wait at Boston Harbor as the *Samaria* pulled in was a crowd of reporters, who assailed her with questions ranging from her thoughts on wartime reparations to the modern woman. "You'll get the shock of your life in America, Lady Astor," one reporter called out. "You'll see people drunk. You'll see girls drunk. Cocktails everywhere." A month later into her trip back home, although she still feigned not to know what a flapper was—"but I suppose they mean a modern young woman"—Lady Astor persisted in defending her: "I may be amazed at the sight of short hair and short skirts, but surely these are far healthier than long skirts and tight waists and curl papers and all the other paraphernalia that we women have had to put up with for years. I haven't had intelligence enough to bob my hair, but I take off my hat to those who have."

The Jazz Age had proven to be a balancing act: the post–World War I New Woman had an independence previously unimaginable, but it was accompanied by widespread indictments of her, as if independence was itself a transgression. The boom in women's residential hotels facilitated this independence, and so they too were open to the same sort of criticism. The Barbizon was however given an added boost of respectability when the National Association of Junior Leagues, the charitable sorority for upper-class women, opened its clubroom on the twenty-second floor of the hotel with majestic views of Manhattan. The room, featured in *Vogue,* was lauded for "retaining its common denominator of modernity" while providing a practical clubroom for young women: an angular white laminated fireplace was the central feature, with an enormous mirror from the top of the mantel up to the ceiling, which reflected the art deco ceiling lights that looked like translucent stacked matchboxes. The posh Junior League was not the only one to set up beautifully appointed clubrooms at the Barbizon. Back in 1922, the Vassar College Club had already rented out a whole floor of the Allerton House because women's hotels were a perfect location for women's college clubs, re-creating the same-sex solidarity ethos that buoyed the suffragette movement and had helped establish these colleges in the first place. Even as the Barbizon was still under construction, the Wellesley Club ordered up a suite of rooms on the eighteenth floor, and signed on for the exclusive use of its southern and western roof gardens. The plan was for a large lounge, a dining room connected with the restaurant down on the first floor by a small elevator for bringing up the food, and a smaller lounge to be used as a writing room or library. Twenty bedrooms were also being set aside for exclusive use by club members. Other women's college clubs quickly followed.

The hotel was quick to capitalize on these associations, placing an advertisement in the *New Yorker*: "The Barbizon has become the latest accepted rendezvous for the art and music-loving young set. In the center of New York's social life . . . no more fitting background could have been chosen by the following organizations for the establishment of their club rooms: Barnard College . . . Cornell's Women's College . . . Wellesley College . . . Mt. Holyoke College . . . League of Seven Women's Colleges." In the January 1928 *Junior League Magazine*, the Arts Council of the City of New York further announced it would have its executive offices on the mezzanine floor of the Barbizon, and the services of its director would be available to the residents of the Arts Wing, who would be kept abreast of all the latest art exhibitions and musical and dramatic presentations. In other words, as the Barbizon was being built, brick by salmon-colored brick, so too was its image. It would be *the* place for the artistic but rarefied young lady, for the respectable but modern woman.

✦

In February 1928, the Barbizon Club-Residence for Women officially opened on Sixty-Third Street and Lexington Avenue. The Unsinkable Molly Brown, back from Paris and no longer with a vast fortune to her name, settled in at the Barbizon in 1931, delighted to find herself with a room of her own—exactly what Virginia Woolf famously proclaimed was vital for a woman's independence and creativity. The Barbizon was the perfect place for the thoroughly modern Molly. Art exhibitions, concerts, and dramatic performances were constantly on the hotel's social roster, many showcasing the Barbizon's own aspiring actors, musicians, and artists. And one never knew whom one might bump into on the elevator. According to the 1930 United States Census, Molly Brown's fellow hotel residents included Helen Ressler, a model from Ohio; Helen Bourns, a singer from Maryland; Rose Barr, an interior decorator from Iowa; Margaret Gallagher, a trained nurse from Pennsylvania; and Florence Du Bois, a statistician from Kansas. Molly reveled in having an airy soundproofed studio for her voice lessons, and corridors filled with modern women like herself, even if she might not have approved of them all, especially the flappers.

But on October 26, 1932, Molly Brown was found dead in her room at the Barbizon. Her death certificate listed her occupation as "housewife," when she had been anything but a housewife. She had been a plucky nineteenth-century woman who had propelled herself into the twentieth century by embracing the mantle of independence and female drive. The press reported apoplexy as the cause of her death: sudden death by aria. They evoked the image of a crazed rich lady who could not sing, eccentrically dressed, belting it out in the Barbizon's practice rooms and collapsing dead from the exertion of it. But Molly could sing, very well in fact, and the real reason for her death was a brain tumor that had been growing since she first arrived at the Barbizon, and from which she would flee to her room, lying there with her eyes closed for days, until the "migraine" went away, and she emerged again for tea.

Molly Brown had managed to outlive the flappers. Three years before her death, *Junior League Magazine* was already noting their steady decline: "Seriously, have you seen a Flapper this past year among your younger sister's friends—or looking in the mirror, has a Flapper reflection smiled back at you? I do not think so." The flapper, the Junior League suggested, had been a crude reflection of the times, "who in her prime, claimed the limelight of the world, and excited pulpits, rostrums, and family hearths, with her sex conscious, self conscious bid for publicity." But she had lost everyone's interest.

Women now were becoming more subtle, shed of "the shabby gestures of Flapperdom, imitating the demi-monde." A younger member of the Junior League summed it up: "The first so-called flapper
was the immediate postwar creation. She was a shocking contrast—
literally speaking—to all the nice girls of 1913. . . . her skirts ended
about her knees, she sneaked her brother's cigarettes, she swore like
a soldier. Her dancing—but who of us could ever forget the inimitable
camel walk and shimmy? Her make-up was as crude as a clown's. She
was like a puppy learning to bark in her new-found independence."
With the flapper, so too went the very idea of the New Woman. All
women of the twentieth century were now new.

As the flapper disappeared from sight, so did the residential hotel.
Hotel owners stormed city hall and demanded of New York mayor
Jimmy Walker that he do something about these "residential clubs,"
these imposter hotels that were cutting into their profits. In 1929,
the Multiple Dwelling Law went into effect, pulling back on the legal
loophole that had made both residential hotels and New York tenements possible. It was the end of the residential hotel boom. But the
Barbizon Club-Residence for Women was here to stay. It was both
a product of its time—born of 1920s New York, an era filled with
illicit booze, speakeasies of mirrored opulence, and a new breed of
women who felt uncaged in both their dress and their lives—as well
as a harbinger of things to come. The Barbizon Club-Residence was,
as the Unsinkable Molly Brown could attest, a place where women
went to reimagine themselves: and in the twentieth century, that
was not about to go out of style.

CHAPTER TWO

SURVIVING THE DEPRESSION

Gibbs Girls and Powers Models

Katharine Gibbs's secretarial school, the gold standard for women seeking credentials that would get them out of the home and into the workplace, housed its students at the Barbizon. The Katie Gibbs certificate became all the more valuable during the Great Depression, especially among former debutantes now looking for work. Here a 1930s catalog for the school shows two young women on the Barbizon terrace, looking out over the expanse of Manhattan and its possibilities.

If someone had told Katharine Gibbs that one day, through her own efforts, she would find herself living in a grand Park Avenue apartment with three live-in servants, she would not have believed it. But she did just this, single-handedly, by creating the Katharine Gibbs Secretarial School. It was not only a school but also a phenomenon, a pathway for young women to find work, especially at the very moment when most everything else was suddenly closed to them. In New York, Katharine would also create a home for her students: a veritable dormitory, across two floors of the Barbizon Hotel, with curfews, house mothers, and lights-out rules. As restrictive as this seemed to some, it was a liberation for others; a chance for her charges to create new lives for themselves, to forge independent livelihoods despite the odds, much like Katharine herself had done, if not on quite the same scale.

In 1909, already forty-six years old, Katharine Gibbs was suddenly widowed and left with two sons and one unmarried sister to support. It was not a good era in which to be a husbandless, middle-aged, penniless woman (not that there ever has been), but Katharine decided that if her husband had failed to leave her a will, at least he had had the good grace to leave her a fine Protestant name. She felt she could do something with that. Borrowing money from friends at Brown University, she founded the Katharine Gibbs School for Secretarial and Executive Training for Educated Women on Brown's campus, in a building that is today the Africana Studies Department. A granddaughter of Irish Catholic immigrants who, despite her married name, would not be looked at twice by the Protestant old-money set, she nevertheless marketed to the WASPish upper classes and their not-yet-married daughters graduating from elite colleges. Katharine, as it turned out, was a born saleswoman. Her advertising suggested that her "private" school would protect America's upper-crust young ladies from the riffraff attending the more commercial secretarial schools, and she did not hesitate to mine the Social Register directories even as she, a single working mother, could never be listed in them.

By 1918, she had expanded to New York. She now advertised in *Harper's Bazaar* because that was what the rich read. The school's 1920 tagline was "a school of unusual character and distinctive purpose," and Katharine offered seniors at top colleges like Barnard and Radcliffe a shot at limited-enrollment intensive courses for young ladies with "High Academic Standing." In 1928, the same year the Barbizon officially opened its doors, the catalog for Katie Gibbs—as the school came to be known—pointed out that inherited wealth was "the most uncertain of all forms of protection," and that the young women who entered Gibbs were looking to make their own living even as they well knew that "a woman's career is blocked by lack of openings; by prejudice; by the fact that business is outside a woman's natural sphere; and finally, that she seldom is granted a just reward by way of salary, recognition, or responsibility."

Despite this feminist ring, a glamorous touch and the whiff of the posh were key to Katharine's business model. In fact, these provocative words about women's career opportunities appeared in a catalog that at the same time mimicked a debutante's dance card—heavy white board, front and back, with a rich white cord as binding. The product fit the very image Katharine was striving for, but it also spoke to the backgrounds of so many of the students themselves, such as Helen Estabrook, who had attended the Bancroft School in Massachusetts, then Vassar College, then the Sorbonne in Paris, all of which she topped off with a Katie Gibbs secretarial certificate—although she knew she would never use it. In 1933, she would marry

Robert Waring Stoddard, a founder of the far-right John Birch Society, and use her vast education to become an "impeccably dressed" Massachusetts-based philanthropist, who could hold her own on any topic, from "bird hunting in Scotland to the art of the Bomboccianti in seventeenth-century Rome."

As the New York branch of Katie Gibbs expanded, it moved its classrooms to 247 Park Avenue, proudly declaring its new location on Manhattan's only green thoroughfare open exclusively for the use of private cars. The young women studying business administration, speed typing, and shorthand, with no time for a formal lunch, ate their sandwiches at the same tables where they worked, which they covered with green cloths, shaking out the crumbs down onto Park Avenue. It was the Roaring Twenties, and the Katie Gibbs School in New York was filled with young ladies like Helen Estabrook. For them, it was part finishing school and part party school, where they could escape for a year between college and getting married and let their hair down—even if the experience did come with some intense typing practice. But then came "Black Thursday," and nothing was ever the same again.

✦

The stock market crashed on a Thursday in October 1929. The future British prime minister Winston Churchill was in New York that day and came upon a crowd of people standing on the street looking up at an unfinished skyscraper. When he followed their line of vision, he saw they had mistaken a workman perched four hundred feet up on the girder for a Wall Street speculator preparing to jump. But it was not so outlandish to think they were watching a man about to jump to his death: that day, Americans had lost what the United States had spent on the whole of World War I. By Tuesday it would be twice as much. Syndicated columnist Will Rogers, also in New

York on Black Thursday, claimed "you had to stand in line to get a window to jump out of." But there were also less public ways to meet the same end. Ignatz Engel, a retired cigar maker in the Bronx, lay down on a blanket in his kitchen and opened all the jets of the gas range. A Brooklyn broker whistled and sang hymns, to the irritation of his neighbors, before he too turned on the gas, opting for his bed over the kitchen floor, dressed sharp in a blue serge suit, gray kid gloves, and pearl-colored spats.

There were those wealthy enough, however, that the crash at first meant only a financial stumble. For them, the fun continued still. The Stork Club, El Morocco, and countless other speakeasies remained filled with socialites, celebrities, and the ultrarich. The lavish Waldorf Astoria hotel opened in 1931—two years after the crash—where its in-house professional hostess, the celebrated Elsa Maxwell, organized costume parties, parlor games, soirees, and scavenger hunts for the rich who needed some cheering up. But with income tax revenues plummeting daily, the United States Treasury was starting to acknowledge that only alcohol taxes could make up for the ever-growing government deficit.

On Tuesday, December 5, 1933, in the late afternoon, a full four years after Black Thursday, the Merry-Go-Round Speakeasy on East Fifty-Sixth Street was packed as usual. The brass-buttoned doorman, looking like some misplaced admiral, was at the door, as always, waiting for new arrivals to utter the password. Downstairs, Omar Champion, the speakeasy's host, was decorating the wrought iron banisters with autumn leaves he had purchased from the Park Avenue hothouses. Upstairs, the circular bar was turning—a full rotation every eleven minutes. Organ music was playing, and bartenders were pouring. Young women sipping sidecars, dressed in Parisian Mainbocher dresses with cinched waists that anticipated the Dior look by many years, perched on wooden merry-go-round horses attached to the rotating bar. Around and around they went.

It was 5:30 p.m. when Omar went to answer the telephone. A few minutes later he returned, his face ashen, his voice shaking: "Ladies and gentlemen, Utah has ratified!" He reached out and pushed a button: the famous merry-go-round bar stopped mid-rotation. The bartenders quietly took off their aprons and put up a sign: NO DRINKS SERVED. Prohibition was officially over: the Twenty-First Amendment had passed, ringing the death knell for New York's speakeasies. The Roaring Twenties had definitively come to a screeching halt, even for the wealthy.

By then, the economic collapse, and its wretched hopelessness, had spread well beyond Wall Street. Within a year of Black Thursday, a quarter of America's workforce had become unemployed. At the worst point, one-third of New Yorkers were unemployed, and the once lush Central Park in Manhattan was turned into a muddy Hooverville, a town of makeshift shanties named after the president who many saw fit to blame. Hustlers and street hawkers were everywhere. Countless men peddled apples on street corners, a philanthropic gesture facilitated by US apple farmers' 1929 bumper crop, which they were trying to unload while also helping out the urban unemployed. These images of men with their apple boxes hoisted high onto their shoulders became synonymous with the family man's plight. But where were the women with their boxes of apples? Nowhere. It was only breadwinners—understood as male, and as white—who got the apples cheap to sell at profit. Women, after all, had men to take care of them. Or so everyone liked to say. But that was far from true—women, like men, suddenly had families to support, or else themselves, if only to ease the financial burden on their families.

+

The Great Depression was now everyone's new reality. It was the Barbizon's too. The Barbizon Hotel had not been cheap to build, costing $4 million in 1927 for its twenty-three floors. With the Great Depression fully under way, in 1931 the Barbizon Corporation, made up of individual shareholders presided over by William H. Silk, who had built the hotel, defaulted on its mortgage. Chase National Bank stepped in and took possession of the Barbizon. The following year, Chase protested the city's assessment of $2,950,000 for the hotel, claiming its fair-market value was almost a third less. Then just a month later, the Barbizon sold at a foreclosure sale for the bargain-basement, Depression-priced sum of $460,000—a quarter of what Chase had just claimed was its real value. The interior fixtures and furnishings went for another $28,000. The lucky bidder for both was Realtor Lawrence B. Elliman, an original shareholder in the Martha Washington but also chairman of a new entity called the Barbizon Hotel bondholders' committee. The hotel, in the most circuitous way, was now back again in the hands of those who had lost it. The skittish among the original shareholders, who did not want back in, were paid off with $400,000 borrowed by the new bondholders' committee for that very purpose.

Throughout the foreclosure proceedings and the resale, the Barbizon carried on as before. Much like its clientele, it needed to survive in the inverted world the 1929 stock market crash had generated, in which many of the previously well-off were now poor, and the poor were destitute. By 1934, there would be seventy-five thousand homeless single women in New York. Just as men had apples to sell, they also had flophouses to go to, dormitory beds for twenty-five cents or less, while the women had nothing. Instead, they rode the subways and sat in train stations, the invisible victims of the Great Depression. With nothing to peddle, many were reduced to selling their own bodies, taking on sex work to balance the scale between life and death. Black women looking for domestic work gathered on street corners, waiting for employers to drive by and make an offer; the women called it their new "slave markets." In the 1920s, some young black women had participated in flapper culture just like their white counterparts; that march forward stopped short. Now both white and black women were expected to hand over to men whatever jobs and self-respect might be left for the taking. More than 80 percent of Americans believed that a woman's proper place was again in the home. There was also widespread belief, which the government's Women's Bureau had to repeatedly quash, that women worked for frivolous "pin money," taking jobs from men. This was of course entirely delusional. The reality was that many young women were now forced to venture out to provide for their families, while women without a spouse to help pay the bills had to take care of themselves.

The Barbizon, New York's razzle-dazzle, exclusive women's hotel, had to take a different tack with the onset of the Great Depression. Its female clientele had changed, and it would have to change along with them. Print advertisements now promised the economic advantage of simple rooms and the earning potential of social networking in glamorous surroundings. On the one hand, the hotel continued to lure in the artistically minded, the upper-class white college graduate whose family fortunes had not taken a sharp downturn, but, on the other, it was also starting to tap into other potential residents. The variety of advertisements that appeared in the *New Yorker* clearly conveyed the shift. There was still the appeal for the sort of resident envisioned when the Barbizon was first conceived:

> **To a Young Woman Who Is a Poet.** Or a musician ... or an artist ... or a careerist in any sphere of activity ... do you realize that THE BARBIZON was created expressly to give you a propitious back-ground for your talents? [...] and that it brings within your present income much of the luxury of your future dreams? [1932]

But the hotel was soon highlighting its networking potential for the ambitious (or desperate):

Intelligent Young Women LIVE Intelligently! Success depends, to a large extent, on your physical comfort, recreations and mental stimulation after business hours. Barbizon young women are alive . . . eager to achieve—because they associate with people active in business and professional life . . . artists . . . musicians . . . dramatists . . . writers . . . people capable of valuable and charming friendships. Be one of them! Learn the dollar-and-cents value of RIGHT ENVIRONMENT! [1933]

The Barbizon advertisements also played to the uncertainty of New York's young female job seekers:

You Woman What Now? You are seeking a career? . . . a little uncertain at times? . . . The Barbizon is for you! Learn the dollars-and-sense value of right environment . . . encourage a zest for achievement by cultivating friendships with the right people. The Barbizon is 'New York's most exclusive residence for young women'—but you can afford to live here. A few charming little rooms now available . . . come in and inspect them. [1934]

What the Barbizon's advertisements did not say, or at least not out-right, was that the hotel now provided a different kind of security than before. In 1927, the Barbizon's salmon-colored brick walls had offered the promise of propriety for its women in a society that was still rife with Victorian condemnations for the New Woman. Now the Barbizon Hotel for Women was offering comfort and protection from a different sort of censure entirely: if women were not meant to hold jobs, if such a luxury was to be reserved for breadwinning men, if women with jobs were now deemed unpatriotic, then any young woman in New York with a salaried job, or else seeking one, was a pariah.

Every time a woman walked down the street dressed for work, or stood waiting at the elevator banks of her office building, she was a reminder of "compromised manhood." By 1932, twenty-six states had made it illegal for married women to hold a job, and in the states where it was not mandatory to quit work upon marriage, it was still mandatory to disclose one's impending married status because it was considered outrageous for a woman to be taking a job away from a "real" breadwinner. The Barbizon provided shelter from such denouncements. It was not just a residential hotel anymore; it was safe harbor.

The winter of 1932–33 was particularly bad. It was not only Hoovervilles and breadlines, but also single unemployed women marching in New York's streets, demanding jobs. Many of them were from "good families," bred on the optimism of the Roaring Twenties. Franklin D. Roosevelt became president in 1933 with the Great Depression at its peak—national income had been cut in half, and nine million savings accounts had been wiped out. As FDR was being inaugurated, home foreclosures reached a thousand a day, thirty-eight states had closed their banks, and many local governments did not have enough to cover relief payments. The stock market crash had exposed the illusion of the earlier optimism in a decade built on what First Lady Eleanor Roosevelt argued had been "a national preoccupation with material gain." No doubt she was right: the 1920s had championed a modernity defined by individualism and consumerism, but it had also benefited women who were allowed to aspire to something other than hearth and home. Now they were being told to go right back there, even as financial circumstances demanded that they do the very opposite.

Nevertheless, some persisted. Many of the young women in search of jobs were recent college graduates, but their chances of getting a job were slim: only one-third of Barnard College's class of 1932 graduates who needed to work found work, and what work was to be had centered on typing. An English literature degree got you nowhere, not unless you could add secretarial school to your résumé, preferably a certificate from the finest: the Katharine Gibbs

Secretarial School. These young female college graduates who had dreamed of sophisticated futures, of fulfilling lives, were now knocking desperately on the doors of the famous secretarial school. If they were accepted, and if they survived the rigorous course of typing, stenography, manners, poise, business training, and more, they became Gibbs girls. The now largely forgotten Gibbs girl, once the pride of the American workforce, who represented nine-to-five glamour and grit, came into her own in the 1930s—exactly at the same time that women were censured for daring to show their faces in the workplace.

Now the Katie Gibbs classrooms were filled not with Seven Sisters alumnae out for a good time but with young women desperate to find a path to real employment. Girls of leisure had turned into girls in search of work. It was harder for Vassar, Smith, and Barnard graduates to get into Katie Gibbs than it had been for them to get into their prestigious colleges. To accommodate the flood of students, in 1930 the sixteenth floor of the Barbizon Hotel became the official Katharine Gibbs residence in New York. Refinement and precision continued to be central to the Gibbs girl training. Mandatory classes in poise, voice, and manner were supplemented by art appreciation lectures by the likes of the famous Hungarian painter and Bauhaus professor László Moholy-Nagy. Prestigious college faculty were tapped for other courses as varied as Health, Posture, and Personal Hygiene (taught by Dr. Dorothy Kenyon, assistant in neurology at Columbia University, and Dr. Faith Meserve, a consulting physician at Wellesley College); Modern Decoration; Banking; Management Problems; Fashion in Business; Income Management; and English Literature, presumably to keep up a conversation about books if the situation arose. Instructions for life after Gibbs suggested that a Gibbs girl always knew best:

> You may find that it is the custom of the firm [where you are now a secretary] to use this form in writing the date, *June 21st, 193-*. Use it

temporarily, at least, with good grace, although you know that the modern trend is to omit the *st* and the period at the end. Do not, however, allow these older methods to become such a fixed habit with you that they actually come to seem correct or even preferable.

In 1934, Katharine's elder son committed suicide, and two months later, Katharine died, but her remaining son, Gordon Gibbs, continued to grow the business, making Katharine's name sacrosanct for its thousands of students. He added the Barbizon's seventeenth floor to the Gibbs girls' dormitory and moved the school once again, this time to the prestigious New York Central Building (later renamed the Helmsley), the tallest structure in the Grand Central rail station complex. Its location was touted for its access to the Grand Central Terminal concourse through "convenient pedestrian subways." The school was on the fourth floor with "modern ventilating and silencing equipment." A private dispensary on-site catered to the students' physical health while their mental and social health were buoyed by a calendar of coffee hours, department entertainments and parties, and a formal all-school dance in the midwinter season.

In addition to the reserved floors of the Barbizon, Gibbs girls also had the exclusive use of "an attractive suite of lounge and recreation rooms" on the twenty-second floor. Their meals (breakfast and dinner) were taken in the private and "picturesque Corot room," with food catered by the downstairs Barbizon coffee shop. They also had their own Thursday teas in the twenty-second-floor lounge, separate from the rest of the hotel. 1930s issues of *The Gibbsonian* routinely featured its young female students in Barbizon's open-air spaces, Manhattan's glorious skyline behind them. The back pages of the Gibbs yearbook—named *Platen* after the cylinder roller in a typewriter that secured the paper—made the connection more explicit still. Sponsoring pages were from "Emile of the Barbizon; Fashion's Dictator . . . All Other Beauty Work Done by Experts," the Barbizon

Pharmacy, and "The Barbizon Coffee Shoppe & Restaurant—Caterers to Katharine Gibbs School."

Gibbs had successfully tied itself to the kind of efficient glamour the Barbizon now exuded. Never mind that many Depression-era students were like Barbara Coulter—and nothing like Helen Estabrook Stoddard, the well-bred Massachusetts philanthropist—who just barely managed to attend Gibbs on money her mother had saved. Living at the Barbizon as a Gibbs girl meant she got breakfast and dinner in the "picturesque" Corot room, as promised, but was always hungry in between with no spare funds for lunch. Any spending money she had went to the hats, gloves, heels, and stockings that Gibbs girls were required to wear at all times. Without them, Barbara Coulter would be fined at best, cast out at worst. Not even on the subway were the Gibbs girls allowed to take off their hats—this remained true well into the late 1960s when the hat, by then a symbol of outdated femininity, had been all but abandoned by anyone under the age of thirty.

While the Katharine Gibbs school's stated mission was to put young women on the business career track, courses in culture and etiquette suggested alternate pathways through the pecuniary jungle. Frances Fonda, the future mother of Jane and Peter Fonda, was determined to go to Gibbs and "become the fastest typist and best secretary anyone could hire." But her plan did not end there. Frances Fonda imagined for herself an ambitious descent onto Wall Street following her Gibbs training, and, soon after, a marriage to a millionaire. She did exactly that, twice over, before taking her own life in 1950. Gibbs job placements were ripe for various possibilities because with no laws, let alone qualms, against outlining exactly what sort of Gibbs girl one desired, it was quite acceptable for executives to request "girls" over five foot eight or only redheads. Charles Lindbergh, famous pilot and well-known fascist sympathizer, requested a secretary who would be in lockstep with his political ideologies. The

Saturday Evening Post quoted an executive who was hiring another Gibbs graduate just two months after the first—because his son had married the first.

But Gibbs girls also used their secretarial positions to start climbing the corporate ladder. The recognition that took root in the 1920s that a woman's career could extend beyond nursing and teaching continued into the 1930s, despite the mixed messages of the Depression era. This recognition was often reinforced at the Barbizon through various teas, talks, and lectures, including a dinner hosted by the Barnard College Club on the topic of women in the professions, with a round of speakers for the night: "Women and Newspapers," "Women in Government," "Women in Medicine," and "Women in Local Politics." Popular culture too in the 1930s, as the movie industry expanded, radio ownership doubled, and newspapers proliferated, often showcased "assertive" women. The 1930s on-screen heroine—played by the likes of Katharine Hepburn, Carole Lombard, Claudette Colbert, Jean Arthur, and others—was "the ambitious career girl, the gutsy entertainer, the sophisticated socialite, the blond seductress, and, leading the list, the worldly wise reporter." (In fact, women had entered journalism in large numbers in the 1920s, and the trend continued into the 1930s, especially with the boost that Eleanor Roosevelt gave them by organizing a weekly women-only press conference to ensure female journalists did not lose their jobs.) These fictional screen heroines became a "repository for some of the lost aspirations of the 1920s."

At the same time, however, these celluloid heroines were also set up to tumble or be tamed, an extreme case being the rape that turned Scarlett O'Hara from lion to lamb in *Gone with the Wind*. Popular culture, in other words, offered a 1930s-type reprimand of 1920s female liberation; and smaller, localized, and less cinematic reprimands were commonplace, experienced by the Barbizon's residents daily. A 1935 handbook *So You Want to Be a Reporter* told it like it was: "In the films you have seen, there have been women who find work as reporters and go on to break the big story. Fairy dust, ladies, fairy dust . . . if you imagine in your dreams that'll be you covering the presidential conference, take a good deep breath, and remember that you are a Susie. 'Susie?' Didn't I mention Susie? All the gang call the new female recruits 'Susie' until they do something outstanding and earn themselves another nickname."

But there were people and places that continued to believe in women's meaningful employment, and the Barbizon was among them. Elizabeth Curtis, social director and vocational adviser at the Barbizon, passionately believed that a women-only residential hotel could offer what society outside its pink brick facade could not. Curtis believed that women had to cut loose from the home, that kitchen chores, compulsory entertaining, and family obligations had to be wiped clean from any modern woman's life if she was to pursue a career: "Women who go to their offices thinking of the dinners they must get or the visiting relatives they must entertain to please mother are only about one half on the job." Curtis was making a point: If you didn't have to cook your meals, let alone cook them for others, if you didn't have to accompany Mother to dinner and instead could visit restaurants and cocktail bars with your fellow female career gals, you would not only have a better time but a better career. And the flurry of white-gloved Gibbs girls that emerged from the doors of the Barbizon each morning was a testament to this very idea.

✛

Gibbs girls were cloaked in acceptability because by the 1930s secretarial work was viewed as exclusively female. But there was also another big-city vocation understood to be singularly female—that of looking pretty. The Gibbs girls occupied a fair percentage of the Barbizon Hotel's rooms during the 1930s, but right behind them were the Powers models. John Robert Powers had arrived in New York in the 1920s as an aspiring actor, but he soon found his real calling as the founder of the world's first modeling agency. One day he overheard a businessman say he needed a group of attractive people to pose for a magazine advertisement. Powers gathered his friends, delivered the goods, and the rest was history. His success story was even turned into a 1943 movie musical, *The Powers Girl*.

The Powers Agency specialized in what was considered the typical Midwestern look: tall, blond, and curvy. A quarter of the agency's earnings came from its models posing for mail-order catalogs such as the Sears Roebuck, rural America's latter-day shopping mall. Some really were Midwestern, but the Powers models came from all over the country, and they inevitably stayed at the Barbizon. As Powers boasted, his unmarried models could of course "find rooms at a lower rent," but they felt it was "worth while to spend a little more money for an atmosphere which offers both prestige and protection." Thus the Barbizon became suffused with their glamour. Elsa Maxwell, the Waldorf Astoria in-house party hostess, liked to say that she could give a party without debutantes but not without at least six Powers girls. Because blond and cute was the look that Powers was after, the models looked so "startlingly" alike that New York's gossip columnists abandoned trying to identify them and simply took to writing "he was seen out with a 'Powers model.'"

These models were not supermodels: they were working models. They were the young women sandwiched in between magazine stories, who, as Mr. Powers liked to explain, "sip your favorite coffee, drive your dream car, display the latest fashion, show you how to cook a waffle." He would look at the girls as they arrived at his offices on Park Avenue and appraise them for their potential in selling everything from "sables to society or groceries to the great American housewife." The "Powers girls" were typically five foot nine inches and a voluptuous 34-24-34—"long stemmed American beauties," illustrator William Brown called them. They came not from the chic Hamptons (although they often ended up there) but from Middle America.

The case of Evelyn Echols was in this sense typical, a journey from the Midwest straight to the Barbizon. Evelyn had always dreamed of New York, and in April 1936, for her twenty-first birthday, she and her best friend bought the cheapest car shuttle tickets to get them cross-country to New York, their luggage crammed into the back seat, driving straight through the night. Upon arriving, the first thing they did was take a room at the Barbizon because that was "where almost every unmarried woman who came to New York in the 1930s resided." The second thing they did was sleep for almost an entire day before they finally ventured out, walking past the men who "hung around the Barbizon Hotel entrance like vultures, 24 hours a day." The first stop had to be Times Square, of course, and the two young women made their way down to Broadway and Forty-Second Street. Once there, Evelyn turned to her friend, clasped her arms around her, and declared that she was never leaving New York.

If she wasn't going to leave, however, she needed a job. She wasn't a Powers model or a Gibbs girl, and so the Barbizon desk clerk, not exactly unfamiliar with the girl-who-came-to-New-York-and-wouldn't-leave type, pulled out the want ads section in the Sunday edition of the *New York Times* and pushed it toward Evelyn. It was still the Depression, but Evelyn fortunately was a trained nurse, and she quickly landed a job in a private maternity hospital six blocks down from the Barbizon. The hospital was owned by an Italian doctor who called every expectant mother "Rosie." Each day, as Evelyn did her rounds, she would hear the persistent chant, a broken record that would not stop, ring through the maternity ward: "Push, Rosie, push!" During her days off, Evelyn, whose best friend had long ago returned home without her, hung out with the hotel's models. They had colorful names that hid their own small-town roots—Dulcet

Tone, Choo Choo Johnson, Dorian Lee, and Honey Child Wilder. They took Evelyn for a mandatory makeover to their stylists, who tamed her blond hair and applied makeup to her birdlike eyes, and escorted her on a shopping trip to Seventh Avenue in the garment district, where women could buy designer dresses at wholesale prices. One day, on the way to the movies, her friends stopped by the Powers Agency to pick up their assignments. While Evelyn was waiting for them, a man walked by and did a double take. "You're the most typical Midwesterner I've seen in a long time!" Mr. Powers exclaimed, and declared Evelyn would be "ideal" for the Montgomery Ward catalog.

While Evelyn's time as a Powers model would be short-lived, Celeste Gheen, who also resided at the Barbizon, was serious about her career. Not for nothing had she won the title of Most Versatile Model, and the list of products to which she had already given her face, her body, and even a limb here and there was long and impressive: Camels, Old Golds, Chesterfields (she smoked only the latter); Krippendorf Foot Rest Shoes, United States Rubber Company, Buick, Hellman's, La Cellophane, Log Cabin syrup, Texaco, Packard, Bayer aspirin, Beech-Nut, Simmons Beautyrest mattresses, Bon Ami, Spam, and the laxative Castoria (which she didn't touch). Mr. Powers had baptized her with his highest compliment: "She is the typical-American-girl-type!" What that meant, the *New Yorker* explained, was that she "hasn't the sort of breath-taking beauty that compels small boys to whistle involuntarily when exposed to it, but she is a decidedly attractive girl, with delicate, neatly arranged features and a lot of poise."

Celeste was just fine with that. Originally from Cleveland, Ohio, she had attended an eight-month secretarial course and then found work as a secretary for the Sherwin-Williams paint company. One day in 1934 she went to a photographer's studio to get her picture taken for her mother, and the photographer said he could try to get her a spot in a General Electric advertisement, which he had been commissioned to illustrate. He followed through, and Celeste was paid five dollars to hold a sixty-watt Mazda bulb—the photograph appearing with the caption "Talk about your bargains!" To her mind, that was it with modeling, but advertising agencies in New York saw the picture of Celeste holding the Mazda bulb and told Mr. Powers they wanted her. Powers took on the challenge and finally tracked her down in Cleveland; for a full year he sent her pleading notes, which she initially ignored because she had never heard of him and was suspicious that he was trafficking in young white women. Which, in a sense, he was.

But after a year of Mr. Powers's unrelenting pleas, she finally agreed to come to New York in the fall of 1935 and meet with him. Celeste, very much the working girl, had by then extracted a promise from him: if she did not hold up to his modeling expectations, he would still have to give her a job as a secretary at the Powers Agency. She came to New York, passed his test, settled into the Barbizon, yet still remained suspicious. When her first photo studio appointment came up, she arranged for one of her Barbizon friends to call the police if she was not back by a certain time. She then went one step further and told the photographer that her friend back at the Barbizon was waiting to report him, which turned him into a nervous wreck, barely able to hold the camera still. But Celeste soon learned that everyone in the 1930s was after the same thing: making a living. Herself included. With this wobbly start she was soon earning about $25 a week, and her room at the Barbizon was $11, which left her with more than enough to live comfortably and even save up a nest egg.

Like every model in New York, Celeste carried a black hatbox with her, which held her makeup, accessories, and anything else a model might need for a shoot, since it was up to the models to do their own makeup and hair. If the hatbox came from the men's hatter John Cavanagh, whose store was in the same building as the Powers Agency, then everyone knew she was a Powers girl. When a rival hatter became tired of all the free publicity for his competitor, he created special hat-boxes with each Powers model's name stamped on the front, but few were willing to switch. Although Celeste had come close to ditching her Cavanagh hatbox after the bottom fell out on the Madison Avenue bus, giving her fellow passengers an intimate view of its contents, includ-ing long woolen underwear and so-called "binoculars," an apparatus that helped to create a bosomy effect if the shoot demanded it. Celeste resented her Cavanagh hatbox in other ways too: when she carried it, people would shout "Hi, Powers!" at her. That said, when she didn't, they would shout "Hi, Toots!" Neither was ideal.

But one of the worst aspects of modeling was tolerating the light-ing lamps that generated an intense heat. Photo shoots were as much about fighting off perspiration and fainting as they were about posing. Celeste learned to do what other models did: she propped herself up against the slim metal support routinely provided by photographers and furiously chewed Beechies gum (which she always had on hand) to fend off a fainting spell. Celeste averaged three to four hours of work a day, but it was a constant hassle to get those jobs. Model-ing jobs were arranged by two average-looking, stressed-out young women who had twenty-three models to take care of and commanded an enormous scheduling chart that hung on the wall behind them and dictated all their lives. Some Powers models were used only for their faces and were never shot below the neckline, but Celeste had a good figure, to which her leather-bound look-book, with her name and Mr. Powers's printed on the front, could attest. She was a dress size 12 (which today would be about a size 4), hat 22, shoe 7½ AAA, hose 10, gloves 7. This translated to 35-inch hips, a 24-inch waist, and a 34-inch bust, with a height of 5 feet 8½ inches, weighing in at 115 pounds. She was a living and walking Barbie before Barbie existed.

When a job was called in, the two office assistants scoured the models' schedules to see who would go. The WP jobs were, in Celeste's opinion, by far the worst. WP stood for "weather permitting," and there had been times that she had had to wait for ten afternoons until the weather cleared up, during which time the Powers schedulers could not book her for anything else.

After two years as a $5-for-one-and-a-half-hours model, Celeste had promoted herself to a $5-for-one-hour model. It was up to the models themselves to decide when they wanted to raise their price, when they thought clients were ready to pay up; of Powers's four hundred girls, only twenty were at the $10-an-hour rate, and Celeste, being a realist, doubted she would get there.

But Celeste was talented, and she could adjust her hair and makeup to look anywhere from eighteen to thirty-five. She had once played the part of a "loving mother giving a cookie to a rather large child," although she did not enjoy working with juvenile models, who were generally badly behaved; once she swatted one when his mother wasn't looking. The jobs called "objectionables" paid double, and included posing with depilatories or deodorants and in bathing suits, brassieres, and step-ins. Celeste's most objectionable "objectionable" was when she had had to bathe in Colman's mustard, after which the proposed advertising campaign, claiming health benefits for sore muscles, was abandoned. Celeste was undoubtedly a workingwoman, no less than the Gibbs secretaries, however different their jobs might appear at first glance. Both the Gibbs girls and the Powers models were in the business of making a living in the professions that had been allotted to them as "women's work" during the Great Depression.

+

It was this shift in the Barbizon's residents during the 1930s—to eager professionals determined to work, even if within the confines of what was not only considered ladylike but also exclusively female—that solidified the hotel's reputation as the premier landing spot for young, ambitious, beautiful women. In 1938, Kathryn

Scola, a prolific screenwriter, booked herself into the Barbizon for two weeks, billing her expenses to 20th Century Fox. Her instructions were to observe, absorb, and write a movie script about what she saw. She soaked up the atmosphere of what *Washington Post* columnist Alice Hughes described at the time as "a fine big secular nunnery," its ornate lobby filled with young men who "all look as though a house detective were about to pitch them into the street on the seat of their best ice-cream pants. And the girls are mighty grand to look at, too, most of them. Models, mannequins, and such-like." It was the models, of course, who would become Scola's focus. The film script she wrote was to be called *Hotel for Women*. The film's director, Gregory Ratoff, at first hired Elsa Maxwell, the Waldorf Astoria's famous party planner, as the technical director for the movie's party sequence, but he soon insisted that she work with Scola on the film's storyline as well.

Elsa Maxwell was an American phenomenon, an unlikely rags-to-riches tale. She had started to cultivate her party-planning skills at the age of twelve when she was told she was too poor to be invited to a friend's party. As she grew, so did her parties, and by the time she was an adult "party planner," an entirely new job category thanks to Elsa, her events were showstopping. Her parties for the rich and famous put Venice's Lido on the map, after which she was hired by Monaco to do the same, and she created havoc in Paris when she organized a scavenger hunt there. A woman who was not in the least attractive and dressed, as the *New York Times* noted, in "mannish toggery," her reputation was still such that when she returned to New York in 1931, in the thick of the Depression, the Waldorf Astoria gave her a suite rent-free to attract clientele to the new hotel and paid her to entertain them. Under her supervision, Kathryn Scola's film was suddenly retitled *Elsa Maxwell's Hotel for Women*.

Elsa Maxwell's helping hand was a heavy one. The movie's heroine, Marcia Bromely, arrives at the Sherrington (a fictionalized version of the Barbizon) from Syracuse. She is in New York to marry her boyfriend, Jeff, an architect. But at dinner that night, Jeff tells her he needs to advance his career, and that means no ties, and no marriage. Back at the women-only hotel, as Marcia prepares to return home, she meets two of her hallmates, both older models. With no train to Syracuse until the next day, she agrees to accompany one of them on a double date with two South American millionaires. At the Pelican Club (a stand-in for the famous Stork Club), she is predictably sighted by her now ex-boyfriend (who, just as predictably, is on a date with his boss's daughter); yet more predictably, he seethes with jealousy upon seeing Marcia with the millionaires. Marcia soon becomes a model herself, and even wins out against a fellow Sherrington model/resident to become the next Cambridge Cigarette girl. Now Marcia begins to date Jeff's boss, whom she meets at a cocktail party at the Blue Room hosted by none other than society hostess Elsa Maxwell (set up to be Elsa's starring moment, a reviewer simply noted that she said her words far too quickly).

Elsa Maxwell's Hotel for Women came out in movie theaters as the air had begun to shift and the Depression was finally starting to recede. The Barbizon reawakened as steadily as the economy, and once again getting a room at the premier women's hotel was a process intended to underscore the hotel's prestige. Serious references were required. So it was that Phyllis McCarthy of Worcester, Massachusetts, submitted an application for a room at the Barbizon and asked a well-connected friend, St. Clair McKelway, the managing editor of the *New Yorker*, to be her reference. The Barbizon's manager at the time, Bruno R. Wiedermann, checking on her credentials, wrote to St. Clair to ask for his "opinion as to the desirability of Miss McCarthy."

Wiedermann's wording was impossible for St. Clair to pass up, and he had a field day, sending the Barbizon's manager a typed four-page letter: "It certainly is a coincidence that you should write me just at this time, when the desirability of Miss McCarthy is practically the only thing on my mind. . . . I never thought I would be confiding in a hotel manager about her but you asked for it, Bruno, so here goes: Miss McCarthy is just about as desirable as a girl can be. She is tall, just about the right height for a six-foot man, blond, with longish hair that has a way of falling all around her face in spite of the efforts of hairdressers and herself to keep it orderly. It is nicer when not orderly." To keep fit, St. Clair continued, "she rides on occasion, handles the jibs and sometimes the helm of a sloop, dances until four and fights her way in and out of the Stork Club, using her escort as a club. . . . She dresses beautifully and is inclined to buy a grey suit for $150 or so when she hasn't got $150, much less a so; she is apt, also, to choose a grey suit because she happens to like that particular grey suit and entirely disregard the fact, in doing so, that she has neither grey shoes, grey hat or grey gloves and consequently will be forced to buy these, too, with what she has left out of the $150 or so she didn't have in the first place."

That this was indeed Phyllis McCarthy's approach to life was quite accidentally confirmed in a newspaper piece written by a George Bushfield about an afternoon he had spent in New York visiting his friend Hank Harleton, an advertising man. Hank lived in a bachelor pad on Lexington Avenue, with a back terrace that looked directly onto the Barbizon. Bushfield kidded his friend about the priceless location of his apartment, and Hank admitted that sometimes things did happen; just that day a crumpled piece of a paper had been carelessly tossed out a window of the hotel and landed on his terrace many floors down. The four-by-five-inch paper was a telephone message from the Barbizon's front desk for a McCarthy in Room 1515. The Carlisle bookstore had called to say that her copy of *How Green Was My Valley* had arrived. On the back, before discarding the telephone message, McCarthy had written up her weekly expenses: *$18.50 Rent; 2.00 Mom; .13 Postage; .23 Books; .10 Fares; .70 Mon. Dinner; .20 Mon. Breakfast; .25 Mon. Lunch; .50 Five & Ten; .25 Breakfast Tues.; .30*

Cigs; .25 Breakfast Wed.; .15 Candy & Coke. From this, George and Hank deduced, or thought they had, that McCarthy was a small-town girl (why else so much postage to write letters home?), not independently wealthy ($2.00 for Mom?), slender (she could indulge in candy and Coke!), independent (not easy to pay $18.50 for a weekly rent), wined and dined by the opposite sex (no need to pay for Tuesday nor Wednesday dinners), and nervous (30 cents got you two packs of cigarettes). It turned out that the stunning Phyllis McCarthy, who had the look of a movie star taking a short break on Cape Cod, and whose desirability was very much on the mind of *New Yorker* editor St. Clair McKelway, was of course a Barbizon-residing Powers model.

While the Barbizon was populated with Gibbs girls and Powers models throughout the 1930s, the hotel continued to serve as a sanctuary for many others too. Robin Chandler Duke, later a Wall Street pioneer and President Bill Clinton's Norwegian ambassador, lived in a room there with her mother and sister after their father abruptly abandoned both the family law firm and the family. Her mother, a privileged Southern belle, took work as a cashier in a New York tearoom, Robin's sister got work as a high-fashion model, and Robin herself found work as a house model at the Lord & Taylor department store after lying that she was eighteen when she was in fact two years younger. Her job was to swan around the store in Balenciaga clothes to pique the customers' interest. In the evenings she returned to their Barbizon room, where the three women in her once well-off family now lived together like "three little bears." It was indicative of the times that these were the sorts of jobs open to these three women, and that they were in fact grateful to have them, and that the Barbizon, as glamorously as it was portrayed by screenwriter Kathryn Scola, was also willing to look the other way when all three made a home in their tiny shared room.

But the economic climate was starting to improve, and in 1940, the Barbizon declared itself "free and clear of mortgage." The hotel was running a profit of $103,476 for the year, significantly up from $63,676 two years before. What had in part made those numbers surge forward between 1938 and 1940 was the millions of visitors to the World's Fair out in Flushing Meadows, Queens. Built on an ash dump, the fair's theme was "Building the World of Tomorrow," suggesting the new sense of hope as the economy improved. On the 150th anniversary of George Washington's inauguration in New York, President Franklin D. Roosevelt gave the opening speech. Two hundred television sets were scattered throughout the fair so the first day's visitors could experience that next revolutionary medium. The fair was open spring and fall, in both 1939 and 1940; a gravy train for New York and its hotels as 44 million visitors searched for a place to lay their heads.

Powers models posing at the 1939 New York World's Fair.

The Barbizon Hotel Corporation, feeling flush, purchased, with cash, the building adjoining it, thereby securing the hotel's light in the future: no one would be able to build there and obstruct the sun. As if to mark this moment of becoming unshackled from its Depression-era debt, the Barbizon also put up a marquee at the main entrance of the hotel, on Sixty-Third Street. Designed by architects Schwartz & Gross, it was made to match the style of the hotel's architecture. The marquee was thirty feet in length, art deco: the fascia built of bronze, with panels of aluminite. The name "The Barbizon" was cut out in the bronze fascia so that the light shone through.

While the Barbizon could assert its future with the guarantee of natural light going forward and an enormous bronze marquee to mark its continued presence, most young women emerged from the Great Depression with a string of broken promises. The better-off among them had imagined, and until that fateful week in October 1929 had been brought up to expect, a leisurely life of ice-skating, horseback riding, outings, cars, dates, and friends. What they got instead was one pair of shoes, perhaps a second as a spare. When the financial dark clouds finally cleared, they wanted to make up for the fun they had missed out on as an entire generation. The war that had just started in Europe, far across the Atlantic—at the same time as Phyllis McCarthy was worrying about getting a room at the Barbizon—at first hardly registered. But that too would come to an end.

Evelyn Echols, whom Mr. Powers had declared to be the most typical Midwesterner, was now married and had just finished lunch on Sunday, December 7, 1941. It was a bright sunny day in New York, and she and her husband were reading the doorstopper-size Sunday edition of the *New York Times* and listening to the New York Giants' game on the radio at home. The broadcast was suddenly interrupted with the announcement that all servicemen and women were to return to their stations immediately. There was nothing more after that, no explanation. Evelyn and her husband sat and waited until finally the next announcement came: Japan had attacked Pearl Harbor, and America was now at war. A third announcement followed: *Cover all windows and do not allow any light to escape. Do not use the telephone, because all telephone lines at this time must be reserved for the government.* Evelyn got up and switched off all the lights, and as she looked out her window in the direction of Times Square—the very place where she had stood as a twenty-one-year-old and sworn she would never leave New York—she could not believe her eyes: there was "not one speck of light showing in the entire city."

Men left for war, and women were now expected to take over their jobs—even as before they had been reprimanded for it. When General "Wild Bill" Donovan put out a call for women to come work for the Office of Strategic Services, the predecessor to the CIA, he explained the ideal employee would be "a cross between a Smith College graduate, a Powers model, and a Katie Gibbs secretary." He might as well have come right over to Mrs. Mae Sibley at the front desk and asked for a Barbizon resident.

CHAPTER THREE

McCarthyism and
Its Female Prey

Betsy Talbot Blackwell and Her Career Women

The remarkable Betsy Talbot Blackwell (far left), editor-in-chief of *Mademoiselle* magazine, who was never seen without a hat, posing alongside two similarly hatted models. In 1944, she decided the winners of the prestigious guest editor contest would stay at the Barbizon, thereby opening its doors to Sylvia Plath, Joan Didion, Betsey Johnson, and many others.

There were two types of office-bound women. There were the secretaries who flooded New York's shiny new skyscrapers in the 1920s and then hung on as best they could through the Great Depression. And then there were the women who had not just jobs but careers. Betsy Talbot Blackwell, or BTB, as she signed herself, was one of them. She wore a hat at all times, without fail, so much so that one newspaper claimed she even wore it in the bathtub. She would pull out the Scotch at 5:00 p.m., "when the sun is over the yardarm," she'd say. She was a Republican amid a sea of New York liberal literati, who were her staff. While women were still climbing their way into the workforce, grasping one widely spaced rung at a time, there was a handful of women in the 1930s and 1940s that already had seats at the men's table. Blackwell, editor-in-chief of *Mademoiselle*, was one of them. BTB directed so many other career women—her employees, her protégés, her readers—to the Barbizon that she would tie the reputation of *Mademoiselle* magazine to the hotel forever, so that the fate of one followed that of the other, and the hallways of both became shelter as well as testing ground for generations of ambitious women.

Betsy Talbot Blackwell was never willing to reveal her true age but her staff guessed she'd been born in 1905, and indeed there is a photograph of her as a small girl, taken around the same year that the Unsinkable Molly Brown survived the *Titanic*. Betsy is dressed in the dropped-waist Edwardian fashion of the time, hat on, clutching her doll, staring at the camera. Her penchant for hats started early. Fifty years later she would fondly recall that same hat: "I remember it well—a kind of golden brown upholstery velvet, trimmed with mink bandings and heather. The coat matched it . . . the whole ensemble was quite elegant. You can see I was fashion conscious at the age of six, or whatever it was. . . ." BTB's father, Hayden Talbot, was a newspaper correspondent and playwright, while her mother, Benedict Bristow Talbot, an artist, was one of the first known stylists and taught her daughter about "all things beautiful and visual."

Everyone needs an origin story, and BTB's included the hat—as well as a pair of golden slippers. She spied them in a shop window and was determined to have them, but being only fifteen, she needed a job to pay for them: for three weeks, during her Easter vacation from New Jersey's Academy of Saint Elizabeth, BTB worked as a comparison shopper for Lord & Taylor on Fifth Avenue. She was hooked. When she graduated high school, she got a job as a fashion reporter for a trade magazine, and in 1923—at the height of flapperdom—she joined *Charm* magazine, eventually becoming the fashion editor there. Two years after joining *Charm*, she got married, but her husband did not believe a wife should work, and she soon had the marriage dissolved. Remarrying in 1930, she chose a man who was not bothered by a working wife, mostly because, she said, his first wife had not been one and so he was clueless about what that meant.

In 1935, Street & Smith, the pulp publishers who put out *Charm*, decided to start a magazine called *Mademoiselle*. The daughter of the vice president of Street & Smith, a student at the prestigious all-girls Emma Willard School in Albany, complained that she and her classmates were fed up with *Harper's Bazaar* and *Vogue*. With only haute couture on the one hand, or else sewing patterns on the other, the existing women's magazines catered either to rich ladies with lavish funds or frumpy middle-class housewives with a sewing machine. The Emma Willard girls wanted a magazine with youthful fashion that cared about the problems of young women like themselves. It was, as BTB would later say, an entirely suicidal proposition: not only was it the Depression, but there was no such thing as a youth market, and young women especially had no status, no leverage, no disposable income, no purchasing power, nothing. If that were not bad enough, the first issue, in February 1935, came out with a front cover featuring a poorly rendered illustration of a girl with enormous eyelashed eyes and a puckered mouth. It was a complete disaster, and the only people to buy it were men who thought it was a saucy girlie mag: soft porn circa 1935. Horrified, Street & Smith employees were sent out into the streets to wrestle the publication back from news vendors.

That's when Blackwell, now around thirty years old, was called in. On a miserable February morning, she was summoned by her old employer, Street & Smith, to the CBS Building and shown offices that were the size of "2¼ rooms." They asked her to come on board this fast-sinking ship. The salaries on offer were low, even by Depression-era standards, expenses nonexistent (pilfering from the stamp box was the only way to reimburse yourself), and the offices minuscule. It was the mid-1930s, and skirts were long and felt hats large and raffish, pulled down over one eye. Trench coats were in too. BTB agreed to give it a go.

There was no March 1935 issue of *Mademoiselle*; the magazine only returned to newsstands in April, revamped under BTB's keen eye and iron hand. She changed around the entire magazine and introduced America to the first-ever magazine makeover (on a Boston nurse named Barbara Phillips). Blackwell directed her staff to avoid "Prize Recipes, Romantic fiction written with a stencil. Articles on how to handle six-year-olds, etc. Stuffed shirts. Sublime acceptance of everything the publicity men tell you, and the apparently general assumption that all young women in America actively interested in fashion are either nieces of J. P. Morgan or slaves to [sewing] patterns." The magazine was entirely geared toward younger women, from seventeen to twenty-five, from high school to early married. Two years later, in 1937, Blackwell was promoted to editor-in-chief, and became "BTB."

Despite the hats, BTB was no fashionista. In fact, she seemed to be perpetually "dressed for a ladies' tea." She was often referred to as homely; and while she was no beauty queen, photographs do show a well-presented woman with dark hair cut to just above the collar, with greenish Bette Davis–like sunken eyes, and a carefully lipsticked mouth. She looked something like a squishy, middle-aged Judy Garland. Her love of shoes, not just hats, was legendary and a central motif in her office, down to the custom-designed shoe wallpaper in her private bathroom and the collection of miniature shoes all about. The office itself was gloriously green: green walls, green carpet, the chairs were upholstered in green, her English desk was painted green, and there was even a green telephone. And then there was the pink, *Mademoiselle*'s signature color. The stationery was pink, the parties were pink, and the invitations to the parties were pink.

Her golden rule was that "the staff must get younger every year, even if it kills them in the process." But even if the directive was meant as a joke, it held a fundamental truth: *Mademoiselle*'s readership was going to remain young, even as BTB and her staff did not. So she came up with the *Mademoiselle* College Board. The idea was to have hundreds of female college students throughout the United States relaying back to the New York offices the latest trends and news and consumable desires. In one fell swoop, BTB not only brought in the voices of the young women who were the magazine's target readers but also, not so incidentally, reaped the enormous financial benefits of having scouts with their ears to the ground who could feed information to BTB. She then held that information hostage over her advertisers, who were desperate for this level of marketing data. No one had ever done anything like it before. After establishing the College Board, she permanently recast the August issue of *Mademoiselle* as the College Issue, soon nicknamed "the bible" because no college girl would deign to return for her fall semester without consulting it for what to wear, read, and think in the coming school year. What BTB had effectively done was turn "dreadful" August, known for its sluggish advertising and even worse newsstand sales, entirely on its head.

She soon followed with yet another ingenious idea: the guest editor program. She hit upon the idea at a meeting with a very contemporary ring to it: a small group of staff members was discussing what to feature for prom-wear in the upcoming August College Issue. The College Board editor, just three years out of Vassar, said, "Well, I can tell you what I wore to the junior prom." A nineteen-year-old who was at the meeting turned to the twenty-five-year-old Vassar graduate and, with a sneer, replied, "How could *you* know what anyone would wear today?" This gave BTB pause: "If the Vassar graduate was on the shelf, what about *us*? That did it." *Mademoiselle*'s guest editor contest was born.

Later, the *Los Angeles Times* would insist that the famous editor-in-chief Blackwell "took plain young women to New York, where she put them in stylish clothes, restyled their hair and makeup and then put their pictures in her magazine." But the guest editor contest was far more complex, prestigious, and powerful. The *Mademoiselle* GE program was the most sought-after launching pad for girls with literary and artistic ambitions. Throughout the 1940s, '50s, and '60s, college dormitory rooms were busy with girls working on essays and short stories and artwork they hoped *Mademoiselle* would publish or, better yet, would make them a summer guest editor. If you were lucky enough to be one of the chosen twenty, you were brought to New York for the month of June to shadow senior editors at *Mademoiselle* and to stay—of course!—at the Barbizon Hotel for Women.

The perfect guest editor (much like the perfect reader) was spelled out in the magazine's tagline: *The Magazine for Smart Young Women*. The "smart young woman" was ready for both a poetry reading and a college party and needed to know what to wear to both. She liked to dress well but without spending a fortune: *Mademoiselle* was the first to turn the spotlight away from Paris fashion, to focus on American designers and actually print the prices of the clothes it featured, most of them midrange and accessible. It did so timidly at first—"GADABOUT CARDIGAN. 100% wool and kid mohair . . . About $4"—but soon enough was defiantly listing the price of clothing down to the last cent. Advertisers went crazy for the College Issue idea, so much so that when BTB was sharing a cab with a fellow editor from another magazine, she asked if they didn't have some fiction in a bottom drawer to sell her so she could fill up the magazine's pages now bloated by advertising. But in fact it was not just the August College Issue; each issue of *Mademoiselle* was hypnotic for the college girl because it was never just about fashion. ABC news reporter Lynn Sherr—herself one of the chosen, in the summer of 1962—summarized its appeal: "If you were young and your head was filled with literary aspirations, you read *Mademoiselle*."

The February 1954 *Mademoiselle* issue would famously have just two headlines on its front cover: "Romantic fashions for spring, for brides, for tall girls" and "Dylan Thomas' Under Milk Wood." The publishers originally refused to let *Mademoiselle* devote twenty pages to the late Dylan Thomas and his verse play, *Under Milk Wood*, never yet published. But BTB put down her foot and argued that, contrary to what they thought, it *would* sell fashion, and if they didn't let her go ahead with it, she would be resigning at 5:30 p.m. that same day. She got her way, and the intellectual value of *Mademoiselle* surged yet again, along with its profits. It was BTB's genius in combining the frivolous with the serious that ultimately hooked readers and differentiated the magazine from all others on the newsstand. BTB reasoned that her readers were studying the literary masters in college and so why insult them with anything less in their favorite magazine? *Mademoiselle* became a prolific publisher of foreign authors such as Alberto Moravia and Eugène Ionesco, as well as creating a space for young avant-garde writers who had nowhere else to go.

But BTB was a businesswoman first and foremost, and taking this intellectual route was also financially expedient: she did not have the budget for bestselling authors, which forced the fiction department to find up-and-coming writers at rock-bottom prices, including Truman Capote, James Purdy, Flannery O'Connor, and Edward Albee. Between the just-discovered writers and the affordable fashions modeled by young collegiate types, the magazine fed the desires of ambitious, pretty, creative young coeds, and the guest editor program was the honey to the bees. In the years ahead, it would entice future writers Sylvia Plath, Joan Didion, Ann Beattie, Diane Johnson, Mona Simpson, Meg Wolitzer, Janet Burroway, as well as actress Ali MacGraw and fashion designer Betsey Johnson. Each of them walked the hallways of *Mademoiselle*; all of them spent their nights at the Barbizon.

It was back in 1944, toward the end of World War II, that BTB decided that the "Millies," as the guest editors would later be called, needed to be housed at the Barbizon. On the one hand, the Barbizon fit the image that *Mademoiselle* projected; on the other, housing the GEs there was also the best way to convince their parents to give permission for their young daughters to go to New York alone, unchaperoned, often traveling cross-country, by plane and by train, to get there. Because when that telegram from BTB arrived, congratulating you on having won one of the coveted spots in the guest editor program and inviting you to be in New York by the first day of June—even if it meant missing final exams and graduations, there was not one college girl out there who would refuse. The Barbizon helped allay the parents' concerns: their daughters would be appropriately accommodated in a highly reputed and well-secured hotel for women, with curfews, stern front-desk receptionists, a watchful doorman, and a strict policy of never letting men, any men—not fathers, nor brothers, and certainly not boyfriends—anywhere near the bedroom floors. The Barbizon was not just a hotel with rooms, it was protection for young women, and just as it had in the 1920s and 1930s, so too in the 1940s still, protection meant freedom. In the case of the young GEs, it meant the freedom to come to New York and get a head start on their own lives as career women.

+

Young women during World War II were being told they could do anything they put their minds to. That promise was cemented by Rosie the Riveter's relentless message. Wherever one looked, there was Rosie, America's favorite poster girl, with a red-and-white polka-dot bandanna keeping her hair out of the machinery, flexing her biceps, urging women that "We Can Do It!" Among the young women she fired up was Nanette Emery, although Nanette had no interest in testing her skills on the factory floor: she was more interested in following in the footsteps of BTB.

Nanette Emery, a dark-haired Bryn Mawr College sophomore from Detroit, approached the 1945 guest editor contest with calculated ferocity. Her first step was to get accepted onto the *Mademoiselle* College Board. Back in *Mademoiselle*'s New York offices, a map of the United States stretched across one wall, with each board member's college location marked by a red pin. That this setup mimicked a war room was no accident; throughout World War II, Blackwell had worked closely with the US government to help recruit her readers for women's wartime services like the Women's Army Corps (WAC), the navy's WAVES, and the coast guard's SPARS, and the magazine, much like America's culture generally, had been affected by the war effort. A flyer for College Board membership announced: *UNDER-GRADS ATTENTION! Mlle INVITES YOU to enlist now for the COLLEGE BOARD. No commissions—but War Stamps and Bonds for silver-barred ideas from collegiate artists, writers and shutterbugs. For details write to the College Board Editor, MADEMOISELLE, 1 E. 57 ST., New York 22, N.Y.*

College Board editor Phyllis Lee Schwalbe had started at *Mademoiselle* in 1942, when she herself was barely older than the guest editor applicants. Just out of college and more accustomed to serious women who taught Chaucer and Shakespeare, she quickly learned "that Arpège [perfume] by the quart and turquoise eyelids were not the only hallmarks of a fashion magazine editor. One had to make provisions, for example, for a cigarette holder worn out of the side of the mouth, the way a flamenco dancer bites a rose." In 1944, as Nanette was preparing to apply to the *Mademoiselle* College Board as the first step toward her ticket to New York, Phyllis Lee Schwalbe wrote to her: "As you probably know, we've organized the College Board on practically every campus in the country. Being a Board member means covering your campus from head to toe, inside and outside the classroom and dormitory. It means reporting on war activities, new courses, charities, volunteer work, hairdos, fads and fashions, in fact, EVERYTHING that's NEW." (BTB had not been exaggerating when she boasted in a speech to the Fashion Chicago Group that "these assignments tell us what she and her schoolmates like; what they dislike; what they wear; what they pay; what they read, think, and do.") By the 1940s, *Mademoiselle*'s influence was so vast among college-age women that America's colleges themselves worried about the magazine portraying them in a good light. Aware of the power of a young College Board member to make that happen, the Bryn Mawr College administration sent Nanette a note congratulating her on her intention to try out for the board but also asking her to meet with a Mrs. Chadwick-Collins who "does not mean to exercise any censorship over what you send in but she does want to explain a few things to you."

Nanette successfully cleared this first hurdle, but her acceptance to the board was followed by various assignments throughout the school year, and her performance on them was crucial for her guest editor contest chances. The statistics were not in her favor. Eight hundred and fifty young women had won a place on the College Board out of a pool of three to four thousand applicants; from that pool, only fourteen would now win the position of GE (in 1950, this number would expand to twenty). As Schwalbe explained to Nanette, "when stock-taking arrives late in April . . . the brainiest fourteen Board members are whisked to New York for the month of June to slide in beside our own Editors, to be Guest Editors and go everywhere and do everything." Schwalbe was right: the winning GEs first had to prove their worth as writers, artists, critical voices, and college students. But they were also going to be photographed throughout the month of June, and they needed to be pleasant-looking at the very least. An addendum to the application discreetly asked for a snapshot, and the board members' final assignment for the year included a quick PS: "Dig up a tape measure and have your room-or-hallmate take your exact measurements." Nanette was five foot seven, 134 pounds, with a (then) 14 dress size and a very narrow 9AAA shoe.

Nanette did not place in the top ten winners for the first two assignments, but the third time was a charm. The assignment was to "plan a college fashion show which will dramatize, in some new and diverting way, clothes to wear on campus and off." This was no casual, off-the-cuff assignment; the magazine's editors were fishing for new ideas they could use. *Mademoiselle* was in the midst of planning one of its key events for June—the so-called College Clinic. It was a terrible name for an otherwise extravagant fashion show held at the Hotel Astor each year, with much of the clothing modeled by the GEs themselves, showcasing merchandise to be featured in the August College Issue. The College Clinic fashion show was intended to be whimsical, even mildly irreverent, to match the style of the print advertisements the magazine was known for, where perky, peppy college-aged young women—sometimes actual college women, other times Midwestern-looking Powers models—posed, leaning against a bridge, or feeding pigeons at the park, or bicycling across campus, with captions such as: "Pausing to window-wish on a street of antique shops, Joan wears a soft-tailored dress of J. P. Stevens' wool-and-rayon, a McKettrick Classic, $10.93" or "On Sunday the Wall Street canyons look like a ghost town (and some smart money says they are). Near Trinity Church, Joan's snapped in Petti's plaid dirndl with a wool-and-rayon top, $14.95." Nanette, even after she had won the third assignment, did not rest on her laurels but quickly submitted a collection of her poems to *Mademoiselle* and let Schwalbe know that in March—strategically close to when the editors gathered in late April to decide on the list of that summer's guest editors—she would be in New York. Might she stop by the offices? she asked.

Her gamble paid off. *Mademoiselle* did not publish her poems, but Schwalbe did invite Nanette to the magazine's April College Forum (it did help that Nanette was just a train ride away and wartime fuel rationing meant no one a plane ride away could be invited). The College Forum was Schwalbe's pet project. Schwalbe, genuinely concerned about America's direction once the war was over, had approached BTB for permission to put together a conference-type workshop on these very questions. The first College Forum, held in 1944, was shaped by Schwalbe's travels from one campus to another as the magazine's College Board editor, where she discovered that even if students appeared to be participating in the everyday life of American college coeds, they "were squirming in their desk chairs," "wondering if they should be studying while others were fighting." With the war now practically over, the 1945 College Forum, to which she invited Nanette Emery, included a mix of experts and students in panel discussions on topics such as "labor, race, prejudice, political action, world security, postwar education." Photographs of the conference show Nanette as an attentive and intelligent, if somewhat self-conscious, pretty young woman dressed in the heavily shoulder-padded jacket of the 1940s, her hair pinned on the sides and curled at the back, pen poised to take notes. But Nanette had ensured she was seen.

Less than a month later, on May 7, 1945, Germany surrendered to the Allies. The very next day the most anticipated of telegrams arrived for Nanette at Radnor Hall, her Bryn Mawr College dormitory: *HAPPY TO ANNOUNCE YOU HAVE BEEN CHOSEN AS ONE OF MLLE'S APPRENTICE EDITORS DETAILS FOLLOW WIRE ACCEPTANCE VIA WESTERN UNION COLLECT AND DATE OF AVAILABILITY CLOSEST TO JUNE FIRST=BETSY TALBOT BLACKWELL EDITOR-IN-CHIEF MADEMOISELLE.* It was tantamount to winning the golden ticket in *Charlie and the Chocolate Factory*, and GE contest winners needed no convincing to come to New York: Lanie Diamond, a 1947 GE winner, would skip out of UCLA without finishing her finals so she could make it to *Mademoiselle* and the Barbizon on time.

Nanette Emery now had less than three weeks to prepare for her arrival. She certainly knew about the Barbizon. Two years earlier, the stunning redheaded screen star Rita Hayworth had posed for a series of photographs for *Life* magazine in the Barbizon's gym. The photos were impertinent, funny, and a bit risqué. One showed Rita looking bored, rolling her eyes, defiantly sitting down on a chair as the Barbizon's resident models exercised around her—doing handstands, playing table tennis. Another had five women bent over, derrières in decidedly granny knickers facing the photographer, while Rita Hayworth towered over them, her head cocked to the side, exuding sarcasm while staring silently at the reader.

The Barbizon had been steadily building up its reputation during World War II, and Rita Hayworth's photo shoot in the basement gymnasium was part of that. The hotel had polished its public relations approach, starting with the habit of feeding snippets of delicious gossip to *Photoplay* magazine about the young, the ambitious, and the desirable women who were staying at the Barbizon. Nanette would miss out on seeing actresses Elaine Stritch, Cloris Leachman, and Nancy Davis (later Reagan) by exactly one year—they would all reside there in 1946. When Cloris Leachman arrived, recently crowned "Miss Chicago," she was only twenty years old, but three months later, she was already gliding through the aisles of the Bergdorf Goodman department store in a tailored green wool suit beneath a full-length beaver coat, with matching green suede heels. She was an understudy in two Broadway plays and feeling like it was "the most exciting moment of my life."

Nanette Emery felt much the same. She planned to make her New York entrance in a knockoff of the latest "it" dress, the Townley frock by Claire McCardell. McCardell was an American designer inspired by American tastes and traditions. She had blossomed under the restrictions of World War II, when American designers were cut off from Paris, traditionally fashion's epicenter. Among her innovations was a modernized dirndl—the full, wide skirt with a cinched-in waist—and in 1944, she created the ultimate patriotic dress by utilizing government surplus weather-balloon cottons. A year later, McCardell, much like Phyllis Lee Schwalbe, was trying to envision what lay ahead following victory over fascism. Her 1945 collection showcased American pioneering values: she made full use of what she called frontier pants pockets, which she placed on both her trousers and skirts, where they jutted out at provocative sharp angles. (Just two years later, this nod toward the liberating life of the American frontier would give way to Christian Dior's iconic "New Look." At first, American women balked at his overt return to restrictive femininity: skirts just inches from the floor, tightly belted, a bosom in seemingly military uprightness, and all the painful foundation garments that that pertness required. Yet the New Look quickly trumped McCardell's earlier postwar vision.)

But it was still 1945, McCardell was very much in fashion, the war in Europe had finally ended, and Nanette was heading to the Barbizon. The air was full of questions that were waiting to be answered and a postwar optimism that was infectious. Joseph Stalin was still being referred to as "Uncle Joe," the Cold War was not yet in clear sight, and it would be five years before Senator McCarthy unleashed his witch hunt for covert communists. In this immediate moment, what the Depression and then the Second World War had taught Nanette and her friends was that fun was fleeting and they should grab it while they could.

Schwalbe wrote to Nanette and the other thirteen guest editor winners that they would be the second group housed at the Barbizon. She noted that "last year our Apprentice Editors enjoyed living a kind of dormitory-hotel life at the Barbizon Hotel for Women," but she also warned that "you must be prepared to accept whatever accommodations there are available." Along with Schwalbe's letter, Nanette received the Barbizon brochure, a thick-paged, beautifully photographed presentation of where she would be living, which looked far from a "dormitory-hotel." The brochure offered glamorous shots of the library, the music room, and the sunny solarium among the hotel's turrets. The hotel stationery suggested both luxury and femininity: the name, *The Barbizon*, topped the sheet of delicate paper, drawn out in a perfect, feminine curly script, with small block letters below for the address—LEXINGTON AVENUE AT 63RD STREET, NEW YORK 21, N.Y. From there on, until the program's end in 1979, every group of guest editors would stay at the Barbizon.

Phyllis Lee Schwalbe advised Nanette and the other contest winners that "your wardrobe will best be cool, dark city clothes for work," and that "MLLE's own pet taboos are hatlessness and white shoes." Schwalbe's message was loud and clear: these fourteen young women, chosen to be guest editors from all across the United States, were to show up in sophisticated New York fashions and *not* their hometown looks. Schwalbe's concern was warranted. The writer Diane Johnson, author of a string of successful novels including *Le Divorce*, guest editor in 1953 at the age of nineteen, was typical in that she had never been "east of the Mississippi." For her, the requisite hat worn by Blackwell and all the other successful New York women was entirely alien: "Hats were known, of course, in my hometown of Moline, Illinois; I can see my mother putting hers on to go downtown or on occasion (Easter) to church." But standing before the *Mademoiselle* staff upon arrival, Diane and her fellow guest editors (including Sylvia Plath), while excellent students and ambitious young women, were not exactly glamour personified: "Twenty girls from California and Utah and Missouri—our clothes turned those editors pale, our hats dismayed, timid churchgoing lids borrowed from our mothers."

While the GEs were expected to have new hats and new clothes, the *Mademoiselle* program was not exactly lucrative summer work, and those without extra means were often left hanging, looking to borrow, while everyone else was writing home to ask for money to be wired ASAP. Nanette, like the others, would receive $150 for the month of June, a sum that—rather cleverly—legally covered "payment for all photographic modeling for MADEMOISELLE, for short stories, articles, ideas or artwork accepted for publication." One hundred and fifty dollars, while more than adequate for girls like Nanette who could afford to bring more for extras, barely covered the month's expenses, especially when many costs came up front whereas *Mademoiselle*'s first paycheck only arrived midmonth. (The sum of $150—before taxes—would not change for another nine years until finally, in 1954, the GEs got a pay raise of $25 when it was pointed out that by then it cost $60 to stay at the Barbizon for the month, and when compared to college graduates starting their first jobs in the city, and getting paid $195 while paying $30 to $40 for small apartments or apartment group shares, it just did not add up.)

Nanette, with the luxury of not having to worry about the $150 paycheck, was determined to make June 1945 exactly as she had imagined it. Nanette stayed in room 1411 at the Barbizon, receiving frequent telephone messages from the operator, which she picked up from the front desk whenever she returned home. Her friends trying to reach her at the Barbizon did not hesitate to say they would call her back at midnight. Late nights were nothing out of the ordinary for Barbizon residents like Nanette, unlike for the unfortunate ones placed on the curfew list by their parents or else for the Gibbs girls, with their own house mothers who ensured they went early to bed, fresh for morning classes.

One of Nanette Emery's many telephone messages from the front-desk staff.

Everything was at Nanette's fingertips at the Barbizon: without ever leaving the building, via a small corridor off the lobby, she could access Nate Scollar's drugstore or buy new novels at Miss Crystal's, and if she had been artistically inclined, she could even have exhibited her work on the mezzanine gallery free of charge. If anything were to go wrong, there was always the Barbizon's new bespectacled manager, Hugh J. Connor, a little like a boring uncle but a caring one. He sent flowers to guests who were sick and offered $5 and $10 advances to those waiting for funds. If parents wanted him to dish out a weekly allowance, he did. His know-how of both New York and business was also on offer, and he had recently helped a Fort Wayne native with a dress shop on East Fifty-Fourth Street set up a second location.

Mrs. Mae Sibley, assistant manager and front-desk monitor, swung between role of mother hen and strict enforcer. It was she who pulled aside any young residents who were returning home to their rooms too late too often; she would ask them what their parents might think, and then if nothing changed, suggest that their room would shortly be needed, which would bring a torrent of tears and pleas for forgiveness. Doorman Oscar Beck was 220 pounds of overwrought enthusiasm, who took delight in holding open cab doors for the Barbizon's resident ladies and welcoming them home as reliably as a puppy. When men would drive by the hotel, hollering at Oscar to give them some numbers, he would call out the number for the hotel's front desk—Templeton 8-5700. One Ohio resident explained that Oscar, with a thick German accent that he had never shed, "burbles and gurgles, and no one knows quite what he says, but the impression is that you're just about the prettiest thing on earth."

Oscar Beck, the Barbizon's longtime doorman.

Nanette did not need Oscar's extra encouragement, nor Sibley's warnings or Connor's advice. As soon as she arrived in New York, she transformed from the serious young woman talking politics at the April College Forum to a girl about town. Assigned to be guest editor of health and beauty ("health" had been added to "beauty" as part of the war effort—a gesture to move away from the frivolous), on the very first day she lunched with her editor, the famous Miss Bernice Peck, whom she found "startlingly wonderful and frank." Miss Peck, who would end up being *Mademoiselle*'s beauty editor for twenty-four years, was not wracked by the need to be or stay beautiful, and consequently injected humor into the battle for beauty, turning her back on "solemn" discussions of "what cream you rubbed into your navel." Nanette finished her first day by dining with three other GEs in the Barbizon's main dining room, which the hotel brochure she had studied nightly before arrival described as "reflecting an Old Charleston atmosphere" with "pastel colors and delightful flower murals of Southern inspiration." Dinner entrées cost anywhere from 55 cents to $1.50. After dinner, Nanette and her new friends went off to explore the hotel's sundeck, then took a stroll to the Waldorf Astoria and made their way up Fifth Avenue, ending with ice cream at Schrafft's, the go-to restaurant chain for women at that time, its interiors intentionally designed to evoke the gentility of an upper-middle-class WASP household. Nanette felt perfectly at home.

In fact, within a matter of days, Nanette had made herself entirely at home in Manhattan. During one breathless evening, she managed to squeeze in a quick trip to Delmonico's Officers' Club, where she and another of the GEs were photographed with their dates for a fashion shoot titled "prize date dress." Next came a formal dance, which the girls left at 10:30 p.m. to grab a cab to the Barrymore Theatre, where Nanette interviewed Katharine Cornell for the "We Hitch Our Wagons" feature, a perennial favorite in the *Mademoiselle* August College Issue, where each GE interviewed someone famous who inspired them. Nanette was photographed sitting with the actress, whose dogs lounged on both their laps. "Flash bulbs flashing, the Cornell Daschunds, Illo and Looney, and scintillating conversation with la Cornell," Nanette wrote breathlessly in her diary. (Other GEs chose more judiciously, one interviewing the artist Marc Chagall—communicating in French and "American" with "wild gestures and leaping eyebrows"—and another the writer and German refugee, Nobel Prize winner Thomas Mann.) Then back to the famed Delmonico's restaurant at 11:45 p.m. and a double date with two brothers, a marine and an army officer, and finally, in the early morning hours, over to "a German restaurant where someone was playing a piano and everyone was singing Irish songs. Knockwurst sandwiches and coffee." Nanette was on a postwar rampage of fun, lightness, and frivolity.

Along the way, she collected memorabilia like an out-of-control tourist—from the Plaza's Oak Room, which, by tradition, was reserved until 3:00 p.m. on Mondays through Fridays for gentlemen only; from the Persian Room, its calling card saturated with sumptuous reds and golds, where Bob Grant and his orchestra played after 9:30 p.m. for a $1.50 cover charge; from the Cotillion Room at the Pierre hotel, where Myrus, the Man with the X-ray Eyes, the Wizard of Mental Telepathy, performed, answering pressing questions that guests wrote out on small pieces of white cardstock. When General Ike Eisenhower rode down Fifth Avenue to mark US victory in the war, Nanette and the other thirteen GEs joined the crowds: "Standing room was at a premium so we hailed the general from atop a garbage truck. Wonderful to see five million persons cheering for the same team . . . ," they reported for *Mademoiselle*. On less exciting days, Nanette ate at the Barbizon, often choosing the coffee shop or else the veranda room ("a balcony with lacy iron work and flower gardens painted against azure sky"), adjacent to the main dining room, where the guest editors could get breakfast for 25 to 65 cents, and lunch 35 to 65 cents. If she preferred to go out, Nanette chose Longchamps, an upscale chain in New York, or else Stouffer's on Second Avenue—when it was still a popular restaurant and not a frozen TV-dinner brand.

Nanette's workload was not demanding because, as the editors explained to the GEs, much of the copy for the August College Issue had to be done long before they arrived. Even so, Nanette managed to squeeze in a byline here and there, reporting on such pressing issues as dieting off those extra freshman pounds by possibly joining or, better yet, starting a diet table at one's college dining hall. Consulting with an expert in the field, who, as she wrote, had "de-fatted something like a quarter million American females," Nanette passed on the advice that chubby college girls should band together and demand from their parents bushels of unrationed fruit and vegetables, which they should divvy up and eat extravagantly before each meal. Clearly the war had done nothing to disrupt the demand—articulated by the corseted Gibson girl and then by the skinny, boyish-looking flapper—that women be slim to be desirable.

On the last Thursday of the month, a day before they were finished with their monthlong program, the guest editors lunched with Blackwell at the Viennese Roof of the St. Regis hotel, where everything—the napkins, the tablecloths, the room—was arranged to be as pink as *Mademoiselle*'s trademark stationery. Nanette returned home to Detroit with her itineraries, her front-desk messages, Barbizon postcards and letterheads and matchbooks, an assortment of ticket stubs, entry tickets, everything really, which she would soon compile into one enormous scrapbook, leather-bound. June 1945 in New York had been everything she could have dreamed it to be. Manhattan of the 1940s, as the writer John Cheever famously declared, was "filled with a river light, when you heard Benny Goodman quartets from a radio in the corner stationery store, and when almost everybody wore a hat." But behind Nanette's breathless descent onto postwar New York, a thrill ride accompanied by the cheerful sounds of the "King of Swing," there loomed the coming Cold War. Career women like BTB, and those in training, like Nanette Emery, would prove to be in the crosshairs of Senator Joseph McCarthy's Red Scare, the series of congressional hearings intent on picking out the traitors in America's midst.

✦

Elizabeth Moulton, then going under the name Betsy Day, was another of the fourteen guest editors in the summer of 1945 who spent her days at *Mademoiselle* and her nights at the Barbizon. Like Nanette, she too had received the same telegram from BTB the day after the war ended in Europe, and with just as much fanfare and excitement, she had packed her bags for New York. When the summer at *Mademoiselle* was over, Elizabeth returned to Radcliffe College and Nanette to Bryn Mawr, but Elizabeth had only one semester left to graduate, and she could not believe her luck when a job as assistant to George Davis, the magazine's associate editor as well as fiction editor, opened up. In the editorial hallways of *Mademoiselle*, he was the only man amid a sea of powerful career women. The GEs found him to be warm and open in a way that the indomitable BTB was not. George Davis urged them to address him by his first name, and each June he "dusted the parochialism off brand-new New Yorkers from Roanoke, Chicago, Key West, Texas, Georgia, Minnesota," helping them achieve style not just in their writing but in their appearance too, sending them home as newly hatched fashionistas who had a way with the written word.

George Davis's reputation preceded him, and all the GEs knew who he was even before they arrived. He had famously dropped out of high school in Ludington, Michigan, and as a sophomore, moved to Paris. There he wrote his first, and what would turn out to be his only, novel at the age of twenty-one (it became a rite of passage that his assistants scoured New York's secondhand bookstores until they found a copy for themselves—and Elizabeth would do that too). George befriended Jacques Prévert, Cocteau, and pretty much everyone else in Paris, returning to New York a decade later to work as fiction editor for *Harper's Bazaar* before moving over to *Mademoiselle*.

Phyllis Lee Schwalbe, when she arrived in the *Mademoiselle* offices in 1942 to work on the College Board, first mistook him for the office porter because he was always gossiping with the telephone operator, leaning in at her desk to keep others from hearing what they said. It was not until the famous writer Carson McCullers arrived one day looking for George that Phyllis was shocked to learn who he was—the very man who had discovered the great writer Truman Capote. George's three-story brownstone at 7 Middagh Street in Brooklyn, bought with a $125 deposit borrowed from the infamous Gypsy Rose Lee, was a thing of legend too: it was a Bohemian-type commune, a famous literary salon, a writers' retreat to rival the famous upstate New York Yaddo, and a funhouse boarding house. George Davis rented rooms not only to Carson McCullers but to other writers such as W. H. Auden, as well as carnival performers, including a monkey trainer.

In 1945, when Nanette Emery and Elizabeth Moulton arrived at *Mademoiselle*, George was a forty-year-old editor who no longer resembled the boyish man from early photographs. He was short, sloping, with a head much bigger than it should have been, with wavy hair on top of it, receding and gray. No looker was he. But his voice stood out: Elizabeth would describe it as "soft, malicious, amused, playful, lucid." She didn't add "malicious" for nothing. In February 1946, Elizabeth joined George's team, which also included his other young assistant, Lelia (Lee) Carson, and assistant fiction editor Margarita (Rita) Smith, the mousy and beleaguered caretaker of her sister, the writer Carson McCullers. Elizabeth's mother, born of an era when female ambition was being stoked, had pushed Elizabeth to succeed, encouraging her to try out for all the contests she could, including *Mademoiselle*'s. That Elizabeth had stayed at the Barbizon, under the careful watch of doorman Oscar Beck, front-desk matron Mrs. Sibley, and hotel manager Connor, calmed her mother's fears: exactly BTB's intention when she decided the Barbizon would be the only place for the GEs to lodge. But when Elizabeth now moved back to New York in 1946, her mother was gripped with terror; on her starting salary, Elizabeth could not afford to move back into the Barbizon. To allay her mother's worries, the only thing she could do was promise to leave Central Park by sundown and to never set foot in Brooklyn: she kept to her promise, missing out on countless parties at George's Brooklyn funhouse.

Working for George was all-consuming. Elizabeth, Lee, and Rita did whatever George needed. It took some time for Elizabeth, even though she was far from sheltered, her father being a playwright, to work out George's sexual orientation. Sex was simply not discussed in those days; it was, Elizabeth noted, "punished or laundered" by the church, the state, and the movie censors. It only started to dawn on her when whoever was on morning desk duty—be it she or Lee—had to shoo away George's French sailor callers from the night before. Lee, a Southerner trained in the subtle art of gracious white lies, diverted and deflected—and taught Elizabeth to do the same.

By fall 1946, George had closed down his Brooklyn commune and moved to a brownstone on East Eighty-Sixth Street in Manhattan with a bad-tempered parrot, "a small, unraveled dog," four to seven cats (it was hard to keep count), and various humans, temporarily camped out. He would call his assistants from there midmorning to say he'd be coming in soon—once he had bathed, shaved, and found enough empty bottles lying around to return for the deposit so he could buy a subway token to get him downtown. Elizabeth and Lee, having made excuses for him all morning, often met him furtively at the back of the building to hand over his paycheck, which he promptly spent on one of his sailors or "protégés."

George's parties remained spectacular, however, and now that they were on the Upper East Side, Elizabeth was able to attend. There were the big parties, paid for by the magazine, that focused on the toasting and fawning of a star guest such as Richard Wright, Henri Cartier-Bresson, or Tennessee Williams, with guests fanned out in concentric circles, the first circle being book and magazine editors, then their assistants, and the last made up of relatives and friends, who were relegated to passing around food and champagne. At one party, a friend with a dog-and-monkey act performed in the standing-room-only back drawing room, leaving a black-turtlenecked Truman Capote and the angry parrot stranded in the front room. Smaller gatherings at George's apartment generally meant seven to ten young *Mademoiselle* staff members espousing leftist fantasies while George, a Democrat, listened in with an avuncular, encouraging smile.

Elizabeth found *Mademoiselle* to be like family, but a family that quarreled at the drop of a hat: in particular, George Davis and managing editor Cyrilly Abels. BTB was a lamb in comparison to Abels, who would soon enough cement her reputation as the ferocious editor who terrorized poet Sylvia Plath into a nervous breakdown. Abels was supposedly an unattractive woman with a large bosom and a closet of haute couture; when once asked in an interview what the fashion editors did, if they ever wrote copy, she laughed: "Write?! They can't even read!" Cyrilly Abels soon became George Davis's "chief—and long-suffering—antagonist," in part because it was her job, as managing editor, to keep everyone to their deadlines, and George wasn't good at deadlines, just as he wasn't good at waking up in the morning for normal workday hours.

There was yet another problem, however: their politics. Abels, a moneyed, highly intellectual Radcliffe College graduate, was defiantly on the left of the political spectrum. It might have been fashionable before the war, but it was becoming decidedly dangerous after.

Their political clashes surfaced in particular when it came time to decide which short stories to include for publication in *Mademoiselle*. George was unwilling to sacrifice form over content; he refused a short story that Abels championed about an embittered African American handyman living on a "filthy basement pallet." She applauded it for its progressive message, and he rejected it for its awkward prose. The battle lines were drawn, and in 1947, a year into Elizabeth's employment as his assistant, George wrote to BTB that he was resigning from his post as fiction editor; it was too much to hold down two editorships, and he would prefer to reduce his job description back down to associate editor of the magazine. Nor did he wish to take part in discussions about the new hire for fiction editor. BTB and Abels agreed and did as he asked; without consulting him, they promoted assistant fiction editor Rita Smith to the job.

For Rita, being the younger sister and emotional caretaker of Carson McCullers was not easy, and everyone in the office knew that it was Rita's particular burden to bear, even as she herself needed propping up. Carson McCullers, pale and sickly, tormented by multiple strokes, eventually smoked and drank herself to death by fifty. The pressure on her was enormous: at the age of only twenty-three, this slight white girl from segregated Georgia wrote the 1940 novel *The Heart Is a Lonely Hunter*. A review by Richard Wright remarked on her uncanny ability as a white writer "for the first time in Southern fiction, to handle Negro characters with as much ease and justice as those of her own race. This cannot be accounted for stylistically or politically; it seems to stem from an attitude toward life which enables McCullers to rise above the pressures of her environment and embrace white and black humanity in one sweep of apprehension and tenderness." Her very vulnerability contributed to her talent.

Rita, her sister, was not without her own vulnerabilities. She was a "plump woman with sad brown eyes," who would go rushing up to Westchester County whenever "Sistuh" called, even as Sistuh had purportedly ruined her life. Rita was afraid of elevators, and instead climbed the stairs to *Mademoiselle*'s sixth-floor offices; nor would she travel on the subway without someone by her side. She left burning cigarettes everywhere she went, and aware of this problem, she feared it spelled the incendiary end of herself and any building in which she had been. It became the job of her assistant to meticulously go through the office at the end of each day in search of any remaining cinders.

Just a year after Rita was promoted to fiction editor, George Davis suddenly wrote an anguished letter to BTB, in which he staked his right to tell the truth on the "sacred duty" of any "serious writer." His "truth" was that "naming Rita Smith as fiction editor is a shameful blot upon your record." Rita was utterly incompetent, he argued, and she was lazy too. Contrary to her claims, she had not worked "months" with Truman Capote: George had. She was perpetually behind in her work, so much so that every few weeks work in his own department ground to a halt as everyone at the magazine was rallied to "read for Rita"—even her friends were called in to help read through the enormous pile of submissions that had accumulated over the weeks. And then there were "the vapors," as George called her alcoholism: "Coffee trailing up ten times a day. Often the poor child was downright drunk and unable to cope. Her part of the office was a nasty shambles, both in appearance and dedication."

Why, George asked rhetorically, was she not fired? He offered the answer himself: because of the fear of what she would do to herself. And then there were the tears—"often boozy and for hours, over the telephone in the middle of the night." And then, of course, there were the family connections. Yet George laid the ultimate blame at the feet of his political nemesis, Cyrilly Abels: "Well, God damn it and to hell, I'm through with that bloody lie. Abels knows full well that Rita is editorially a mess." As to Abels having done a song and dance about how well George had trained Rita: "My answer to that is: I vomit." He finished his letter to BTB, "To repeat: I vomit." That was the nail in the coffin. George Davis resigned from his remaining position of associate editor before he could be fired.

But Abels remained under his skin even after he had left *Mademoiselle*. He could not hold back and wrote to BTB again, explaining that he still needed to vent some more. He wanted to tell his story. He had first met Abels when they both worked at *Harper's Bazaar*, and after he came over to *Mademoiselle*, she had stayed in touch with him, a "shy, warm, idealistic woman"—or so it seemed to him at the time. When BTB said she was having trouble finding a managing editor, he had suggested Cyrilly Abels. He had always known that politically she stood more to the left, but he hadn't thought it mattered. Not until later did he realize that it mattered very much, in fact. At first, George had congratulated himself on how he had helped BTB make a wise choice, and then "Miss Abels began wistfully— and, oh God, how wistfully—to ask if she might occasionally suggest a writer or an idea." The writers were all, George realized, Communist Party members or "fellow travelers," liberals approved by the party. George thought he could keep it under control, but "as it turned out, I couldn't." A veritable cold war had erupted between her department and his, with Abels getting the girls in his department involved in "Commie front committees." But he hadn't said anything; he "dared not risk being called a renegade liberal." He was caught in a trap, as he saw it.

George Davis claimed he was repulsed by Abels's politics, but the nature of his complaints suggested another, unspoken, cause: her female ambition. He wrote: "Understand, I am sure Miss Abels does not belong to the Communist Party. I believe her now to be a woman of staggering ambition, who knows how to use the materials at hand." She had, according to him, adopted all the Communist Party tactics of infiltration to fuel that ambition, including "sweetly and uncomplainingly taking over executive dirty work, of being the first to show up in the morning and the last to leave at night. That way, she makes you, me, everybody, feel guilty as hell. . . . Gradually the loyal drudge is rewarded. More and more power falls into her hands." George explained that the previous year he had held back from saying anything because he did not want to add to the "squalid Red baiting." But, finally, with no other recourse, he had "decided to run, to get out, to back down from the whole rotten business. Yes,

yes, I would write, I would be free again," he had convinced himself as he finally decided to quit.

But as soon as he had given his notice to BTB, George watched Abels "ruthlessly take over my department. I saw the mask of sweet timidity fall." Still caught between a rock and a hard place, as George saw it, there was nothing Abels "would find more exploitable than to have me play the Whittaker Chambers to her Alger Hiss. I shall not do so; the issue is her personal ambition, not her politics." George warned that *Mademoiselle* was being "turned over to a leftist clique," and that it was the talk of New York's literary world. According to him, an editor of the leftist *New York Star* had even said: "Isn't it wonderful what that little Miss Abels is slipping past that stuffy old firm, and that reactionary husband of her boss?" BTB's husband, James Madison Blackwell, referred to by *Mademoiselle*'s staff as "the Colonel," was known to be ultra-conservative, even anti-Semitic and racist. But George was ultimately afraid of women's power.

+

George was really only echoing the zeitgeist of the time. In 1945, the Cold War was still barely on the horizon. Three years later, in 1948, Harry Truman won the presidential election by channeling the growing anti-communist mood in America. Red-baiting became fully entrenched in everyday life, and the family—with wife and mother in the home, and not at the office—was understood to be the most effective safeguard against this new ideological threat emanating from Moscow. In 1949, the Soviet Union showed off its atomic muscle, China joined the communist camp, and America's House Un-American Activities Committee warned Americans about communists, fellow travelers, subversives, and "perverts" (homosexuals) lurking among them.

The "Red Scare" quickly became intertwined with a postwar fear of the feminist. Many wondered if women would be willing to relinquish their wartime "men's jobs" and return to the kitchen. Those who didn't became suspect. Schoolteachers, in particular, being traditionally female, were suddenly seen as potentially dangerous and most likely to spread Soviet propaganda. One Columbia University professor theorized that "the girls' schools and women's colleges contain some of the most loyal disciples of Russia. Teachers there are often frustrated females. They have gone through bitter struggles to attain their positions. A political dogma based on hatred expresses their personal attitudes." And what then could one say about women-staffed women's magazines, these unique enclaves of female employment and empowerment? Let alone women's hotels?

Unsuspecting Nanette Emery had done everything she could to win a place in the 1945 guest editor program, including participate in Phyllis Lee Schwalbe's April College Forum. But by 1949, at the same time that George Davis was lobbing accusations at Cyrilly Abels, Nanette was indirectly under suspicion too. In *Counterattack: The Newsletter of Facts on Communism*, *Mademoiselle* and its publisher, Street & Smith, were put on notice: "Memo to the top people at Street & Smith: You'd better really take a look at your *Mademoiselle* forum, really find out what goes on there. Ask a few questions: Who picks the speakers? What standards are used in making the choice? Does anyone ever investigate what they really stand for?" Referring to the dime novels that Street & Smith was once famous for publishing, particularly a series called the Frank Merriwell Stories about an athletic undergraduate at Yale University who fights crime and rights wrongs, *Counterattack* suggested it would "sadden [Merriwell fans] to think the top men of Street & Smith, in their modern offices at 122 E 42nd St., NY, didn't have enough of the old Merriwell spirit to clean up the Mademoiselle forum and make it gleamingly virtuous." Another Red-seeing newspaper explained that the fifty-five college girls brought over from forty-two colleges for the 1949 forum were viewed as student leaders but, if misled, would become "MISLEADERS."

Yet George Davis was, in theory, just as suspect for his sexual preferences. Truman Capote, in his unfinished novel *Answered Prayers*, did not draw an attractive picture of George Davis, whom he turned into the character of Boaty: "a certain kind of queer who has Freon refrigerating his bloodstream. Diaghilev, for example. J. Edgar Hoover. Hadrian. Not to compare him with those pedestal personages, but the fellow I'm thinking of is Turner Boatwright— Boaty, as his courtiers called him. Mr. Boatwright was the fiction editor of a women's fashion magazine that published 'quality' writers. He came to my attention, or rather I came to his, when one day he spoke to our writing class. I was sitting in the front row, and I could tell, by the way his chilly crotch-watching eyes kept gravitating toward me, what was spinning around in his pretty curly-grey head." In 1951, Davis suddenly married the famous singer Lotte Lenya, the widow of Kurt Weill. George helped revive Weill's remarkable *Threepenny Opera*, as well as Lotte Lenya's career. The notoriously gay editor, a Democrat, beloved by the GEs who saw him only how he wanted to be seen, had become, at the height of McCarthyism, a married man and a borderline Red-baiter. Again he could not hold back and wrote to BTB: he wanted her to know that his life was back on track through "the inspiring support of a remarkable and dear person, my wife," and he felt ready to confess something. He wanted to have it remain between him and BTB, although he did not mind if she shared it with her husband, "the Colonel." Five years earlier, he explained, back in 1948, he had been "horrified by the color of such phrases as 'witch-hunting' and 'red-baiting,'" and even today, in 1953, he was decidedly "opposed to what is called 'McCarthyism' . . ."

"*Yet.*"

Yet a month earlier he had—he confessed now—made an unso-licited visit to the FBI "to tell them everything I know about the Communist infiltration of publishing. What I know is limited to the activities of one person, whom you know." He was of course talking about *Mademoiselle*'s managing editor Cyrilly Abels. His story was listened to "attentively" by the FBI, and when he was asked if there were any doubts as to BTB's loyalties, he answered no—he assured her—"*As positively as you can imagine.*" Yet unable to leave Abels alone, he added a postscript: "I do realize that our friend, in accor-dance with the party line, must now pose as a 'poor-confused liberal' who was taken in intellectually during the Spanish Civil War, etc. etc." BTB was no fool, and she knew she had to launch a preemptive strike. McCarthyism was not generous to career women. She con-tacted Street & Smith's legal team, and two weeks later they wrote to her in Paris to let her know that they had decided it would be best to go see the FBI themselves, "voluntarily."

George Davis's swift slide into McCarthyism, even as he swore he was against the Red-baiting, clearly conflated communism with a distaste for ambitious women. In this, George, albeit a bohemian, a homosexual, and a New Yorker, was not so very different from many other Americans. As BTB sat in her green office, a glass of Scotch in her hand, and then another, reading George Davis's written missives that stretched over five years, perhaps she understood the real target of George's rage and suspicion. She was no stranger to the assault on women like herself. She would be accused of many things, and hiding "her iron hand under a charming and extremely feminine satin finish" was the least of it. Street & Smith had made a killing with *Mademoiselle*, discarding its pulp fiction operation and turning exclusively to magazine publishing. Yet BTB fought to get rightfully compensated. Gerald Smith, the president of Smith & Street, was a friend and confidant, and one day in 1952, she had again had lunch with him on a Friday to discuss her resentment. Clearly she had not gotten through to him. On the Monday, once the workday was done and the office had emptied, she sat down to write to him, reiterating the argument she had been making for years. The inequality was getting under her skin. What bothered her most, she wrote, was the lack of "recognition" she received, which she broke down into two categories—"professional (title) and money." "There seems to me little doubt," she said, "of my having been made an officer of the company had I not been a woman." Yes, sure, she'd been thrown a bone, she had been made the only woman on the board—where, on her first day, bewildered by the presence of a woman and fumbling for a friendly gesture, the men had passed her a box of cigars. But the board appointment proved to be more show than substance: she had no real say, no title. And as for salary, she had sacrificed pay raises for the good of the company—the same could never be said of the men at her level, or even below, who felt perfectly entitled to take raise after raise. "I believe I have been the victim of discrimination. If not that, then what?"

By 1950, Dior's postwar New Look silhouette had been modified with layers of added crinoline and petticoats to weigh down movement, much like the nineteenth-century bustle. But there were those who refused to be weighed down. Nanette Emery had left the Barbizon with her suitcase packed with New York memorabilia and returned to Bryn Mawr, graduating in 1947. She would lead an unconventional life, working all around the world, marrying late, at the age of forty, to a man in the State Department. There is a photograph of her wedding in 1966, in Paris, France, where she wears a stunning Jackie O.-style white knee-length coatdress and pillbox hat. She would adopt a daughter, Maria, while living in Paraguay. Elizabeth Moulton, her fellow guest editor, who could not afford to stay at the Barbizon the second time around, became a writer and artist, the author of several novels. Editors Cyrilly Abels and Rita Smith would continue to find and publish the best of new and cutting-edge fiction, for which *Mademoiselle* would become ever more famous. Black-well would continue to reign over the magazine until 1970. There is no doubt that the typical image of American women in the 1950s pushed back into the home, behind the white picket fence of a new postwar suburbia, was in part true. But there were also enormous variations, including career women who defied the trend, and whom McCarthyism wanted to punish for daring to do so. Some of them sought shelter and found it in the hallways of the Barbizon and the corridors of *Mademoiselle*.

CHAPTER FOUR

THE DOLLHOUSE DAYS

Grace Kelly and the Beauty Queens

Photographs of the beautiful Grace Kelly wearing glasses are less common, but that is exactly how Grace looked when the model Carolyn Scott first encountered her in the room next to hers.

Throughout the late 1940s and early 1950s, requests for rooms at the Barbizon grew exponentially, coming in all the way from New Delhi in India to Bournemouth in England. Meche Azcarate from Mexico, for example, was forbidden by her mother to stay anywhere other than the Barbizon. But even if left to her own devices, she would never have wanted to stay anywhere else; she loved "the atmosphere of a sorority house," where "you can never run out of bobby pins." The hotel manager Hugh J. Connor, with the help of assistant manager Mrs. Mae Sibley, was now finding it a challenge to coordinate all the various reservations and check-in/check-out dates. Together they calculated that close to "100 famous fashion models, radio and television actresses" along with many more "stage and screen hopefuls, girls studying art, music, ballet and designing" were residing at the Barbizon at any given time.

Phyllis Kirk, lead actress in *The Thin Man* television series, stayed at the Barbizon at her mother's insistence. Shirley Jones, later to star as David Cassidy's on-screen mother in *The Partridge Family* (as well as become his real-life stepmother), was dropped off at the Barbizon by her parents with $200 in her pocket. She had spent a year as "Miss Pittsburgh," followed by a year acting at the Pittsburgh Playhouse. The next step was of course New York and the Barbizon. Sure enough, she walked into the weekly open auditions for all the Rodgers and Hammerstein Broadway shows, and the casting director, upon hearing her sing, sent everyone else home. Judy Garland insisted her daughter, Liza Minnelli, stay at the Barbizon and drove the staff crazy by calling every three hours to check up on her Liza, and if she wasn't in her room, they were ordered to go find her.

The postwar Barbizon now staked its claim as New York's "dollhouse," as the place to spy shapely young females, made all the more alluring by being tantalizingly out of reach in their sequestered, women-only lodgings. The dollhouse was a place many men dreamed of. Even J. D. Salinger, the elusive author of the 1951 novel *Catcher in the Rye*, hung about the Barbizon coffee shop to pick up women. He was often there after his girlfriend, Oona O'Neill (daughter of the playwright Eugene O'Neill), married Charlie Chaplin without warning. Charlie Chaplin could make her laugh; J. D. Salinger could not. But Salinger had other attributes. One Barbizon resident recalled that "I'd never encountered such intensity in a person," while another noted his odd sense of humor: she returned to the Barbizon fully convinced she had just been on a date with the goalie of the Montreal Canadiens—which Salinger had pretended to be.

Many men tried to breach the Barbizon's security cordon. Mae Sibley was used to being called to the reception desk to speak to someone claiming he was a doctor on call to see one of the hotel guests: "No doubt he'll be twenty years old and will take care that I see part of a stethoscope sticking out of his pocket. It's the oldest gag in the Barbizon."

Carolyn Schaffner was the kind of young woman that a man might dress up in hospital scrubs to try to see. Carolyn, of Steubenville, Ohio, looked a lot like Audrey Hepburn, with pale skin and black hair that shone as if it had been brilliantined. She wanted one thing: to get out of smog-covered Steubenville, to say goodbye to her stepfather, who considered her an unpaid caretaker to his children with Carolyn's mother. Carolyn understood that dreams needed to be worked at. She studied fashion magazines, models' expressions, hand gestures, and when it was time for the town to choose its Queen of Steubenville in celebration of its 150-year anniversary, Carolyn canvassed. She

Not permitted to go beyond the lobby, young men lined up by the telephones to call their dates.

went door-to-door making her case, even as she was known to be the prettiest girl in town. She understood one cannot leave dreams up to chance. As the winning queen, riding in the parade, hoisted high, waving to the people of Steubenville, she was offered the choice of a trip to Hollywood for a screen test or five hundred dollars. Carolyn wanted escape, not stardom, and chose the cash. It was 1947, and she was nineteen years old when she boarded the train to take her to New York; no one in her family came to see her off because her mother had to stay home to make dinner for her stepfather.

Carolyn's exit strategy was similar to that of so many other late teens at the time. Throughout the 1940s and 1950s, local beauty contests were tickets out of small-town America. In 1945, Lorraine Davies won the title of Tangerine Queen of Florida, traveling to New York by train. She passed out tangerines while her picture was taken. She arrived in New York on December 1, and saw her first snow before being escorted to the citrus industry's official banquet at the Roosevelt Hotel. Fifteen hundred people watched as she floated in while the band played "Tangerine." The evening finished with the famous bandleader Guy Lombardo buying her a drink and serenading her with "Sweet Lorraine." Lorraine's prize, like Carolyn's, offered the local "pretty girl" an opportunity for a better or at least more exciting future, if she was willing to grasp it. Even as Lorraine was contractually obligated to hand out tangerines wherever she went, part of her prize was to meet with Harry Conover, who had gotten into the modeling business after seeing John Powers succeed. Conover declared Lorraine had what it took and invited her to return to New York after she finished high school. At eighteen, she did just that, making a beeline for the Barbizon.

✦

It took Carolyn Schaffner one full day to travel by train from Ohio to Penn Station in New York. She did not know much about New York, but enough to flag down a yellow cab and ask for the Barbizon Hotel for Women. It's what all the fashion magazines she studied so earnestly told her: the Barbizon was the only place to stay for a young girl new to the city. There she would be safe. She went in through the revolving doors and looked about her. Walking up to the front desk, she asked to see someone about a room. Mae Sibley appeared and asked for Carolyn's references, which—being as well organized about her life as she was—she had brought with her. With the Depression long over and the postwar boom in place, Mrs. Sibley, at the Barbizon since 1936, was heavily invested in her vetting system. A former front-desk employee recalled that Sibley's "first test of getting in, after she knows you can pay, seems to be how pretty you are. Later on, after the September school rush, she's not so discriminating. And if a lady over 40 wants to come to the Barbizon, she'll have a tough time unless she's only staying a few days. The older ones and the plain ones appear to be there on sufferance." Sibley would say she looked out for the hotel's exclusivity; others would say she commodified the young women who came through the Barbizon's doors, knowing full well that their attractiveness added to the notoriety of the hotel.

Mrs. Sibley laid out the rules to Carolyn: no liquor in the rooms, preferably no late nights out, or certainly not enough of them in a row to set off alarm bells about possible improprieties. Fire-hazard cooking appliances in the rooms were also banned, as evidenced in the backroom closet full of confiscated appliances, enough with which to open a store: "hot plates for cheap meals, bottle warmers for morning coffee or midnight bouillon, hair driers and sun lamps." (The extent of Mae Sibley's power was such that it was not unusual for a young resident to begin a sentence with: "Mrs. Sibley would kill me if she heard this. . . .") In the afternoons, free tea was served, particularly handy for those low on funds—although Mrs. Sibley did not say as much—and there were card games, backgammon, and lecture series in the evenings. Carolyn knew about the no-men-allowed rule but was surprised to hear that after sundown, male elevator operators were switched out for female ones.

Carolyn found her room sparse and small. But although the tiny room felt "like being in a closet," she did not mind; the floral drapes and matching bedspread gave everything a homey feel. She took off her shoes, sank her stockinged feet into the green carpet, and reached for the speaker box above the bed: she turned the knob, and classical music hummed through the room. She had found escape at $18 a week. Instead of cleaning for her younger half siblings, the hotel maids now tidied her room while she was out. She had her savings and then of course her looks. But her savings and prize money, even if an impressive two thousand dollars, could not last forever.

Young women of varying backgrounds and means slept within the walls of the Barbizon. There were the Carolyns, the girls from nowhere, both literally and figuratively, but there were also the debutantes. In the infamous documentary film *Grey Gardens*, as Little Edie Beale and her mother Big Edie Bouvier, cousin of Jacqueline Bouvier Kennedy, battle it out in their derelict Hamptons home among far too many cats, Little Edie longingly reminisces of her time at the Barbizon. She lived there from 1947—when Carolyn also arrived—to 1952, dabbling in modeling, waiting for the chance to make it in show business. Just as her lucky break was about to happen (or so she believed), she was yanked back to the Hamptons by her mother, who claimed she could no longer afford the bills but in fact feared being left alone. (The notorious cats first began to accumulate while Little Edie was staying at the Barbizon. Years later, she would write to a friend: "They were given to mother by a client of my lawyer brother who lived near us. Mother trained them—they were house pets. I was living at the Barbizon and had a job at the time. The cats had nothing to do with me though everyone always blamed me for everything!")

But it was the Carolyns, not the debutantes, who truly understood that their time at the Barbizon offered a finite window of opportunity—while they were still young, pretty, desirable, driven. Those assets could lead to secretarial positions, to modeling gigs, to acting jobs. Yet all the women at the Barbizon, from the debutantes to the Carolyns, shared the same goal: marriage. As bold as one might be, however big one might dream, as a young woman you knew that the pot of gold at the end of the rainbow was marriage. Had to be marriage. Even if a part of you longed to be an actress, a writer, a model, an artist. The debutantes did not have to travel far to meet eligible bachelors (there were plenty enough within their own milieu—from

Papa's country club to the annual balls), and so the Barbizon meant a little fun, perhaps some notoriety or success before marriage. But the Carolyns were there to make it in New York: to become something and meet someone. Back home was the life that the Carolyns' mothers had, and that was the last thing they wanted for themselves.

From the first day in New York, Carolyn Schaffner dressed as if she were going to work even as she had nowhere to go. Wearing white gloves, like the Gibbs girls, she headed out into the streets alongside the droves of other young ladies of the Barbizon, but whereas they headed to offices and studios and training schools, she wandered the streets, exploring. It was during her city wanderings that Carolyn came upon the Horn & Hardart automat on Fifty-Seventh Street and Sixth Avenue. The automat, originally a German import, was the fast-food chain restaurant equivalent of its day, and the Horn & Hardart automat was the most famous in New York, filled with silver banks of art deco, coin-operated vending machines. Carolyn loved it immediately. She would change a dollar for nickels and then stroll among the many glass boxes, peering in to see what tempted her. Once she had finally decided, she dropped in the nickel, turned the dial, and pulled open the glass door. Coffee came out of a dolphin-head silver spout, and the steam table offered up Salisbury steak with mashed potatoes. She took her food upstairs to one of the tables by the windows and ate slowly, lingering, looking out onto West Fifty-Seventh Street.

It was only a week after arriving, as she sat and daydreamed at Horn & Hardart, that a man came up to her and asked to sit down. He told her he was a photographer and that she'd be perfect for the camera. He asked if she had ever considered modeling, and if she would like to meet the famous modeling agent Harry Conover. Carolyn, being the small-town girl she was, but also the young woman who knew she had a finite window at the Barbizon, said she would indeed like to meet Conover. The photographer wrote down an address—52 Vanderbilt Avenue. She took the slip of paper.

Carolyn had been getting to know the city and also the Barbizon's residents. Every Monday, she carefully studied the week's events of social teas and lectures, typed out by the hotel's social director, a former Barbizon resident herself, and slipped under each hotel room door at the start of the week. She had spoken to some guests; others she recognized only by sight. There was one young woman she had seen leaving the Barbizon: a round-faced teenager with light brown wavy hair, in a black coat and matching hat with blue flowers attached. She saw her again as she was unlocking her room on the ninth floor. In fact, the young woman was in the room right next to Carolyn's: they were neighbors.

Carolyn reached out her hand. "I'm Carolyn from Ohio, Steubenville," she introduced herself.

"I'm Grace, Grace Kelly, from Philadelphia," said the other girl. She said she was studying acting at the American Academy of Dramatic Arts.

Grace and Carolyn became fast friends. Grace had arrived at the Barbizon two months earlier, in September. Yet she already seemed like a New York native, in part because her uncle was a playwright in Manhattan and she had often come up from Philadelphia to visit him, to see the latest Broadway shows, from which she kept all the ticket stubs and *Playbill*s, organized by date, pasted carefully into a scrapbook alongside her meticulous notes. Grace followed theater obsessively, just as Carolyn did fashion, studying sewing patterns and making her own clothes—a wardrobe of skirts and blouses and a pair of gloves that were, admittedly, a bit too tight but still manageable if she didn't try to move her fingers about too much.

They were a case of opposites attract. Counter to the always fashionable Carolyn, Grace Kelly wore horn-rimmed glasses, without which she could not see; later in her short but enormously successful film career, by taking off her glasses, she exuded a sensuous dreaminess that was in fact plain old myopia. Her favorite go-tos were tweed suits, skirts, and cardigans, echoes of her upper-class Philadelphia upbringing.

Yet the two friends also dressed in opposition to their personalities; while the fashionable Carolyn was quiet and shy, the frumpy Grace was poised and boisterous. Her parents had wanted her in college instead of the American Academy of Dramatic Arts but, as luck would have it, the influx of GIs back from the war meant college placements were in high demand, and the GIs got priority. So when Grace failed to get into Bennington College, it was her chance to break away from her parents' expectations. She eventually convinced them to let her go to New York. Her father, Jack Kelly, stipulated one condition, which was nonnegotiable: she would have to stay at the Barbizon Hotel for Women.

Each day, Grace headed to class, intent on impressing her teachers. Carolyn had to do something too. The day after she met that photographer, she made her way to 52 Vanderbilt Avenue, just behind Grand Central Terminal. It could have gone terribly wrong: part of the reason for staying at the Barbizon, even if you paid a bit more, was that the doormen, along with the rest of the staff, protected you from "wolves," those men on the prowl on the streets of New York. But when Carolyn came into the office, she was indeed introduced to Harry Conover, his dark black hair slicked back (was it dyed? she wondered). She had heard he'd once been a disc jockey, and then a model-actor with the Powers Agency, who had figured out the real money was in the management of models—not in being one. Much like his former boss, John Powers, Conover sought out the natural "clean-scrubbed" beauties, not the emaciated models of the runways. He famously advised his models to eat what they wanted because "returning servicemen want a good, well-rounded bundle, not a matchstick." To find the all-American girl, he had scouts at all the East Coast college campuses during fraternity weekends and relied heavily on regional festivals and beauty contests.

Carolyn, at five foot four inches, was too short for high fashion, but her petite size and delicate features made her perfect for modeling "junior fashion," a segment of the market that was just then exploding. Teenagers and young adults had begun to define themselves separately, distinct from those a decade older, a phenomenon very much fueled by *Mademoiselle* and editor-in-chief BTB's discovery of the lucrative "youth market."

Harry Conover sat Carolyn down and explained to her that there were pretty girls all over New York, but it was those who were willing to pound the pavement, to do the time, who had a chance at getting somewhere. Carolyn already knew how to persevere; that's how she had gotten herself out of Steubenville. And so she gladly did the rounds, taking anything that was given to her, making her way through dark halls, narrow staircases, eerily empty lobbies. It didn't faze her; none of it felt worse than home. At the client's office or showroom, or wherever they had asked the Conover agency to send her, she presented herself for a no-holds-barred evaluation. It would have broken down a dozen other young women, hearing what they had to say about her, speaking as if she were not standing right there, but Carolyn listened carefully and learned what to correct, such as the dark circles under her eyes.

Her first serious job was a two-page spread in *Junior Bazaar*, where she was surrounded by the accoutrements deemed necessary for a young wife—dirty laundry, laundry basket, iron, ironing board. This first big modeling job quickly led to more bookings, until she was working steadily. Carolyn's comp card, the card she handed out to clients with her exact sizes and measurements, had a photograph of her in a fitted suit and hat looking up at a shop window of Lord & Taylor's department store—and in that window was another photograph of her, wearing a wedding dress. It was very clever. When she again encountered the photographer who had first approached her at the automat, he asked her point-blank if she would go away with him—not for a date, but for a weekend.

"No," she said, avoiding his eye, thinking how she had been both right and wrong when he had sat down next to her at Horn & Hardart. She hurried home to the safety of the Barbizon.

Carolyn Scott in a photo shoot for *Mademoiselle*.

Christmas arrived and Grace went home to Philadelphia while Carolyn stayed behind in New York, attending the Barbizon's afternoon teas with the other young women too far from home to return for the holidays, or else with reasons not to want to go home. Grace had advantages Carolyn could not even imagine; Grace's father, a self-made millionaire, paid for her room at the Barbizon as well as her acting classes. Unlike so many other residents, Grace did not have to sit herself down every week with paper and pencil to figure out where to cut corners, particularly after Mrs. Sibley had confiscated one's hot plate. Residents' frequent budgetary self-reprimands included promises to cut down on room service, cabs, and phone calls (they were an exorbitant eleven cents each from the rooms). One trick was to wait until 9:00 p.m. to see if you got a dinner date invite, which helped significantly with monthly meal costs. Another penny-pinching tactic was to hold off shopping at Bloomingdale's, even though it was down the street, and wait for an in-house clothes swap or auction, which was particularly thrilling when it was a model who was clearing out her closet or, better yet, leaving the Barbizon to get married: the models had designer clothes purchased at wholesale prices and were more likely to give them away for minuscule sums.

While Grace Kelly did not have to worry about money, she did have to worry about her parents, who were clearly waiting for her to fail or give up. When she returned from the holidays back to the Barbizon, Grace thus made doubly sure she did not do either. Her voice was a problem, she was told by her acting teachers, too high-pitched, too nasal; but like Carolyn, she knew how to fix a problem. She bought herself a wire recorder and sat in her room next to Carolyn's, speaking into the machine and playing back her voice until she had corrected her speech and acquired that oddly transatlantic British-like accent mandatory for all actors of the time.

Altogether, there was something genuinely resourceful about these postwar young women. Many residents were putting money aside for further training, such as seventeen-year-old Helen Sinclair, with "a drawl as broad as her native Texas," who was working for $300 a week as a fashion magazine model so she could save enough to return to college for a fashion art degree. Kathleen Carnes, from Detroit, sang jingles to pay for voice lessons, and San Antonio's Dorothy White taught music appreciation in New York's suburbs to pay for her piano studies. Joan de Bey Murchison, from Kewanee, Illinois, started a publicity firm with earnings from a television gig, and Clair McQuillen from Pennsylvania used her modeling fees to study art and head out as a freelance advertising artist. Barbizon manager Hugh J. Connor took all these accomplishments and promotions as shared victories, sending flowers to those who had gotten their break, particularly if he knew how tough the road getting there had been. He smiled widely when sharing good news of Barbizon residents who went from sales clerks to buyers, from receptionists to magazine cover girls, from secretaries to company executives. The Barbizon dollhouse might well have been full of young, beguiling beauties, but there was much more behind their attractive facades. Even if many of these young women would indeed end up as wives and mothers back in the towns from which they had come, their goals while in New York were as ambitious as Betsy Talbot Blackwell's.

Hugh J. Connor of course knew the intricacies of the hotel residents' budgets and financial constraints. Carolyn now had one modeling job after another, but that did not immediately translate to money in the bank; Conover was notorious for not paying his models on time (in fact he would lose his New York license in 1959 for just this reason), and after two months of working for him, she had yet to receive her paycheck. And it wasn't just Carolyn. New York's working models were getting fed up with not being paid on time, or paid at all, and they were soon whispering among themselves about a new agency run by women. Two women, in fact: top-notch model Natálie Nickerson and her friend Eileen Ford. Natálie, a tall, leggy blonde, had been a successful Powers model. But, like almost everyone else, she became tired of the payment runaround. She began to plot with Ford, a model booker. They had met in 1945, soon after Natálie had walked away from her wartime job as a drill-press operator at an aircraft assembly plant in Phoenix, Arizona. She had left for New York after her supervisor took the credit for an innovation she had invented that would improve the production of an airplane's altitude meter, and which the company then profitably adopted. She was determined to become a model, but one agency after another took a look at her five-foot-nine-and-a-half-inch willowy frame, and said, "No, thank you." She simply did not have the look that was selling then, or that anyone thought would sell. So Natálie, who, like Carolyn, was no stranger to hard work, got a job in a hotel where she punched an adding machine from midnight until 7:00 a.m. She would rush back to her room, get a few hours of sleep, and then continue to canvass photographers. She finally persuaded one to see her potential, and the shots he took immediately sold; within two months, Natálie was pulling in $25 an hour, making the enormous sum of $25,000 by the end of the year as a top high-fashion model.

Natálie had started out in New York at a church hostel, but as soon as the modeling work stepped up, she did as well: to the Barbizon. She wanted everyone to know it too, and had special stationery ordered to announce her place in the world: NATÁLIE, THE BARBIZON, 140 EAST 63RD STREET, NEW YORK 21. Eileen Ford, who had booked her for a job and then befriended her, would stay the night on a cot in Natálie's Barbizon room when it was too late to return home to her husband on Long Island. She and Natálie would lie there and chat for hours about the modeling world they both knew so well. And just as Natálie had improved the production of altimeters, so now she would improve the world of modeling (and, just as happened at the aircraft plant, she again would not get the credit that was due, nor really the payout).

Plotting well into the night, Natálie, on the narrow Barbizon bed, and Eileen, on the foldout cot the hotel provided at request, decided to overhaul the New York modeling industry. The first step would be an entirely new payment method for the models. Eileen would work for the models, and not the other way around, as the three top agents, Powers, Conover, and Hartford, all men, assumed it should be. Now the photographers would pay the models at the end of the shoot, and the models would then pay the Ford Modeling Agency its 10 percent. There would be no more worrying for working models like Carolyn about when they'd get paid. Natálie put herself in charge of recruitment, ushering her favorite models over to Eileen. While the ideal Ford model later became a facsimile of Natálie's blond, healthy, tall, leggy profile, during the late 1940s and then 1950s especially, the Ford agency handled all three categories of models: the junior model, up to five foot five and 106 pounds; the misses model, an inch or two taller and up to 110 pounds; and then the elite high-fashion model, who towered over the rest yet weighed around 112 (and if they didn't, Eileen would badger them into it).

It was Natálie who approached Carolyn about joining their agency. Natálie and Eileen had set up shop in a brownstone sandwiched between a funeral parlor and a cigar store on Second Avenue, between Fiftieth and Fifty-First Street. Three flights up the stairs and behind a red door were the official headquarters of Ford Models. When Carolyn walked in, there was no receptionist, only a small, curly-haired woman surrounded by six black telephones. This was Eileen. She sat, a telephone or two hoisted to her ear, and wordlessly pointed to an old red sofa. Carolyn sat down and listened to Eileen argue into the phone. Natálie was the face of the agency, the one who picked the girls with good working reputations and brought them in; then Eileen worked her magic, her Rolodex. Eileen booked shoots, banished photographers who crossed the line, and instructed "her girls" on how to style their hair. Eileen was particularly conversant in the new junior market, and she immediately saw Carolyn's potential: petite, slender, small-waisted, with large eyes and a great smile. Eileen took matters into her own hands and renamed Carolyn on the spot. Carolyn Schaffner would not do, she said: from here on, she would be Carolyn Scott.

Eileen delivered on what she promised. Carolyn was soon on the cover of *McCall's*, photographed by a still relatively unknown photographer by the name of Richard Avedon. He was able to capture Carolyn's intelligence: holding a parasol, in a lacy dress, a spring bouquet of flowers and a yellow satin ribbon in her hair, Carolyn could have come off as vapid or mundane. But in shot after shot, Carolyn stares out at the viewer in a way that makes one want to see more of her, even as (or because) so much in fact remains hidden behind her expression. (It helped that Avedon, unlike so many other photographers, treated the models humanely, playing music, letting them choose the music, in fact, and ordering in their favorite food during shoots.)

It seemed Carolyn had made it; she had accomplished what she had set out to do when she boarded that train from Ohio to New York. She now made the kind of gesture that marks the triumph of a small-town escapee: she sent her mother the latest refrigerator model to replace the ice block in the larder. It was also a four-letter gesture to her stepfather, of course. She was saying it loud and clear: she, the newly renamed Carolyn Scott, barely twenty, could provide what he would never be able to, or be willing to.

+

Lorraine Davies, the Tangerine Queen, like Carolyn, had found her niche as a junior model, even as she idolized the tall high-fashion models. She specialized in live television commercials, print work, Sears Roebuck, and even managed to land a lucrative gig handing out prizes on the television game show *Try and Do It*. Like Celeste Gheen, Barbizon resident and Powers model during the Great Depression, who had even bathed in a tub of Colman's mustard for the extra pay, Lorraine considered herself an artist of disguise. This was the secret to her success: she would switch her hair from long to short, blond to dark—anything the job demanded. But also like Carolyn, she was always having to worry about getting paid on time and settling her weekly Barbizon bill. Tired of Conover's tricks, she first moved over to Huntington Hartford, an agency started in 1948 by the heir to the A&P supermarket fortune. He did it so he could "be with the girls." When he said girls, he meant it too; he had a penchant for the particularly young, and thought "way past her prime" Lana Turner and "too pushy like a high-class hooker" Marilyn Monroe were too old for him. They were certainly too mature for him. A decade earlier, he had had a son with a twenty-three-year-old chorus girl, who then left him for the actor Douglas Fairbanks Jr. By some accounts, his reputation for sleeping with his models was all hot air. Certainly Lorraine never had a problem, and she was thrilled to be paid each week by Hartford; her salary did not depend on whether the clients had already paid Hartford because he had deep pockets full of A&P money. Even so, Eileen Ford's promise of getting paid on the spot beat out getting paid at the end of the week, and soon Lorraine also switched over to the Ford modeling agency.

✛

Eileen Ford was already married back when she spent the night on a cot at the Barbizon because it was too late to take the train home to Long Island. Now her husband, Jerry, joined the company too, and the familial, nurturing aspect of the agency was amplified. It was a family business now. When *Life* magazine featured Jerry and Eileen in a five-page photo essay, it was hard not to contrast the low-level sleaziness of the modeling world, epitomized by A&P playboy Huntington Hartford, former actor and disc jockey Harry Conover, and former model John Powers, with the homespun charm of the Fords, their first baby crawling across the floor of the agency office. The agency also caught the eye of Sherman Billingsley, former speakeasy proprietor and now owner of the famous and glamorous Stork Club, who invited the Fords to bring their young charges to eat and drink for free as they hobnobbed with the rich and famous who were always ready to dine with a pretty face or two, or three.

But the Fords' fussing over their young models was not just a publicity stunt. When new girls arrived, particularly from abroad—and with Natálie's look as their guiding light, the Fords dipped heavily into the Scandinavian gene pool—Eileen would first have them live with the family, and then move them over to the Barbizon, often at her own expense. It was safe, it was respectable, it was exactly what she needed to keep them in check and keep their reputations intact. After Nena von Schlebrügge, actress Uma Thurman's future mother, was discovered by Eileen Ford in Sweden at the age of seventeen, she made her way to New York. She arrived by ocean liner in March 1958 to a snowstorm and, as she remembered, to the sorry sight of American women hobbling their way through piles of snow in impractical high heels and beige stockings. She too first stayed with Eileen, Jerry, and their children at their new home on Seventy-Eighth Street before transferring to the Barbizon. The Fords supplied their models with "diets, dermatologists, hairdressers and housing"—as Phyllis Lee Schwalbe, former College Board editor at *Mademoiselle*, would write for the *New York Times* in 1958. It was not unusual for the models to spend their days hanging around the office on Second Avenue. Lorraine Davies, the Tangerine Queen, was therefore sitting in the office in the dingy brownstone, on the red sofa, when a tall blonde walked in.

The blonde said her name was Janet Wagner. Lorraine, five foot five and a half inches, always wore heels, and on Eileen's advice told clients she was five six. Janet, over five foot nine inches, would be told by Eileen to never admit being over five nine, and to keep her footwear low-heeled. Janet had never modeled before, and in fact her path to Eileen Ford's red door was entirely unique.

It started with Janet desperate for a job: her parents had just written that all the summer jobs back home in Galesburg, Illinois, were taken up while Janet was away in New York as a guest editor at *Mademoiselle*. There was no question Janet was the prettiest GE that summer, although Sylvia Plath was a close second. They were both radiant blondes, all-American, but Janet was taller, and her features were more vivid. She was standing in the Barbizon lobby with Neva Nelson, another guest editor, when a small, pudgy man approached them with a camera and asked if they wanted to be models. Neva, who had had to make her own way through life, was street smart and wanted nothing to do with him, but Janet followed him into the Barbizon coffee shop, where she signed a contract on the spot. He now had what he needed. He took that flimsy written agreement to *Mademoiselle* and informed them that Janet was under contract with him, and he would not let her appear in the magazine without sufficient compensation.

Betsy Talbot Blackwell was now in a bind. Janet had already been photographed for the August College Issue alongside the other GEs, and they could not exactly brush her out of the pictures. So with her hands tied, BTB struck a deal, first with the man with the camera, and then with Eileen Ford. At BTB's suggestion, Eileen would buy out his contract with Janet to avoid any further embarrassment. To make it seem as if Eileen had indeed discovered Janet accidentally, BTB "happened" to be sitting with her guest editor at the Stork Club when Eileen bumped into them and "discovered her."

So there was Janet, in a dark-blue-checked gingham dress, the same in which she had arrived at the Barbizon three weeks earlier. Eileen handed her a map of New York City and some pancake makeup, and told her to learn both. Janet was clueless, but Lorraine, who had some time to spare, jumped in to help. She later recalled Janet as tall, blond, with a large smile and perfect teeth, a mix between "Goldie Hawn and Grace Kelly," with "the bounciness of Hawn and the classiness of Kelly." The two spent the afternoon together while Lorraine explained to Janet the essentials of modeling, and Janet chatted about *Mademoiselle*. By the end of the afternoon, with Janet's makeup done to perfection by Lorraine's practiced hand, Janet had officially gone from *Mademoiselle* guest editor to Ford model.

✦

Back at the Barbizon, Grace Kelly had watched with some envy as Carolyn became financially independent, certainly not rich but with enough to pay her weekly hotel bill, as well as buy lunches and dinners out or at the coffee shop and all the various things that models needed to stay looking good. Although she had nothing to worry about because her room at the Barbizon was paid for by her parents—always in full, always on time—Grace wanted to know she too could support herself. And it wasn't just Carolyn; there were lots of other young women at the Barbizon who were benefitting from Madison Avenue's demand for a pretty face and a slender figure. Advertising was one of the fastest growing industries. Carolyn understood what Grace was yearning for, that she didn't need financial independence but wanted it, and she encouraged her to give modeling a try. Behind the prim, proper, and rather unimaginative outfits that Grace preferred, and the ever-present thick glasses, Carolyn saw a hidden beauty. So she sent her off to Eileen Ford, where Grace took a seat on the red sofa while she waited for judgment. It was not positive.

Eileen thought there was "too much meat on the bones" and that Grace's look was too commercially run-of-the-mill, not to the Ford Agency's high standards. (Eileen would later say this was the biggest mistake of her career.) So Grace took the opposite route of her modeling friends who were making their way from Powers over to Eileen; she headed to Powers instead, who hired her on the spot. As Eileen Ford would later pretend, her girls—she said—should advertise beautiful clothes and not products, and she had turned

Grace Kelly down for having done bug spray and cigarette commercials. But in fact these were among Grace's first modeling jobs with Powers—after Eileen had already rejected her for the extra meat on her bones.

Grace should have merely played to Eileen's ego just like the famous Dolores Hawkins, who had already had some success when she walked into the Ford agency, which meant Eileen could not lay claim to having discovered her. She didn't like that, and she rejected Dolores, complaining that at 108 pounds, she was overweight. Dolores shrugged. She understood the business and its personalities. She returned to Eileen a week later, declaring she'd lost the weight (which she had not). Nothing more was said. She had let Eileen save face. In 1957, in between apartments, Dolores stayed at the Barbizon, where she had a brand-new dove-gray convertible Thunderbird delivered right to the front door of the hotel, with a big bow on its hood, as Oscar stood on the sidewalk directing the gawkers to move away.

While Dolores Hawkins used her new Thunderbird to drive up to her parents' horse farm in upstate New York for weekends, Janet Wagner reveled in the perks that came with New York City modeling. She would often go—although not nearly enough, she later regretted—with her friend Lorraine to the Stork Club, where instead of a bill at the end of the meal, the waiter would bring them a small gift, often perfume, or perhaps a lipstick, and a small note: "Compliments of the house." Janet also befriended Lily Carlson, another of Eileen Ford's top models. At five eleven and of Swedish stock (her father was a Lutheran minister in Iowa, who often sermonized in Swedish), Lily Carlson had put the Ford agency on the map when she signed with them shortly after they opened. She had come to modeling in her late twenties when her husband lost his job in the midst of the Depression, but her rise under Eileen's direction was meteoric. In the famous 1947 fashion photograph *The Twelve*

Beauties, photographer Irving Penn posed Lily in the very center of the ensemble, almost as if she were standing alone, basking in her own reflective light, in a simple white ruched floor-length gown.

Lily introduced Janet Wagner to Gita Hall, another famous New York–based Swedish model and actress. Delighted to be in her company, Janet took up Gita's rich boyfriend's offer to join them for a weekend at his mansion in Southampton on Long Island, the summer playground of the fabulously wealthy. What Gita—whom Janet would soon refer to as "one of the biggest prostitutes in town"—had not told her was that her boyfriend's cousin was already there at the mansion, waiting for Janet and a sex-filled weekend. But Janet was clueless, and when he came into her room that night, she sat up straight, horrified, and nervously explained, fumbling for the right words, that she had never slept with a man, which sent him into fits of laughter. For him, her virginity was not only a point of great mirth but, fortunately, also an automatic deterrent.

Perhaps Janet was too unworldly for a world that pretended to be virtuous, even puritanical, but behind closed doors was far more complex. And perhaps Janet, her experiences thus far spanning no farther than Galesburg, Illinois, really was unusually naive and inexperienced. But because the 1950s were rife with contradictions, especially when it came to women and sexuality, looks could deceive. Those who appeared pristine and proper might be masking another layer, whereas the overtly sexy could be hiding a guileless virginity— like Janet. Indeed, Grace Kelly was the poster girl for that decade's perfect woman, a persona solidified later by her on-screen role as the luminescent Lisa Fremont, the sophisticated, smart, modern woman patiently waiting for her man in Hitchcock's *Rear Window*. Yet Grace Kelly, forever identified with sweetness and chastity, was fond of dancing to Hawaiian music down the hallways of the Barbizon, and given to shocking her fellow residents by performing topless. Rumors of her sexual appetite and promiscuity abounded.

Few spoke about these contradictions with which young women at this time battled daily. But Malachy McCourt had a front-row seat to them. On May 12, 1958, the actor, professional storyteller, and relentless bon vivant (and brother of the schoolteacher Frank McCourt, who would later write the famous memoir *Angela's Ashes*), opened up Malachy's bar on Third Avenue between Sixty-Third and Sixty-Fourth Street. Formerly called O'Rourke's, the place was a "rundown saloon" but Malachy and his partners slapped some cream paint on the walls, put down red carpet on the floor, and put up a sign over the canopy. One final touch was a brightly lit fish tank, and the other was Earl Walker, "trained in the art of food preparation and service at Rikers Island," as Malachy McCourt liked to say. Malachy's would become known as the first singles bar in New York. Its location within two blocks of the Barbizon was no accident.

Opening the bar required navigating land mines of regulations and codes that spoke to the era's emphasis on propriety and all its implications. In every bar in New York, food had to be served (from a kitchen on the premises), with one dining table available for every two feet of bar counter installed. Lighting, it was stipulated, needed to be bright enough by which to read a newspaper. (When Malachy would later be hauled in for this particular violation, the judge asked the officer the name of the paper he had tried to read. "*The Daily Mirror*," the cop replied. The judge ruled against him: bad choice of reading material, he said, and if the cop wanted to read so badly, there was always the public library.) There were also unspoken rules, such as the one about women not being allowed to sit up at a bar alone. Malachy got rid of that one.

Soon after opening night, the Barbizon's young women started to wander in, curious at first, a little hesitant, but once they had discovered it, they let their friends know that Malachy's was a respite from what was otherwise "a pale, green preserve up and down Third

Avenue, with shamrocks, and Irish bars, and green fluorescent lights." Malachy, who could be counted on to spin a good yarn in his Irish brogue, was a regular on the *Tonight Show* with Jack Paar, then broadcast live from New York. The jet-setters—charmed by Malachy and "prone to the lemming syndrome," in his words—started to flock to the bar: the Whitneys, the Reynolds (of tobacco money), the Hitchcocks, and the socialite Berlin kids, whose father was chairman of the Hearst newspaper empire (Brigid Berlin would end up as Andy Warhol's confidante). The actors that Malachy McCourt ran with—Richard Burton, Richard Harris, Peter O'Toole, Albert Finney—also joined.

Everywhere else across Manhattan women were still being banned from sitting up at the bar by themselves, just as once they had been banned from checking in to a hotel by themselves after 6:00 p.m. If a girl was up at the bar, the thinking was, nothing good was going to come of it, and in fact there was probably nothing "good" about the girl to begin with. At first, Malachy had thought it must be a citywide regulation of some sort, but after searching for the ordinance, he realized this rule was nothing more than a tradition, and a bad one at that. He invited the Barbizon's women to come sit up at the bar alone. At Malachy's, anyone could sit "wherever the hell they wanted." "The beautiful young women, and handsome guys—they'd talk to each other. And then all of a sudden there were lines outside the bar." When finally a cop came and pulled out his ticket pad to write out a violation because there were unaccompanied women sitting at the bar, Malachy dared him to name the ordinance. The police officer could not.

What Malachy's offered to the Barbizon residents, if not the best of decor, was a chance to speak to whomever they wished or else to sit quietly alone if they wanted to. Because that was the one single rule at the bar: in there, "you were under the protection of the house," and no one was allowed to harass anyone else. Even the Gibbs girls, otherwise under the strict restrictions of dress codes and mandatory lights-out, would come home from their classes, put on their night-dresses, then throw on a raincoat and come over to Malachy's. His brother Mike called them the "Raincoat Brigade." He even claimed some of them had forgotten their nightdresses under their raincoats. Sometimes, Malachy noted, his bar offered real sustenance too, and he was not above feeding the Barbizon girls: "Sometimes you could tell if they were counting their pennies." If the young woman ordered a beer or a soda, and then began to count out her money, placing each coin carefully onto the bar, he would cheerfully offer her a burger on the house, making it seem like the most offhand of gestures.

One night, Malachy himself caught a fancy to one of the Barbizon girls. He was "on the booze then," and drunkenly he escorted her back to the hotel. With the alcohol giving him confidence, and rugby training a fast run, he made it up to her room while she distracted the front desk receptionist. He vaulted up those stairs "faster than a fiddler's elbow." He did not find the hard single bed exactly condu-cive to lovemaking, but he made do. A few hours later, he crept back down and waited until the "eagle-eyed woman" at the front desk had temporarily stepped away. Then he made a run for the door, figuring that if she saw him, she could not catch him; and even if she caught him, she would still not know which cramped narrow bed he had been in when there were "seven hundred rooms of throbbing virginity" to choose from. Malachy would try it again many times after but always fail, even as he met half a dozen men in his time who claimed that they had vaulted up those stairs too and lived to tell the tale. If they were telling the truth, according to Ford model, Barbizon resident, and fashion icon Carmen Dell'Orefice, it might have been that they were masquerading as John MacGuigan, a good-looking Upper East Side gynecologist who was called in often enough that the staff became used to waving him on through. As for inviting them in, even actress Cybill Shepherd, rather good at "sneaking 'em in, sneaking 'em out," refused to give it a try at the Barbizon because it "was an *institution*," not to be messed with.

The intricate balancing act played out in the 1950s by both women and men was eased by the martini culture of the time. The training started early in one's college years, if not sooner. In 1958, the future actress from *Love Story*, Ali MacGraw, also at the Barbizon as a guest editor at *Mademoiselle*, illustrated a witty account of a typical Ivy League college weekend for the August College Issue of the magazine. Fellow guest editor Colette Hoppman, its author, described her anticipation for a weekend filled with "witticisms, milk punch, Frisbee on the lawn." One friend, she noted wistfully, had recounted "hopping off a train in Cambridge [Harvard] on a Friday and being told that she was to be in a reading of *The Cocktail Party* that evening." Thus Colette headed to Yale for her first Ivy League college weekend full of excitement and hope: a blind date with a boy who came recommended as "tall, clean-cut and well liked." As was traditional for the college weekend, her blind date would pay for her lodging, food, and entertainment, and she would only need to cover her train fare.

But what she found there was nothing like her friend's adventure in Cambridge. Colette's experience was more like an alcohol-soaked frat weekend under the guise of genteel elegance. She arrived in New Haven with a girlfriend who was similarly set up. They were picked up in a convertible, taken to their boarding house, and told to be ready for dinner in an hour. Fence, the fraternity to which her date, Bill, belonged, was hosting the dinner, and they all sat down in "some fat leather chairs," attempting conversation. Colette asked Bill if he was interested in advertising, as she had heard. He said he would most likely follow his father's footsteps into it, eventually, but for now, "Drinking's good enough for me."

As if on command, "a white-coated waiter plopped a Martini down in front of me," Colette wrote. Taking one sip, she decided gin was not for her, but for the rest of the weekend it was hard to avoid. Dinner was followed by yet more binge-drinking well into the early morning hours. Saturday was the big football game, the stands filling with Yale students and alumni, "old grads carrying 1919 balloons, tweedy boys in porkpie hats and camel-coated girls and girls and girls." Public drinking was part of the game itself: liquor right out of the bottle, beer out of the can. One group chugged wine from "old Spanish wineskins, obvious souvenirs of a summer abroad." The game was followed by another string of parties, these separated by theme, as if to stave off the growing ennui. When the night was finally over, the floor was "littered with cigarette butts, beer cans and an earring sprinkled here and there." It was a disappointing Ivy League weekend for Colette, but an initiation into college life and after. Equally so, it was a peek into what life as an upper-middle-class young wife might mean, and the rounds of stultifying social rituals that came with it. Because it was the 1950s, and that would almost inevitably be her fate. The "dollhouse" was merely an interlude in a young woman's journey toward the end goal: to become the mistress of her own home.

✦

By the time Colette was coming to terms with her Ivy League weekend in 1958, Grace Kelly was already living in Monaco as its princess. In 1956, she had married the prince of Monaco in a wedding that dominated world news. In a few short years, she had gone from acting student staying at the Barbizon Hotel for Women to famous actress and Academy Award winner to love interest of Prince Rainier III of Monaco. In marrying him, she officially retired from acting at the age of twenty-six. Thinking back on the 1950s, one of her bridesmaids would say: "Did I think at all about the future? Not at all. Not a bit about ours nor even Grace's . . . it was the Fifties. From where we stood, we were pretty sure that as long as we looked the right way, married the right man and did and said the right things life would unfold before us as easily and enjoyably as it always had." Marriage was still the goal, and the Barbizon, the dollhouse, was its most coveted antechamber.

During the 1950s, one in three women were married by age nineteen, and by 1957, fourteen million girls were engaged by the age of seventeen. Eileen Ford would famously gather her models nearing their expiration date and arrange for meet-and-greets with wealthy Americans and titled European suitors. She was proud of marrying off "her girls" to successful men and excellent providers. While Grace Kelly moved out of the Barbizon to Monaco's royal palace, her friends, now also getting married, moved out to the chic suburbs of New York. That too was a 1950s thing. Suburbs were growing six times faster than cities. Carolyn Scott would move to Long Island, while Lorraine Davies and Janet Wagner became neighbors in Westport, Connecticut.

The 1950s is a decade sometimes remembered with rose-colored glasses, a time, some say, when America prospered as it never had before nor has since. Yet the 1950s were bursting with contradictions, with the unspoken, with pretense, some of which would lead to tragedy. Grace Kelly, actress and princess, would famously die as her car pitched over the side of the mountainous, winding road in Monaco. Carolyn Scott, the model, would succumb to mental illness and live out the rest of her years in a homeless shelter in Manhattan. Janet Wagner, *Mademoiselle* guest editor and model, would marry a man who caught a flight to a business meeting one day and never came back: he would be accused of exploding the commercial plane he was on in a desperate act of suicide, taking everyone with him. Lorraine Davies, Tangerine Queen and model, would write a fictionalized account of her friend Janet's fight to clear her late husband's name. The prevailing wisdom for women of the 1950s, the notion that marriage meant success or at least security, often proved false. For many 1950s residents of the Barbizon, their small rooms, hard beds, frantic dress-ups before a date, late-night conversations with friends, even chidings by Mrs. Sibley, would become touchstones of nostalgia. They had understood their time at the Barbizon as a short window of opportunity that would usher them toward the ultimate goal of marriage, but in fact, looking back, that window—and the female camaraderie and independence that defined it—turned out to be a high point.

CHAPTER FIVE

SYLVIA PLATH

The Summer of 1953

This iconic photograph of Sylvia Plath holding a rose was taken
on her first day as guest editor at *Mademoiselle* by an impatient
Hermann Landshoff, who complained he was more used to models
than dilettantes.

Sylvia Plath was also caught up in the push and pull of the 1950s. She would become one of America's greatest twentieth-century poets, as well as the author of one single but famous novel, *The Bell Jar*, entirely based on her time at the Barbizon Hotel. In that novel, she documented her ambivalence toward the promises of the decade: "So I began to think maybe it was true that when you were married and had children it was like being brainwashed, and afterward you went about as numb as a slave in some private, totalitarian state." But in the spring of 1953, Sylvia was still fixated on the window of time offered to a young woman like herself and not on how short that window might prove to be, even for the most beautiful, ambitious, and talented. Sylvia had not yet finished college and already she had a reputation that preceded her. She was the one they whispered about: that young woman who was going to be a writer, with a bright blond pageboy haircut and a penchant for parties.

Sylvia Plath was in her third year at Smith College in Massachusetts, and since she was already on her way to being the writer she planned to become, it was inevitable she would apply to *Mademoiselle* for the guest editor contest. In April, the College Board editor came up to visit the Smith College applicants, and Sylvia wrote forlornly to her mother that over tea, she watched her chances slip away as it became clear the other contestants had "tremendous" talents too. But, still, Sylvia could not resist a dig; she was, she wrote, especially sure one of the other girls would win because (unlike her) "none of them have received prizes yet." Sylvia of course had a drawer full of them, and was not shy about saying so. She had just won *Mademoiselle*'s College Fiction Prize ($500, which was no small change then) and also sold three poems to *Harper's Magazine* for $100.

But she did not let the visit from the *Mademoiselle* College Board editor get her down: Sylvia was intent on enjoying life, and she approached it with the same determination as she did her poetry. A medical student had just invited her for a whirlwind weekend in New York; another student had invited her to the Yale University spring dance for the weekend after (and, unlike Colette, she would not be disappointed). If anything, it was clothes that were on Sylvia's mind: "I now have a white bag and white shoes, a red bag and red shoes, and some day am going to get a black patent leather bag. I am so proud of myself now, in my judgment in clothes. I know what I want and just what I need, and feel most positive and good about it all."

The New York weekend with the medical student proved to be the quintessential Manhattan experience circa 1953. Sylvia arrived at Grand Central Terminal with her friend Carol, who had been fixed up with her own date ("a short, balding but simply wonderfully kind and intelligent first year man," Sylvia summed up). The four of them immediately headed for dinner at La Petite Maison, where Sylvia was dazzled by the linens, the French waiters, and, most of all, the food (for she loved food, as she loved clothes), tasting her first raw oysters that very night. Then a Checker cab to see a play, *The Crucible*, by Arthur Miller, followed by intense conversation at the famed nightclub Delmonico's—the very place where eight years earlier Nanette Emery had had an 11:45 p.m. double date with a marine and an army officer. A piano played in the background as Sylvia, her friend, and their dates bent their heads low and discussed race relations, communism, and religion. And that was only the first night.

So when the sought-after telegram finally did arrive for her from Betsy Talbot Blackwell of *Mademoiselle* to say that she was in fact one of the winners of the guest editor program, Sylvia felt she had just tasted a sumptuous bite of what was to come. She wrote to her mother after receiving all the requisite *Mademoiselle* forms, lists, and instructions, letting her know she would be staying at the Barbizon "at a reduced rate of $15 a week."

"Never stayed at a hotel before!" she wrote. Sylvia listed the clothes she was advised to bring to New York, including a swimsuit, a formal dress, and "cool, dark clothes 'which will look as fresh at 5 p.m. as at 9 a.m.'" In fact, *Mademoiselle* had been more specific still: they warned (as if they already knew that the summer of 1953 would be a record-breaking heat wave) that "it can get *very* hot in New York in June." For managing the daily combination of office work, luncheons, and outings to various manufacturers, they recommended "dark cottons, nylons, shantungs, silks or light-weight suits—cool, dark clothes preferably . . . and don't forget hats."

Sylvia was twenty years old, blond, a tall five foot nine inches, and a trim 137 pounds. She arrived at the Barbizon on Sunday, May 31, where she would stay until Friday, June 26. *The Bell Jar*, published ten years later, is an almost literal account of her life in New York in June 1953. In it, she renamed the Barbizon "the Amazon," turned herself into the protagonist Esther Greenwood, and reduced (and conflated) the other nineteen guest editors to twelve.

Sylvia was forever tabulating, and in preparation for her trip to *Mademoiselle* and the Barbizon, she calculated that she had spent more on clothes during her current junior year in college than she had on everything combined during her first year. But both mother and daughter understood the potential of New York. Sylvia's father, a professor, had died when she was young, and with no life insurance policy left behind, her mother, with the help of her parents, was keeping the household afloat, even with the lifestyle that someone like Sylvia and her brother, Warren, who had just received news of a scholarship to Harvard, expected to have. But money was a constant source of stress, and Sylvia's letters home sometimes read like an accountant's tally. The clothing expenses were justifiable, Sylvia noted as much to herself as to her mother, because the guest editorship was a rare opportunity to skip a few rungs of the professional ladder on her climb to the top. Moreover, as Sylvia explained (combining her ambition with her love for shopping), "I've always wanted to try 'jobs on like dresses and decide which fits best,' and now I'll have the chance to see what it's like living in the Big City. . . ."

New York in the summer of 1953 held the promise of a fairy tale. Sylvia, excited for her brother, now a Harvard man, and for herself, now a *Mademoiselle* guest editor, a "Millie," wrote to him: "Being one of the 20 winners in the U.S. of this month in New York is a dream of an opportunity. . . . I feel like a collegiate Cinderella whose fairy Godmother suddenly hopped out of the mailbox and said: 'What is your first woosh?' and I, Cinderella, said: 'New York,' and she winked, waved her pikestaff, and said: 'Woosh granted.'" The fairy tale continued reassuringly into Grand Central Terminal. Sylvia had traveled from her mother's house in Wellesley, Massachusetts, with Laurie Totten, another GE who, serendipitously, lived only two blocks away from Sylvia. But in her letter home, Sylvia was living the fantasy alone. *She* was helped off the train by "two lovely muscular members of the US soldiery." *She* was guided through the "predatory crowd" by the two uniformed men. It was *she* they accompanied in the cab to the Barbizon, depositing her and her luggage at the front desk.

Sylvia looked about her and decided that the Barbizon was "exquisite—green lobby, light café-au-lait woodwork." Checked in, Laurie and she took the elevator to the fifteenth floor, where all the GEs except for two would reside for the next four weeks. Sylvia was delighted by her "darlingest single," with a "wall-to-wall rug, pale beige walls, dark green bedspread with rose-patterned ruffle, matching curtains, a desk, bureau, closet and white enameled bowl growing like a convenient mushroom from the wall," handy for wash- ing white gloves and undergarments. Like Molly Brown more than two decades earlier, Sylvia was especially thrilled by the "Radio in the wall," but also the "telephone by the bed—and the view!" She could see gardens, and alleyways, and the elevated Third Avenue El train, and the new United Nations building, and even the slightest bit of the East River. But it wasn't even the view as much as what it signified, for when Sylvia sat there many following evenings, work- ing overtime, burdened with more work than the other GEs had—a perversely literal interpretation of the "woosh" to be Cinderella, the put-upon sister who did all the work while the rest pranced around town—below at least was the magical New York of lights and car horns.

But on that first night at the Barbizon, the guest editors gath- ered to look each other over, to start to forge relationships at the accelerated pace that the experience demanded. Sylvia found the others "intriguing," four of them so stunning they "could be Paris models" (and of course fellow GE Janet Wagner would, however accidentally, become a model by the end of the month), and everyone vivacious and smart, with even a Mormon in the mix. They all sat in Grace MacLeod's room, number 1506, which would also become the group's unofficial lounge throughout the month because her room brought in the most light.

Their hotel rooms looked out onto Lexington Avenue, or Sixty- Third Street, or the alleys in the back on the east and south sides of the building. No one knew how the rooms had been divvied up, but the luckiest got the best views, the most light, or both. In the center of the fifteenth floor were the shared bathrooms, an inadequate num- ber: two with a tub and toilet each, and another two larger ones with a shower and two toilet stalls each. Considering Sylvia's obsession for long, drawn-out baths, she was lucky to have her room near the tubs, whereas those GEs on the other side of the floor found themselves having to make do with the showers more often than not. There were twenty GEs in total; nineteen of them single, but one already married with a young son. The married GE commuted in from the Bronx, while guest fiction editor, Candy Bolster, opted to stay with friends, the Larkins, in Manhattan. Margaret "Peggy" Affleck, a Mormon, also chose not to stay at the Barbizon. The Mormon Church did not allow it, and so instead she would take a bus back and forth from the Mormon mission to the Barbizon and the magazine.

As they chatted, sizing each other up, geography was on everyone's mind. In the 1950s, air travel was still expensive enough to be rare, and until they were invited to New York by *Mademoiselle*, most GEs from the West and the South had never set foot in New York. In the national imagination, it was understood that the East Coast was the country's intellectual hub while the rest of the country remained its backwater. Guest editor Dinny Lain, who would become the writer Diane Johnson, author of *Le Divorce* among other novels, was then a sophomore at a women's college in Missouri. She had grown up on the banks of the Mississippi and had never been anywhere, let alone New York. Hotels were strictly places to dine for special occasions; just like Sylvia, she had never actually stayed in one. Yet Sylvia, the Smith girl from Wellesley, Massachusetts, commanded a much higher status. Sylvia was East Coast; Dinny was backwater.

Geography could be made up for, however, and the Barbizon was a potent site of reinvention for young women. It offered an alternative imagined life, even if it was as short-lived as one's room rental. A young woman who had abandoned Wellesley College to come to New York to become a writer observed, "It is *the* place where you go when you leave something—college, your family, your old life. And for that it's perfect—as long as you don't stay too long."

While Sylvia Plath arrived with the full recognition that she was at the top of the heap, and Dinny Lain arrived relatively ignorant of what this opportunity meant, Neva Nelson arrived that evening from San Jose, California, with determination. On the plane, during the last leg of the trip from Texas to New York, she had had the good luck to be seated next to a Mr. Ross, the CEO of the Neiman Marcus department store. Neva had not put much thought into how she would get from the airport to the Barbizon, half expecting a welcoming committee that never arrived. Mr. Ross rescued her by declaring she should share his cab. Clearly taken by this girl from San Jose, he had the cabbie drive a circuitous route so he could show Neva the paradoxes of the city. The cab crisscrossed Manhattan under Mr. Ross's direction as he pointed out not the sights of New York but its demographics, the ways in which wealth existed side by side—separated by a block or two—with New York's poor, how race was clearly demarcated across the short stretch of the Manhattan island.

Neva could not believe her luck in having Mr. Ross show her the lay of the land. Yet she had recently had a string of adventures, and this seemed just one more to add to the list. The year before, Neva had been part of a geology course in Death Valley, where they rushed to the top of a mountain at 4:00 a.m. to watch the atomic bomb test sixty miles away. The explosion burned her face, creating small, angry red spots that she would have to hide under makeup for the next seven years. Then, on a dare, and before the professor could rush over to stop her, she had swallowed, whole, a shimmering sardine-size fish from a two-thousand-year-old inland sea. Tanned, laughing, she posed for a photograph with the little fish, now saturated with atomic fallout, dangling over her open mouth, moments before its destructive entry. (Neva would later blame the radioactive fish for her thyroid cancer.) And now here was another adventure, set at the Barbizon, so soon after.

Neva Nelson swallowing the small and now radioactive fish.

By Neva's standards, her room at the Barbizon, number 1536, was magnificent, even as it looked out on a back alley. There was a sink immediately on the right as she entered, a narrow bed on the left, as well as a closet, dresser, desk, and even a comfy chair by the window. She loved the radio over the bed, which piped in music that could be interrupted any minute by the front desk with a personal message. She would have been less excited if she had known that the Barbizon bill would be arriving shortly, even though the GEs were only paid after the first two weeks of work, and Neva's check would in fact be held up even longer, until the third week, because of a mix-up with the airline ticket reimbursement.

That first night, and in other nights to follow, as the guest editors gathered for late-night discussions, Neva, who had forgotten her pajamas, would sit in a T-shirt with her reversible raincoat flung over her like a cape. Sylvia, fully prepared and meticulously packed, with preparatory shopping sprees prior to arrival, had two sets of blue pajamas, a nightgown, and a robe. But Neva was used to making do. She had come from Stanford but would return home to attend San José State University because the *Mademoiselle* opportunity also meant she could not take up her usual summer job at the cannery. But even with that reliable summer paycheck, Stanford's tuition was only piling on debt, and she had arrived in New York already knowing she could not go back there. Her parents were alive but erratic; she had been a ward of the state since she was a baby. By high school, she was living in an efficiency motel by herself, fighting off the presumption that only prostitutes were forced into such accommodations.

As the GEs stayed up past midnight on that first day, sitting in Grace MacLeod's room, awake but barely so, they discussed many things, such as their surprise to find college editor Marybeth Little, their "house mother" who would shepherd them through New York, was so very visibly pregnant. Someone suddenly asked: "Who here is a virgin?" No one was really sure who had asked the question, but everyone now waited to see the show of hands. Not a single hand went up. Eventually they turned to look at Neva, the youngest in the room, a college sophomore, but she only turned a deep red. Grace looked at her with shock, but, then again, perhaps it was feigned shock, the kind that young women in the 1950s practiced regularly. In Neva's experience, by the age of eighteen—regardless of what anyone actually said or admitted—most young women had been "seduced." In fact, when Neva arrived at Stanford, she had been surprised to find she was one of the few remaining virgins and much in demand for the traditional Stanford "jolly-up" dance, which called for a virgin date.

On Monday morning the GEs breakfasted together at the coffee shop downstairs, just off the Barbizon lobby, and Sylvia was pleased to find she could buy a coffee, juice, an egg, and two pieces of toast for fifty cents. She had dressed in a light suit to make a good first impression, but at the last minute a voluminous nosebleed ruined it, and she quickly had to go change. Janet Wagner thought she looked sharp for the first day of work dressed in a blue-and-white gingham dress, belted, a small white hat, and matching white shoes (despite *Mademoiselle*'s yearly implorings to its guest editors *not* to show up in white shoes). Janet's hat, the size of an extra-large tea saucer, appeared to be weighed down by a farmer's market share of artificial fruit. When Sylvia saw it, she sniggered. The day before, Sylvia had been itching to size up the competition, especially Janet Wagner, the winner of *Mademoiselle*'s nonfiction prize. Janet looked like a threat—tall, naturally blond, and with a big smile—but as soon as she opened her mouth, there was an unmistakable (and unsophisticated) twang. Janet watched disappointment flood Sylvia's face. Nor did Sylvia try to conceal her disdain; she would throughout the month refer to Janet as "hayseed," and confuse her Knox College in Galesburg, Illinois, with Knoxville College in Tennessee. It did not matter how many times Janet corrected her. In *The Bell Jar*, Sylvia would remake Janet Wagner into Betsy, the "Pollyanna Cowgirl." But one's place in the quickly established hierarchy among the 1953 guest editors was always precarious and relational: Sylvia's "white straw beret," which she wore unfailingly and proudly throughout the month in New York, resembled an old abandoned Frisbee and easily gave Janet's fruit saucer of a hat a run for its money.

Another guest editor, the dark-haired, bright-lipsticked Laurie Glazer, a budding singer from a small town in Iowa, was also on the low rung of regional hierarchies. But Sylvia seemed more fascinated by rural Iowa than Galesburg, Illinois, and only expressed regret that Laurie's parents had not chosen to settle on a farm, because in her view that was far more romantic. Laurie had dreamed of being a guest editor all through her junior year at college, but not until she was a senior had she finally mastered the contest essay form. Now in New York, she was overcome with the excitement of it all. As she would remember it, on that first morning, all the GEs, these "Eisenhower-era innocents," marched abreast, arms linked, from the "glamorous" Barbizon all the way down to the "glamorous" offices of *Mademoiselle* on "glamorous" Madison Avenue (Mad Ave). Of course there was no way that seventeen girls could actually walk arm in arm down the streets of New York from their rooms at the Barbizon to Mad Ave. But Sylvia was not the only one who wanted to convince herself of fairy tales in June 1953.

When the "guest eds," as Sylvia called herself and the others, arrived at Street & Smith Publishers at 575 Madison Avenue, they took the elevator to the *Mademoiselle* floor and gathered in BTB's office, "hugging ourselves as if to contain the private ecstasy of winning." Betsy Talbot Blackwell was in a black-and-white flowered dress with a low boat neckline, looking buxom, perhaps a little dumpy, but nicely groomed. Following BTB's traditional exhortations to remain healthy, in between long inhales of one cigarette after another, which she lit with her own personalized matchbooks (startling silver with "BTB" printed in black), they were introduced to the other editors and given more forms to fill out in the mirrored conference room.

For lunch, the guest editors were split into groups and sent off with various editors, and Sylvia must surely have realized then, if not earlier, that she was among the very chosen; she was marched off to the famous Drake Hotel with editor-in-chief BTB and managing editor Cyrilly Abels, where they sipped sherry, ordered chef salads, and discussed writers and magazine life. Certainly others realized: it was clear to Dinny Lain because of the way the editors fawned over Sylvia. All of which made the first working day's faux pas all the more excruciating.

Sylvia and Neva were waiting for the elevator down in the building lobby, where they had gone to grab a coffee during a break. They were chatting about the morning so far, surprised that the *Mademoiselle* editors were perhaps not as glamorous as they'd expected: instead they were real workingwomen, put together well but clearly less interested in the matters with which the beauty and fashion departments, considered rungs below editorial, occupied their time. Sylvia noted they were "a motley crew," and Neva picked up with the observation that BTB looked like a hardworking Irish washerwoman. For Neva, it was intended as a compliment; for BTB, who soon heard about it, it was not a compliment (in years to follow, instruction sheets for guest editors included a stern warning to never talk about company matters in the lobby or the elevator). Neva and Sylvia were immediately called into her "boudoir," as her shoe-themed office was called, and read the riot act. BTB railed against the two of them, calling Neva a charity case and Sylvia talentless, here only due to her mother's relationship with Cyrilly Abels, for whom she was a reliable supplier of well-trained secretaries. Sylvia locked herself in the bathroom, and her sobs could be heard all the way out in the *Mademoiselle* lobby. Neva was crying too, and in this sorry state both of them were eventually called on by a very impatient Hermann Landshoff, who complained he was used to photographing professional models and not these whimpering dilettantes. Ready or not, he snapped their official photographs for the August College Issue.

Sylvia, still determined for this to be the fairy tale she imagined rather than the nightmare it was fast becoming, held a limp rose in one hand, and between tears, tried to smile convincingly into the camera. In *The Bell Jar*, she wrote: "At last, obediently, like the mouth of a ventriloquist's dummy, my own mouth started to quirk up. 'Hey,' the photographer protested, with sudden foreboding, 'you look like you're going to cry.'" Landshoff's photograph of Sylvia as guest editor would become the iconic and most often reproduced image of Sylvia Plath.

More unpleasant surprises were in store. Back in May, *Mademoiselle* had asked the GEs for a handwritten statement about what they hoped to achieve in New York—"Write us a note *in your own handwriting* and tell us in not less than fifty words nor more than a hundred what you expect to gain from your month at MLLE and what you think you can give the magazine. Sign it—*your full signature*." Tagged as a top priority among the bundle of paperwork the GEs had received ahead of time, these handwritten statements were sent, without consent, to a graphologist. The "gimmick" was that his handwriting analyses would be integrated into each GE's "bio" in the "Jobiographies" feature, alongside the photograph taken by Hermann Landshoff, in which each GE would pose with something of significance to her bio. Sylvia's was the downturned rose, and her "jobiography" promised that "Sylvia will succeed in artistic fields. She has a sense of form and beauty and an intense enjoyment of her work." But the more interesting and much less flattering part of the graphologist's analysis had been left out: while Sylvia's sense of form and beauty would be "useful in fields of fashion and interior decoration," she needed to "overcome superficiality, stilted behavior, rigidity of outlook."

Sylvia had read the whole report, and perhaps she was trying to reverse this crushing analysis when soon after, as the GEs gathered for a special luncheon at an upscale restaurant, she brazenly reached for the large bowl of caviar set out for everyone to share. She pulled it close toward her, took the tiny silver caviar spoon propped next to it, and proceeded to eat it out clean, seemingly oblivious to anyone's stares. But of course she was fully conscious of what she was doing because the scene would appear a decade later in *The Bell Jar*: "I'd discovered . . . that if you do something incorrect at table with a certain arrogance, as if you knew perfectly well you were doing it properly, you can get away with it and nobody will think you are bad-mannered or poorly brought up. They will think you are original and very witty." Sylvia was wrong about believing that "nobody will think you bad-mannered." At least one of her fellow GEs, watching Sylvia hoard the bowl of caviar, wrote her off that day. She understood it was not an innocent gesture, the kind that someone like Janet Wagner or Laurie Glazer—"the hicks"—might have accidentally made.

During this first week, even as so much was on the social schedule, all the guest editors' work assignments were due if they were to make it into the August issue. Sylvia was chosen as the guest managing editor, shadowing Cyrilly Abels. She tried to hide her disappointment at being passed over for guest fiction editor, working alongside the famous Rita Smith. She dutifully moved her typewriter and desk into Abels's office, where she would listen in on her conversations and stay late working. Neva Nelson, like the others, would pass by and "see her peck, peck, peck away at the typewriter, frustrated, ripping up pages and starting over, as she sat at the small portable typewriter table, her back to Abels's desk, facing out toward the door that opened directly into the passageway that everyone took between the various editors' offices." Sylvia's talent made the stakes that much higher; she was expected to do great things that summer while a clueless Dinny Lain and a giddy Laurie Glazer were able to direct readers to the season's top lipstick shade and attend the extensive list of voluntary opportunities to be wined and dined, always with swag handed out at the end by fawning manufacturers and advertisers.

As the days passed, the GEs settled into a routine. Everyone tried to offset the oppressive summer heat with "below-calf cotton skirts," and Laurie Glazer and Sylvia would pass each other in the hallways, smiling, "our teeth white against the magenta lipstick of 1953." Neva adopted a pleasant routine of starting her day at the Barbizon coffee shop, right off the lobby, where she would usually find another GE already seated at the counter. Neva would sit down beside her and order a milky coffee in a big white ceramic mug and a Danish, preferably a bear claw. Dinny Lain, who had arrived already engaged, spent her weekends in search of her wedding dress, which she eventually found—a simple, elegant white organdy. They all discussed how Sylvia was missing out when she worked late, not just on the social events but on the details of their everyday lives, part of which was the sociability on the fifteenth floor of the Barbizon, where the girls kept their room doors open as much to let in the air during the stifling heat of June 1953 as to consult with one another on what to wear.

When it was time for the group's official photograph, a couple of weeks into their stay, the GEs were driven to Central Park and arranged in star formation, dressed in identical tartan skirts, shirts, and caps. Sylvia, as always, gave a positive spin to it in her letter home: she pronounced the tartan outfits to be "very cute." But they were not. They were itchy-looking, unbecoming. The girls were herded to the park in a van, made to stand in 94°F sun "in identical woolen tartans and 40-inch bust-producing longsleeved button-down boy-shirts . . . our arms flung wide, while a mad photographer aimed at us from a footbridge." Laurie Totten, Sylvia's neighbor in Massachusetts, hated the "silly beanies" they were forced to wear on their heads even more than the awful kilt and blouse. Sylvia secretly resented the infantilizing baby-blue blouse that finished off the preposterous look. Nevertheless, in the group photograph, Sylvia is at the top of the star formation, smiling widely.

Another five days later and Sylvia was still trying to convince herself that losing out on being guest fiction editor didn't matter, even as her letters revealed her unusually heavy workload: "Work is continuous . . . I'm reading manuscripts all day in Miss Abels office, learning countless lots by hearing her phone conversations, etc. Reading manuscripts by Elizabeth Bowen, Rumer Godden, Noel Coward, et al. Commenting on all. Getting tremendous education." Even if somewhat disingenuous, she *was* thrilled to send a rejection letter to a *New Yorker* staff member after having suffered countless rejections from them.

Yet Cyrilly Abels had thought she was doing Sylvia a favor by offering her the prestigious role of guest managing editor. Moreover, Abels was in fact Sylvia's greatest advocate at *Mademoiselle*. It was she who had tagged her short story as a standout, writing in her signature blue: "Imaginative, well written, certainly superior: hold." It is unclear whether Sylvia understood that Abels was championing her, but more lies to her mother followed. And they were just as much lies to herself as to her mother: "All the other girls just have 'busy work' to do, but I am constantly reading fascinating manuscripts and making little memo comments on them, and getting an idea of what Mlle publishes and why . . . I am awfully fond of Miss Abels, and think she is the most brilliant clever woman I have ever known." And while Plath continued to insist in *The Bell Jar* that Esther liked Jay Cee, her boss, "a lot," she described her as "plug-ugly," although with the qualifier that it didn't really matter because she had brains and spoke multiple languages.

Carol LeVarn, who had the room on the right of Sylvia's at the Barbizon, would become Sylvia's comrade in arms that summer. Carol too had submitted a short story for consideration; in the *Mademoiselle* offices, she found it hidden inside a file, with one word scrawled across it in Abels's blue pencil: "UGH!" But Carol, when she found the file, probably laughed. She was very blond, very tan, very flamboyant, and very witty, much like Doreen in *The Bell Jar*, who "had bright white hair standing out in a cotton candy fluff around her head and blue eyes like transparent agate marbles . . . and a mouth set in a sort of perpetual sneer. I don't mean a nasty sneer, but an amused, mysterious sneer, as if all the people around her were pretty silly and she could tell some good jokes on them if she wanted to." When Carol was sent news of her acceptance to join the 1953 GEs, her college, Sweet Briar, "the Smith College of the South," was also notified of the good news. Instead of congratulating Carol, they immediately contacted BTB and suggested that *Mademoiselle* reconsider its decision because Carol was not a typical, representative Sweet

Briar student, and they did not want the magazine thinking she was. (Carol was at the time dating the future writer Tom Wolfe, then at Yale, and would later also show up in one of his novels.) But Sylvia, who was not getting enough of the New York adventure she craved and that she had fully anticipated after her spring weekend with the medical student, was thrilled by her new friend's wild nature. One time, unable to cross a congested street in New York, Carol walked up to a cab, rapped on the window, and asked the passenger inside if he might scoot out so they could climb through the cab to get to the other side. He obliged, but she and Sylvia never made it across the seat and instead found themselves at a bar with him.

As much as these few adventures were fun, what Sylvia wanted most was to meet some eligible men in New York. She had set her sights on *Mademoiselle*'s formal dance at the St. Regis hotel's rooftop, where she was hoping to meet "some interesting guys so I can go out without paying for it myself and see New York." The St. Regis event was as glamorous as it could get, with two live bands that alternated throughout the night, one rising up from the floor as the other descended, one finishing off the tune of the other, the whole place aglow in rose, down to the *Mademoiselle*-pink tablecloths. There is a photograph in the August issue (of which Sylvia wanted a copy for herself, lamenting it would show up in the magazine too minuscule to see) with Sylvia and fellow guest editor Anne Shawber laughing raucously alongside two men: Sylvia's date had sat on the glass-topped cocktail table, as instructed by the photographer, and it had shattered just as the photo was snapped.

Despite the festive mood, the evening had not brought forth any eligible young men for Sylvia. In part the problem was height; both Janet Wagner and Sylvia Plath were tall, and the men rounded up for the evening were lamentably short. Sylvia, still hopeful when she set out for the ball, had worn her strapless silver lamé gown, the same one she wore to the Yale dance following her whirlwind spring weekend in New York, but it seemed now to have lost its magical quality in hot, dusty, and enervated June. In *The Bell Jar*: "And when my picture came out in the magazine the twelve of us were working on—drinking martinis in a skimpy, imitation silver-lamé bodice stuck on to a big, fat cloud of white tulle, on some Starlight Roof, in the company of several anonymous young men with all-American bone structures hired or loaned for the occasion—everybody would think I must be having a real whirl." The photograph, the one that appeared in the magazine and of which Sylvia wanted a copy, also made it look as if she were having "a real whirl." But she was not.

Sylvia was irked that some GEs had managed to end up with "eligible New Yorkers" when she had not. Neva Nelson was among the lucky ones. Neva wrote to her mother, temporarily back in her life, that, "Everything was free last night, so of course we had champagne cocktails—three before dinner, then shrimp and dancing with a Herold Hawkey from Wyoming, five feet four, then salad, then dancing with John Appleton, five feet seven, a young book publisher, then chicken with barbeque-type sauce." After finishing off a third pistachio ice-cream dessert, she danced with John Appleton again, and then again as he sipped his ninth Scotch on the rocks. Afterward, that same night, he took her to the Stork Club to prove to her it was not worth its hype, and when she finally agreed it was not, they moved on to the far trendier Salle de Champagne in Greenwich Village. The next day an enormous bouquet of exotic flowers arrived at the *Mademoiselle* offices, with a note for Neva: "With love, from John." She was forced to carry that bouquet, almost like a scarlet letter, back to the Barbizon, with Sylvia and Carol in tow, who did not hold back the whispered remarks about how this was code for "thanks for a good time." Neva could not help but notice that Sylvia's tone was the more judgmental of the two.

To add insult to injury, as far as Sylvia was concerned, Neva was then invited to John Appleton's country home on the Hudson, where he greeted her dressed in tennis whites and had dinner served at the ungodly Mediterranean hour of 9:30 p.m., with a meager (and, Neva decided, WASPish) menu of lettuce salad and steak. Yet these were the very sort of men that Sylvia was after, and so when Neva returned, skulking back to the Barbizon on Monday morning, Sylvia was ready. In the bathroom she cornered her, but Neva breezily explained she had spent the weekend in the country. To Neva's surprise, Sylvia seemed to accept that, or at least pretended to. But Sylvia clearly wrestled with the way Neva flouted the very social codes she herself hated but by which she nevertheless lived. Days later, Sylvia was still "wishing that I knew Men in the city that could take me the places that I couldn't go alone at night."

Indeed, in the 1950s, New York without a male companion was a restricted experience. Being a woman alone, without a date, limited where you could go and what you could do. Sylvia's hankering for a man, both for romance and for practicality, was further emboldened by her *Mademoiselle* best friend Carol LeVarn's shenanigans. The day after the St. Regis dance, with almost everyone nursing a hangover, the GEs piled into three Checker cabs for yet another mandatory *Mademoiselle* outing to one of the magazine's advertisers. Stuck in traffic, sitting in the first of the three cabs, Neva was hanging out the window, as much for air as for entertainment. Well-known disc jockey Art Ford happened to be standing out on the sidewalk in front of a bar, and he walked up to Neva's cab, inviting the GEs to get out and join him and his friends for a drink. They shook their heads, laughing, and Neva playfully suggested they might have better luck with the next cab down. It was the one with Sylvia and Carol inside. Neva and the others watched, incredulous, as Sylvia and Carol opened their cab door and marched out, disappearing into the bar across the street, abandoning their *Mademoiselle* obligations. In *The Bell Jar*, Sylvia, as Esther, recounted her view from the sidewalk: "The man . . . handed a bill to the driver in the middle of a great honking and some yelling, and then we saw the girls from the magazine moving off in a row, one cab after another, like a wedding party with nothing but bridesmaids."

Of course it was Sylvia who had felt like the bridesmaid and not the bride at the St. Regis dance, and she continued to feel that way, despite her and Carol's unorthodox, even risqué, decision to follow Art Ford. But in fact, things got only worse. Following an advertising agency's luncheon for the guest editors, Sylvia, who adored avocados, gorged herself on the crabmeat salad much as she had devoured the caviar. But the avocado-crabmeat-mayonnaise concoction had been sitting out too long in the test kitchen while they waited for the GEs to arrive. In the cab on the way home, Sylvia was already feeling the first waves of nausea that would soon come crashing in. By late evening, almost all the guest editors were taking turns dashing to the shared toilets, knocking desperately, wrenching door handles in agony, lying on the floor, some laughing helplessly as yet another girl, new to that evening's sport, darted in, the stench of vomit spreading. Sylvia marked her calendar for June 16 and 17 with red capital letters: PTOMAINE POISONING.

+

Sylvia, who was otherwise a prolific journal keeper, made only one single entry for June 1953. It was about the execution of the Rosenbergs, the Jewish American couple charged with spying for the Russians. In her journal, Sylvia wrote that she felt "sick at the stomach" because even as "headlines blare" news of the execution that night, no one out and about seemed affected by what was going to happen at 11 p.m.: "no yelling, no horror," instead merely a "complacent yawn." This is also how *The Bell Jar* begins. In many ways, her novel ten years later is a substitute for Sylvia's missing journal entries for June 1953.

Neva Nelson, not knowing any better, was herself guilty of the nationwide "complacent yawn" that decimated Sylvia. On the morning of June 19, Neva entered the Barbizon coffee shop as she did every morning. She saw Sylvia at the counter, joined her, and ordered her fail-proof breakfast of a bear claw Danish and a milky coffee. It was clear that Sylvia was agitated, and when Neva asked about it, Sylvia gestured at the newspapers on sale. But Neva was clueless: clueless about politics, clueless about who or what exactly was a Jew, clueless about the trial and the impending execution. Sylvia swept out, calling her "stupid," deservedly. Neva rushed after her, following Sylvia down into the subway just as a train was approaching out of the tunnel. She stood frozen midway down the subway stairs and watched Sylvia turn her face away from the screech of the subway as it barreled in through the pitch-black tunnel, electric sparks flying.

The Bell Jar describes this day more accurately still: "It was a queer, sultry summer, the summer they electrocuted the Rosenbergs, and I didn't know what I was doing in New York. I'm stupid about executions. The idea of being electrocuted makes me sick...." But why did she not turn to Cyrilly Abels, the leftist fellow traveler (if not completely the card-carrying communist that George Davis, the former associate editor who had gone to the FBI to report on her, tried to suggest)? Abels would have understood Sylvia's horror on June 19 that the Rosenbergs were to be executed that night.

Sylvia was distraught by her job, her workload, the Rosenbergs, the lack of eligible men, the lost dream of New York. *The Bell Jar*: "Only I wasn't steering anything, not even myself. I just bumped from my hotel to work and to parties and from parties to my hotel and back to work like a numb trolleybus." The other guest editors regularly found her crying. Janet Wagner had tried to help, but by the third week, like the others, she would walk away. It was too much.

Sylvia largely hid her inner turmoil from her mother in her letters home, offering a glimpse here and there, hidden within the descriptions of clothes and the overly enthusiastic pronouncements of her love for Cyrilly Abels. On June 8, she wrote to her mother, "Life passes so fast and furiously that there is hardly time to assimilate it. I'm going to bed early tonight . . . ," and then again she repeats, in the same letter, "Life happens so hard and fast I sometimes wonder who is me. I must get to bed." In *The Bell Jar*, she writes, "I was supposed to be the envy of thousands of other college girls just like me all over America who wanted nothing more than to be tripping about in those same size-seven patent leather shoes I'd bought in Bloomingdale's one lunch hour. . . ."

By the end of June, Sylvia could sense that something had shifted inside her, that New York had changed her, but not in the way she had hoped. She would need time to process what she had seen, heard, felt, and experienced—and also what she had not, even as she had desperately wished to. Writing to her brother a week before she was to leave New York, she admitted, "I haven't thought about who I am or where I come from for days. It is abominably hot in NYC . . . the humidity is staggering . . . I have learned an amazing lot here: the world has split open before my gaping eyes and spilt out its guts like a cracked watermelon. I think it will not be until I have meditated in peace upon the multitude of things I have learned and seen that I will begin to comprehend what has happened to me this last month." And it wasn't just the drama at work, or at the Barbizon: part of what happened, quite possibly, was sexual assault, or at least attempted sexual assault. Just the day before she wrote to her brother, Sylvia had been at a country club dance in Forest Hills, where she met a Peruvian man named José Antonio La Vias. Her calendar shows she returned to his apartment on Manhattan's East Side. Elsewhere, she notes he was "cruel." Janet Wagner, who was at the country club with Sylvia that night, had an entirely different recollection: their double date was with two *Brazilian* men, and it was Janet who had had to fight off a brazen, daytime sexual assault; she smashed in his white fake veneers. According to her, they had been trailed by an editorial assistant sent out by *Mademoiselle* to keep an eye on them after they mentioned where they were going, and it was he who rescued them in his convertible, dropping them off at the Barbizon, whose walls they joyfully ran toward, exhausted, laughing about their lucky escape.

But it is difficult to believe this version, especially when read alongside *The Bell Jar*. In the novel, Esther, Sylvia's protagonist and alter ego, is at a suburban country club in Forest Hills, where she is assaulted, almost raped, by Marco, a wealthy Peruvian and friend of the disc jockey (whose name is changed from the real Art Ford, whom Carol LeVarn was now dating, to the fictitious Lenny Shepherd). The assault is powered by explosive misogyny from the very start: Marco clasps her arm so hard that it bruises, which he then shows her with delight.

Whether or not Sylvia suffered a sexual assault, her time in New York left her out of sorts, discombobulated in a way that was unsettling for someone who was always planning her life. Sylvia summed up her month in New York to her brother: "I have been very ecstatic, horribly depressed, shocked, elated, enlightened and enervated...." After writing to him, she said she was planning to head down to the Barbizon's swimming pool and then out onto the sundeck, in a feeble urban attempt to replicate one of her most favorite places—the beach.

In *The Bell Jar*, Esther famously tosses her clothes from the Amazon's rooftop on her last night at the hotel and the evening after Marco's assault at the country club. But in "real life" at the Barbizon, Sylvia's emptying of her wardrobe onto Lexington Avenue was less poetic. Just as on the very first night, so too on the last all the GEs gathered in Grace's room at 9:00 p.m.: it was her birthday, in fact, and there was champagne, wine, leftover liquor, and cake. They had planned to perform a round of limericks for the *Mademoiselle* editors as a jolly goodbye the next day, but that plan soon evaporated in the wake of cake and alcohol. To everyone's shock and amusement, Neva related a story from her time at the cannery, about a dark-haired girl in short skirts who used to turn tricks in the parking lot, using Coca-Cola to douche herself as a form of preventative birth control. Others would line up in front of the vending machine and count off how many Coke bottles had been bought that night. Sometimes it was as many as twelve.

It was in this state of intoxication that Sylvia and her best friend Carol headed to the elevator and up to the roof with armfuls of Sylvia's clothes, stopping Neva to ask if she wanted any of it. Neva said no, thinking Sylvia would need them just as much as she did, having no idea of their plan. Sylvia and Carol shrugged, pushed the elevator button up, and walked out onto the roof. There was a slight breeze and a dark sky, the sun had already set hours before, and Sylvia extracted articles of clothing from the pile that she had accumulated with such care and cost, and tossed them, one by one, off the side of the Barbizon. Neither Sylvia's letters, the other guest editors' recollections, nor *The Bell Jar* offer a satisfactory explanation, but the gesture can be read in multiple ways: bravado, romanticism, resignation, madness.

Sylvia would return to her mother's house in Wellesley, Massachusetts, wearing Janet Wagner's green dirndl skirt and white eyelet peasant blouse. In return, Sylvia gave Janet her last remaining piece of clothing: her green striped bathrobe. In her suitcase, instead of clothes, Sylvia carried avocados and a pair of plastic sunglasses in the shape of two starfish. She had purged herself, or so she believed.

A month before, as she had readied herself for the adventure of her life at the Barbizon and *Mademoiselle*, Sylvia had thrilled at the idea of leaving Smith College, of experiencing so much more than she had ever before. She understood that exposure to the outside world was what she needed for her writing: "More than anything now, I realize I have to Live and Work with People . . . instead of forever being sheltered in this blissful academic environment where all the girls are the same age and have the same general range of nervous tensions and problems. My summer experiences have proved most versatile in story-background data." But the "real world" had shown itself to be more than Sylvia could handle, and her fairy godmother "woosh" fantasies must have seemed grotesquely naive by the end of June.

+

Two weeks after leaving the Barbizon, on July 15, Sylvia came down the stairs of her mother's home, legs bare. Her mother saw right away the scars on her legs that were neither fresh nor healed. It was clear that her daughter had done this to herself. Sylvia pleaded with her mother: she wanted them to die together right there and then because "the world is so rotten!" Within two hours, Sylvia was being ushered into psychiatric counseling, and at the end of July 1953, electroshock treatments began, in the crudest and cruelest way possible, without anesthetization, so that each shock reverberated through Sylvia's body, splitting her open just as she believed New York had done to her. In the days that followed, Sylvia wrote to Peggy Affleck, the Mormon in her guest editor cohort. She wanted to know more about the Mormon view of the afterlife, which staked its bets on a parallel life for the soul after the mortal body had perished.

At the end of August, back home again, Sylvia pried open her mother's metal locker, removed fifty sleeping pills, wrote a note to say that she was going for a long walk and would not be back for a day or so, and folded herself into the crawl space under the house with the pills and a glass of water to help them go down. What happened next would be splashed across national newspapers: a nationwide manhunt for the Smith girl, the talented writer, the *Mademoiselle* star. It was her brother who would finally find her, beneath the house, still alive despite the pills she had swallowed. It was Sylvia's first suicide attempt.

She had returned from New York a different person—just not in the way she had hoped. On the one hand, Sylvia adorned herself with all the privilege that came with her particular kind of life; on the other, she eschewed it, tossing all her carefully curated possessions over the side of the Barbizon. Nothing ever lived up to the hype, nothing was ever as good as it should be; the perfection she craved was indeed a fairy tale.

CHAPTER SIX

Joan Didion

The Summer of 1955

This might well be the earliest and least-known public photograph of Joan Didion. With one year left to graduate from the University of California, Berkeley, Didion was in New York in 1955, staying at the Barbizon as a *Mademoiselle* guest editor. Looking very young and very happy, she poses for the camera while interviewing Pulitzer Prize–winning novelist and short story writer Jean Stafford.

S ylvia Plath keenly felt the contradictions of the 1950s. She embodied them and she battled them; she was neither able to comply with the demands made on women nor bravely shirk them. Yet two years later another set of guest editors would arrive in New York, with more than one future writer in their midst, and while they too experienced their summer at the Barbizon and *Mademoiselle* as a time of reckoning, it would bring them to different conclusions from Sylvia Plath's.

Joan Didion, who would become known as one of the finest writers and chroniclers of America's political and cultural shifts, checked in to the Barbizon in 1955. She arrived, just like Sylvia had, with a drawer full of prizes and awards and a reputation that suggested great things were to come her way. She had received the enviable telegram from Betsy Talbot Blackwell, but so too had Peggy LaViolette, one of her closest friends at the University of California, Berkeley. It was unusual for the magazine to choose two students from the same university, but Joan and Peggy were delighted to have each other along for the ride. As sophisticated as they felt, they were both California natives after all, and in Peggy's words, their circle was limited to WASPs, girls dressed in "cashmere sweaters, and skirts, and saddle Oxfords, with shiny hair." They knew little of the larger world.

Flying to New York, it was Joan Didion's first time on an airplane. It was 1955, late May, and air travel was a pleasure and not yet an ordeal. Flights had names as if to suggest they were the start of a journey. Their American Airlines flight was called the Golden Gate, and it was taking them from San Francisco to New York. Didion was only twenty years old, very small and fine-boned, with dimples and light brown hair cut to just above her shoulders. It was much the same hairstyle Sylvia Plath had worn two years earlier when she traveled to New York as a guest editor. As for Peggy LaViolette, this was not her first trip in an airplane (she had flown the summer before to Mexico City), and she became the unofficial expert as Joan gripped the seat.

The stewardesses, as they were called then, served the passengers Beltsville roast turkey with dressing and giblet sauce. Apparently it wasn't only flights that had names back then; turkeys did too. The Beltsville was an invention of the 1930s—a turkey that was finally small enough to fit an apartment-size oven. As Joan and Peggy leaned over their roast turkey, they made sure not to spill. Both had dressed up for the plane ride, as was expected of any airline passenger in those days. Peggy's mother had insisted that she go to San Francisco's best store, I. Magnin, for her travel suit. Upon entering, they made a beeline for the "moderate" floor. It wasn't "couture," one floor up, where they seldom ventured, but nor did it mean thumbing through the racks. The "moderate" floor came with a "clothing adviser," who greeted Peggy's mother by name, led them over to a damask-covered love seat, and asked Peggy to describe the purpose of her outfit. She was going to New York, she explained, for the month of June, staying at the Barbizon and working in the *Mademoiselle* magazine offices on Madison Avenue. She would need to appear sophisticated while she mingled with editors, advertisers, and the New York literati. Nodding, the clothing adviser disappeared behind a mirrored door and then reappeared with an armful of items that she spread out on the love seat. Peggy, her mother, and the clothing adviser put their heads together, touching the fabrics, remarking on the cut and style, until the outfits were narrowed down to those worth trying. Peggy left I. Magnin with a navy two-piece dress in summer wool: a long tunic top that buttoned up the front and a pleated skirt underneath. There was even a detachable white collar.

With lunch over, the stewardess passed out postcards. One pictured a DC-7, the same airplane that they were on; another some passengers toasting the flight over cocktails in the airplane lounge. This was in-flight entertainment in the 1950s: the opportunity to write to friends and family to let them know you were flying high up in the clouds. But once the postcards were written, the boredom of sitting took over, as did the droning of the metal carcass in flight. The Golden Gate stopped twice along the way, dropping off some passengers and picking up others. In Dallas, Peggy and Joan got off and bought a boxed meal while the plane refueled. Next was Washington, DC, and with it being Friday of Memorial Day weekend, the plane now filled with congressmen. The final leg of the trip to New York was by far the worst, and Peggy sat next to a quivering Joan, reassuring her that the air bumps did not translate to imminent nosedives, even as she was losing faith herself.

Joan Didion was a junior at Berkeley, and had another year of college left, but Peggy was a senior missing her graduation, which her mother had found difficult to process. What her mother did not understand, no matter how much Peggy had tried to explain, was that there wasn't a girl in America who wouldn't choose *Mademoiselle* over her graduation ceremony. New York beckoned as California receded, and Joan and Peggy confided to each other how they were glad to be free of their boyfriends (Joan would take hers back upon returning to Berkeley, even as she felt their relationship was "hopeless," leaving her "bored" and "apathetic"). Peggy felt little loss in leaving her boyfriend behind, was in fact perfectly content without him, but the pressure to have a "steady" was intense. As a college senior over the past year, Peggy seemed to spend almost every weekend at some friend's wedding—checking off yet another girl who had dropped out of Berkeley to accompany her new husband to Fort Benning for his mandatory military service.

Peggy's desire to buck the trend was as intense as the pressure to conform. Her parents had reared her to work: her mother had always had a job, and in the early years, her father, a teacher, thought nothing of spending summers at the local pea cannery to supplement their income. (Even so, one day, as Peggy was helping dry dishes, her mother turned to her: "Peggy, you know you don't have to stay at Cal all the way through. You ought to be able to find a husband in two years." The rest was all noise and haze: Peggy began to shout at her mother that she loved Berkeley and why would her mother suggest she prostitute herself?!)

When Peggy graduated from Berkeley High in 1950, most of her friends received a hope chest as their graduation gift. A cedar-lined chest filled with linen guest towels and bedsheets. Peggy didn't want a hope chest, she wanted a typewriter, preferably an Olivetti portable typewriter with a travel case. Joan Didion turned up at Berkeley with that very typewriter and travel case; moreover, as Peggy enviously learned, Joan had gotten hers without a fight. Now they both carried their typewriters onto the plane with them. A handbag in one hand, and gripping their typewriter in the other.

To try to be who they were, or who they wanted to be, was not easy. The United States was at war again—first Korea, and now slowly Vietnam was beginning. The Cold War fears with which George Davis had grappled, lobbing accusations of female ambition at Cyrilly Abels, were being inflamed all the more. The solution for most women was retreat. The feminist Betty Friedan, in her famous book, *The Feminine Mystique*, would write that this era was marked by women's "pent-up hunger for marriage, home, and children," "a hunger which, in the prosperity of postwar America, everyone could suddenly satisfy." America's expanding suburbs were a witness to this, where one-income families and two-car garages were the new normal. The quiet rebellions against these values were inevitably individual, unassuming, and—in the case of Peggy and Joan—cashmere-clad. They carried their typewriters, boyfriend-less, unencumbered, dressed in their cardigan sets, ready to tackle New York. Joan had already been picked as the guest fiction editor, the most prestigious of all the posts, and the one that Sylvia had so desired. Peggy would be guest shopping editor.

Both wore nylon hose and one-and-a-half-inch heeled pumps on the plane, but Joan had dressed more lightly in anticipation of New York's summer heat; being from Sacramento, she understood hot weather better than Peggy. Nevertheless, when Joan finally got off the DC-7 at the Idlewild Terminal (as JFK International Airport was then called) in Queens, New York, she felt her new dress, chosen for this moment of propitious arrival, and "which had seemed very smart in Sacramento," was "less smart already." New York overwhelmed before it even came into full view.

There was, however, nothing "smart" and stylish about the bus ride from the airport to Manhattan. Joan opened the window wide "and watched the skyline," only to see instead "the wastes of Queens and the big signs that said MIDTOWN TUNNEL THIS LANE." But upon entering Manhattan, everything changed. Their first sighting of the towering skyscrapers and sidewalks crowded with people injected Joan with the "sense, so peculiar to New York, that something extraordinary would happen any minute, any day, any month." When they finally arrived at the Barbizon on Lexington and Sixty-Third Street, they looked up at the salmon-colored multi-turreted building that they'd only before seen in photographs. Its architecture was a playful mixture of Moorish, Neo-Renaissance, and Gothic Revival styles but tastefully arranged in art deco lines and angles that had held up over the almost thirty years since it was built. Oscar, the doorman, stood at attention in his regalia.

Joan and Peggy entered the hotel lobby, the most impressive part of the Barbizon (the hotel keenly understood that first impressions mattered), and looked up at the mezzanine, from which groups of young women peered down, keeping an eye out for their dates or, just as likely, everyone else's. Peggy and Joan went up to their rooms on the fourteenth floor, pleased to discover that theirs were adjacent to each other, at the end of the hall next to the elevators, and right next to the shared showers. As per *Mademoiselle* tradition, on their beds they each found a single red rose and their itinerary for the month of June. But one thing had changed since Sylvia Plath's stay at the Barbizon: now there was air-conditioning to ward off New York's humid summer heat. Joan had caught a cold when she opened the window on the bus into Manhattan, and she would lie in her bed at the Barbizon for the next three days, curled up, fighting a fever, hating the air conditioner that was cooling the room to a wintry 35 degrees, unable to switch it off, too scared to call the front desk because she had no idea how much to tip if they came to help. It was better to freeze and save face. Instead, she called her on-again off-again boyfriend Bob, the son of the owner of Bakersfield's Lincoln-Mercury dealership, and told him she could see the Brooklyn Bridge from her window. It was in fact the Queensboro Bridge.

+

That same day, guest editor and also future writer Janet Burroway was traveling in from Arizona. She called herself Jan because she thought this way she'd have editors guessing her gender (a feminist reflex before she even knew the word). She was a self-described "Arizona greenhorn," but, like a protective shield, she carried with her to New York a preemptive world-weariness. She wrote to her parents—almost as if she were yawning into the page—that her first ever airplane ride was "exciting and beautiful" and yet "surprisingly unamazing." In fact, it turned out to be exactly as she had imagined it: she could pick out her college dorm as they flew over Tucson and "the rockies looked like a salt and soda map, the midwest like a gigantic patchwork quilt, and lake michigan like an ocean." But just as happened to Joan Didion, the mask that Janet had carefully prepared fell away as soon as the plane touched down in New York. Janet had planned to look "cold and beautiful," but upon arriving at the airport she was sure "that arizona was stamped in neon letter[s] on my forehead." Like countless arrivals to New York before her, she immediately felt "ALONE." She stood bewildered in the middle of the terminal, unsure of where to go, standing in the way of others who did. Finally, she spied a young woman with a hatbox, and confident that anyone with a hatbox knew where they were going, she simply followed her through the concourse and onto a bus heading into Manhattan. It was only once she was on the bus, sitting across the aisle from her, that Janet saw her luggage tags: *Ames, Iowa.*

The bus eventually emerged from what Didion had called "the wastes of Queens" and deposited its passengers in Manhattan. Janet hailed a cab. As she sat in bumper-to-bumper traffic, the cabbie eyed her through the rearview mirror. Perhaps he saw that "Arizona" stamp on her forehead.

"New York," he said, turning around to face her, "is like a big ice cream soda—try to eat it all at once, it nauseates you: a little at a time, it's wonderful."

She would soon learn just how right he was. Once checked in at the Barbizon along with all the other GEs, she took one of the hotel postcards out from the desk drawer in her room and wrote home: "Rm 1426—pretty far from the pavement." The next day she elaborated, dismissing the Barbizon's "typical room" as it was featured on the postcard; it was bogus, a lie. Her room—a *real* Barbizon room—was in fact "brother's-size and old." She called it brother's size because back home, in the middle-class, sunlit ranch house in Arizona, it was Janet who had the largest bedroom of everyone and she was used to space to move around in. Still, she had to admit the Barbizon itself was "beautiful, very impressive." And even if one was quick to judge, as Janet Burroway was, it was impossible to deny the hotel's pull, its mythology.

Peggy LaViolette met Janet, and immediately pegged her for a greenhorn. Janet had arrived wearing Indian moccasins and other colorful things that Peggy suspected might very well be everyday wear in Arizona, but certainly not in New York. One outfit in particular deserved to have been left in Arizona, she believed: a very gathered and flared turquoise cotton skirt. That said, there were things Peggy admired about Janet. Peggy thought she was probably the kind of fun-loving Western gal who could jump on a horse at a moment's notice. Janet was not particularly wowed by any of the other guest editors either, Peggy included. She wrote home that she had found them to be "nice but so far not spectacular." A few days later, however, things were looking up and three or four were now "wonderful," two or three were "absolute drips," and "the rest o.k. but not as outstanding as I'd expected."

+

Where the future writer Gael Greene stood within this hierarchy in the early days of June 1955 is hard to say, but by the end of the month she was not about to win any popularity contest. Gael Greene was a senior at the University of Michigan when she applied for the *Mademoiselle* contest. With graduation looming and nothing yet in place, she set to work, as Nanette Emery had done ten years earlier, jumping through the various hoops for a coveted guest editor spot. She worked on her application while assorted friends and people traipsed in and out of her kitchen, where there was a free-flowing keg on twenty-four-hour standby: "Beer suds flowed, somebody's favorite professor cooked up a batch of manicotti in the kitchen, the phonograph played Pakistani love songs and voodoo rain chants while I—slouch-hatted for inspiration as well as privacy—sat at the typewriter preparing replies to MLLE queries." When she received the telegram inviting her to New York (not surprised by it, because "I knew I was good"), she fussed over her wardrobe, much like Sylvia Plath had done. Gael solved the problem by raiding her dad's dress shop in Detroit, though she'd later regret she had not arrived a few pounds lighter to fit the photographed fashions better.

Perhaps to compensate for her few extra pounds, perhaps to mimic the intrepid reporter she planned to be, Gael Greene wore a trench coat: "a great big girl in a great big trench," recalled one guest editor. At Michigan, Gael had been a campus stringer for *Time* magazine, and now she lorded it over the rest of the 1955 GEs. When Gael would mention *Time*, Joan and Peggy would just roll their eyes and back off. Gael gave the impression that she did not like any of the other nineteen GEs—and, in fact, she did not particularly like them: she had no time for their half-hearted ambitions, as she saw them. She suspected that while they might well have come out all the way to New York, their final dream destination was a suburb with white picket fences and a house full of children. Gael, on the other hand, was unabashed in her disdain for such things. She wanted a career, and she was not afraid to say so.

Regardless of what the GEs thought of one another, these were the ambitious girls of their generation, the crème de la crème of their campuses. The day after arriving at the Barbizon, the twenty guest editors gathered nervously at the *Mademoiselle* offices: among them, Joan Didion, her friend and confidante Peggy LaViolette, and the future writers Gael Greene and Janet Burroway. They eyed each other with a heightened sense of competition. Leading this 1955 crop of GEs was Jane Truslow, guest editor-in-chief and a senior at Smith

College, Sylvia Plath's alma mater. It was Jane's job to breathlessly describe to the magazine's readers their first day at work: "'Sesame,' said the hero in Arabian Nights and a door opened for him upon a treasure that was incredibly dazzling. The magic words for twenty very excited Guest Eds. were less exotic but just as effective: 'Sixth floor please . . . the MLLE offices!' As the elevator door slid open on that most anticipated of days, our first with MLLE, we entered a new and glittering world, ours for four fantastic weeks. Editors Blackwell, Abels and Fechheimer, once only mythical names on a masthead, welcomed us in the conference room. They and the rest of the staff set us at ease, and so the whirl began . . . Creative energy crackled like summer heat lightning in the atmosphere over 575 Madison Avenue and the Barbizon as each of us attacked our assignment for the August issue. . . ."

It was not quite like that. Truslow left out the part about how Margaret Fechheimer, the College Board editor, took one look at them and sighed. She wanted to "bomb the Eastman Kodak people," who were responsible for the "underexposed snapshots" on the basis of which—along with the mandatory submission of writings and drawings—she had picked this group. Upon seeing what she was dealing with, Fechheimer immediately called down beauty editor Bernice Peck, who quickly summoned all the assistants, and together they circled the twenty girls, tweezing, clipping, advising, and hurriedly handing out sample-size placenta creams in the hope that improvement would be sudden. Gael was subjected to a "four-layer face paint job" and unceremoniously informed that she needed to diet, as of this very moment, with a goal weight loss of twenty to thirty pounds.

But much as the guest editors had eyed one another critically, they were hardly less judgmental about the staff. Gael Greene found it ironic that BTB lectured them on health, punctuating "her talk with deep drags from a cigarette and a rasping cough." Janet Burroway first caught sight of BTB as she "sailed between the mirrors of the editorial room" "in black sheath, with pearl choker, a very long cigarette holder, which she did indeed handle as Audrey Hepburn would have," and which she lifted into the air while instructing all twenty to "'Believe in Pink'!" Janet's automatic distaste for BTB was no doubt bound up in her Methodist upbringing: her family prided itself on never socializing with people who drank or smoked. Betsy did both, copiously. Unlike the others, Peggy LaViolette liked BTB; she found her to be quite a character, "in the same way that all those women were who ran those magazines." And she got a kick out of watching her slowly eat one single boiled egg for lunch.

Following the beautification of the twenty GEs, *Mademoiselle*'s editorial staff interviewed them, a process that ended with a closed-door meeting where they argued over who would get whom as their guest editor, if not already assigned. The office-held consensus was that, despite the popularity of the program and the financial success of the August College Issue, the GEs were more of a hindrance than a help. During the interviews, Janet Burroway had found everyone, except for Ida McNeil, the merchandising editor, to be very nice, and of course it was McNeil who ended up as her editor—"these new yorkers are very strange people," Janet concluded. On that first day, Janet was invited to lunch at the Ivy Room of the Drake Hotel with Pat Weaver, careers editor, where she consumed a "French and gold-leaf ritzy filet of sole 3.95, coffee .50, ice cream .70." *Mademoiselle* picked up the bill, she assured her mother.

New York, however, even as it was "noisy, muggy," did not disappoint. On the second night, Janet walked from the Barbizon at Sixty-Third and Lexington down to Forty-Fifth and Broadway and "was so overcome" that she cataloged her walk that night as a breathless list of landmarks: "saw saks, bonwit teller, tiffany, i miller, grand central, times square, u.n., rko, rca . . . broadway, broadway, and more broadway." A few days later she spied Harry Belafonte crossing Broadway: "just beautiful!" She had even more to say about her first Sunday service at the famous and affluent St. Patrick's Cathedral on Fifth Avenue: she described an ornate ceremony with an audience of "15,000 women in fur coats; massive unbeautiful pillars; 3% emotion, 91% PRODUCTION, 5% capitalism, and probably, surely somewhere 1% religion. If Jesus had seen it he would have puked...." Under Janet's scrutinizing gaze, the Museum of Modern Art did not fare much better. Until money arrived from home, she was on an "Eat for $2 a Day" diet, which she found to be manageable, if she was careful; she therefore did not appreciate the $1.50 MoMA admission fee that cut so deeply into her food funds.

Peggy and Joan, next door to each other at the far end of the fourteenth-floor hallway, and with an easy friendship, did not join Janet on these adventures. In fact, they did not feel the need to socialize that much with the other guest editors. Gael Greene found Joan Didion to be somewhere "between shy and scared." Peggy LaViolette liked to head off early and alone to the *Mademoiselle* offices, making her way slowly down Fifty-Seventh Street, filled with upscale art dealers, until she reached The Tailored Woman on the corner of Fifth Avenue, a women's clothing store that had opened right after World War I, and whose owner believed less was more, refusing to stock anything with too many "doodads, furbelows, sequins and beads." She would stop and window-shop, and by the time she arrived at the offices, even if it was early, models were already sitting in the lobby, holding on to their hatboxes, waiting to be reviewed, hoping to land a photo shoot. One time, while Peggy was waiting for the elevators, the Secret Service suddenly appeared, followed by President Truman. "How the hell are you, Harry?!" people started to shout out, and he waved back, "Fine!"

The floor of the main lobby at 575 Madison Avenue was beige marble, its banks of elevators art deco brass and ornate metal frames. In the back of the lobby was a small coffee shop with stools and a few tiny tables; you could order your lunch from there and a waiter with a trolley would bring it up to your office. The *Mademoiselle* offices had air conditioners in some of the windows, so on hot summer days, one lingered. The offices were very simple, with sparse decorations and venetian blinds. Most of the staff sat in carrels and only the top editors like BTB, Cyrilly Abels, and Rita Smith had real offices with doors. The art department was right there too, next to editorial—which was unusual—with space next to the windows for natural light. The GEs, when not off at photo shoots for the College Issue or at carefully choreographed luncheons with the magazine's advertisers, were working, or trying. By June 7, Janet Burroway wrote home that she was tired of being asked to write unimaginative magazine copy that then got ripped to shreds by the editors, and that in fact *"all* the GE's" were feeling frustrated too. They were drowning in untapped ambition, as unrecognized by the *Mademoiselle* editors as an unrequited love.

In the evenings, back in their small rooms with blue floral bedspreads and curtains, the GEs resorted to being the college girls they still were despite their yearning to become more. Peggy ate crackers and cheese in bed while she read. Not one to go out much, she was often there when the maid came around at 10:00 p.m. to do the first bed check of the evening: Peggy was ticked off the list as present. But for those who weren't, the bed checks continued hourly until 5:00 a.m. Joan ventured out for the night more often than Peggy, taking up party offers wherever and whenever she could. If the light was still on in Peggy's room, she'd come in and regale her with stories of her evening.

One such night Joan came roaring into the room—Peggy had never seen her like that before: "as if she were set on fire."

"I've met someone!" Joan declared. She explained he was a Southerner, a Catholic, and married.

"Perfect," Peggy drawled.

It turned out that "Mr. Perfect" was Noel Parmentel, writer and enfant terrible, who later helped arrange for the publication of Joan's first novel, *Run, River,* which she dedicated to him. One night, later during Joan's second stint in New York, she promised to take him—bored with the New York scene—to a party with "new faces." As he entered, he burst out laughing: "Of the fifteen people in the room, [. . .] he had already slept with five of the women and owed money to all but two of the men." In fact, if any man could penetrate the Barbizon fortress that restricted men to the lobby, it was probably Noel Parmentel.

✦

As Joan began to spend more nights out with him, Peggy was left to explore New York on her own. She often ate dinner at the Barbizon coffee shop, or else right across the street, on Sixty-Third, at the street-level steak restaurant with a patio out front. Whenever someone offered to take Peggy to dinner, she suggested they go there. For Peggy, the restaurant epitomized New York as she had imagined it: red-and-white-checkered tablecloths with indifferent waiters serving eager customers testing out their new New York selves. All of New York drank Manhattans and enormous martinis, and an eggplant parmigiana dinner cost only a dollar anywhere on Third Avenue.

Back at Berkeley, where Joan and Peggy had both worked on the *Daily Cal,* they had never mentioned to each other that they were applying to *Mademoiselle*'s guest editor contest. Peggy didn't say anything because she was sure her application was a lost cause. The only reason she was even applying was because she'd promised Tom, a young man who had taken an interest in her the previous summer in Mexico. Peggy had wanted to go with some of her sorority sisters to Europe, but her mother said they had just had a war over there and she couldn't go, and so Peggy cooked up the idea to do a tour of Mexico, which came with chaperones to guarantee her parents' consent. The American students on the program all stayed at different *pensiones* but would gather at a central hotel in the afternoon for drinks. One day she met Tom, whose classmate at the University of Pennsylvania was an heir to the *Saturday Evening Post*, and after chatting, Tom convinced Peggy she'd be perfect for the GE program. He made her promise that she would apply. He said he would write and check on her. He did. That June, he would also drive up to New York and take Peggy to the steak restaurant across from the Barbizon, or else for lunch to the Penn Club, where he stayed when he was in town, so she could observe the Ivy Leaguers in their natural habitat—as she liked to say.

Peggy assumed all along that Joan Didion would be chosen as a GE. She already had a "truckload" of literary prizes, and while her grades at Berkeley were not top-notch, the professors loved her work. Indeed, just like Sylvia Plath in 1953, Joan Didion in 1955 was treated differently by *Mademoiselle*'s staff, and in particular by fiction editor Rita Smith, who made a point of introducing her to New York's literati. Joan, in turn, was fascinated by Rita and ready to do anything she asked. One night, when it was already past ten, Joan came running into Peggy's room: Rita had just called, very drunk, saying over and over how she had left the window of her office open and she was afraid that if it remained open, she might be tempted to jump (clearly this was a case of Rita's "vapors," about which George Davis originally complained). She asked Joan to go to the *Mademoiselle* offices immediately, close the window, and then report back that she had done so. "But I'm not going alone," Joan declared as she dragged Peggy out of bed. Peggy, always the faithful friend, accompanied her from the Barbizon down to Fifty-Seventh and Madison. A night watchman was at the Street & Smith building, and Joan lied that she had left something in the office. Under this pretext, and with the guard watching over her, she dashed upstairs and quickly scanned Rita's office: the window was closed shut. It had all been her imagination. That was the moment Peggy decided they were all crazy at *Mademoiselle*.

+

Like Peggy, Janet Burroway was finding her way. At first she was always writing home for money to be sent, but after a while she learned how to skip cab rides whenever possible, even though she'd damaged her heel (an unexpected medical cost—she noted crossly). As the guest editor in the merchandising department, a position she felt was entirely mismatched with her real interests, Janet was going from one fashion show to another and wrote gleefully at first: "Loot from shows is mounting up." Lunches too. After a tour of the Bates plant, they were given a "lush lunch," although Janet would have preferred fabric samples since she designed many of her own dresses—those that Peggy frowned upon. For the Brother sewing machine unveiling, it was lunch on the roof of the Hotel Pierre. But even the swag couldn't make up for the tedium of the shows after a while: "I'll take New York, but you can have the fashion industry, from the eyebrow pencil on NY's highest-paid models to the suspiciously sweet smile on [editor] Ida McNeil." Like all the GEs, Janet had come expecting to do serious literary work. None of them wanted to be in promotions, or advertising, or publicity.

But gradually, Janet began to embrace the glamour of her *Mademoiselle* summer. As the days went by, her Barbizon room no longer seemed so small, she decided, and she liked having a phone and a basin inside the room where she could wash the New York grime off of her white gloves. The front desk had given her $10 of credit toward her meals until her first paycheck arrived, and she loved that the maids left her room looking spotless however badly she'd left it for them that morning. She had learned to enjoy being alone. She had also discovered a magical place in Greenwich Village called the Champagne Gallery—"a favorite haunt of the young strugglings." It was decorated like a very large living room with sofas, carpets, paintings, floor lamps, and a grand piano which anyone could play, and where "Chopsticks" would have elicited no complaints, even as there was a steady stream of classical music, and two boys argued over the score of a piece they were working on. Others sketched but not in a "pseudo-bohemian or arty" way, while a black man, a ventriloquist, wandered around with his dummy, everyone engaging it in conversation and argument about politics and aesthetics. The two waitresses occasionally got up to sing. It certainly rated better than her trip to the Stork Club, which she found to be "very very" and where the "lousy lemonade" left her wondering why some places got to be so famous. Janet's false world-weariness was at least becoming more discriminatory.

Midway through the month, Sylvia Plath showed up. She already had a well-recognized name, certainly among young college coeds, in part because of her nationally publicized suicide attempt. The East Coast guest editors especially "were gaga over her." The hushed talk of her nervous breakdown, of disappearing under her mother's porch with a bottle of pills, the manhunt that followed, merely added to her mystique in an era, Peggy later realized, "when neuroticism among women authors was almost a necessary badge of membership in the women's creative community." The day Plath came to the *Mademoiselle* offices, guest editor-in-chief Jane Truslow, of upper-crust Adams lineage, insisted that Peggy come meet the almost famous young poet. Peggy, an unimpressed Californian, had a pleasant enough conversation with Sylvia, finding her to be a typical American college girl, dressed nicely, with a quiet demeanor. But she didn't understand what all the fuss was about. Janet, who did not get to meet her that day, understood what all the fuss was about and harbored a serious case of envy; she would joke, somewhat defensively, that Sylvia's last name was really "Plass," but that Sylvia had a lisp.

✦

Multiple generations of GEs would go on to debate the eternal question of whether they did have to work, really work, while at *Mademoiselle*. Was the work already done for them so that they were only required to cross the t's and dot the i's? In this sense, Sylvia Plath was an anomaly. She had worked to the point of a nervous breakdown, with an unrelenting stack of assignments always on her desk. But the other GEs would ask themselves: Was their real job to pose for photographers and detail their tastes and desires to a bevy of merchandisers and advertisers keen to know what America's college girls wanted? Much of the contention centered on whether "parading all over the garment district so that manufacturers could analyze our consumer inclinations" was work. Gael Greene thought it was.

Of course Gael might have looked more kindly upon the exploitation had she been the one chosen to walk the runway in the latest fashions at the magazine's College Clinic at the Hotel Astor. But while a guest editor from Utah led the runway show with a twirling baton, Gael Greene was asked to sit it out, watching from the sidelines up in the balcony area. Guest editor-in-chief Jane Truslow wrote in the August issue: at the Astor, "where fashion scored a touchdown," the "Millies" were "offered . . . new hope for a slim-hipped future" by being introduced to Warner's elaborate, long line corset called the "Merry Widow," named after a Lana Turner movie. Janet Burroway's single goal for the College Clinic was straightforward: she wanted to finagle a free haircut (worth an exorbitant $10.50) from the famous Enrico Caruso, hairdresser to the stars and top models, and director of hair and makeup for the College Clinic. She managed to get her free haircut, and also a front-and-center view of the runway show, whose production, she wrote her parents, made St. Patrick's Sunday service look like a provincial sideshow.

That year, 1955, the College Issue carried more advertising than any fashion magazine had ever before. All the merchandise was on display in the Hotel Astor grand ballroom in front of a sea of "buyers, store owners, retailers, wholesalers, promotion managers, window display artists, advertisers, designers," with "scene changes, gimmicks, staging extravaganzas," and a crystal chandelier that opened up to release three thousand balloons of various colors. Gold and upholstered clipboards were given away as party favors; canapés, and Scotch and sodas were served; and while everyone got "hilariously tight ... the 20 innocent young G.E.'s circulate amongst the crowd murmuring sweet nothings about the sincerity of the *Mademoiselle* promotion department and trying to keep from getting picked up." Gael Greene was right in that this part at least *was* work.

Company lunches and photo-opportunity parties certainly took up as much of the young women's time as any kind of editorial work. There was the annual June gathering at the home of skin-care mogul Helena Rubinstein, where Peggy was surprised to find "a tiny, chubby Russian Jew in 5-inch heels, a large chignon, and an incredible afternoon dress" (Rubinstein was actually Polish). Her outrageously decorated Midtown apartment had a floor, reached by elevator, that was a hidden gallery of master works behind dark velvet drapes. While Peggy delighted in being so close to art that no one else would ever get to see, Janet looked at the Picassos and Chagalls on private display, wondering how it was possible to amass the worst paintings by the best painters and then cram them all into one room. Betsy Talbot Blackwell also hosted a party for the GEs in her enormous apartment on Fifth Avenue, a gathering Peggy found to be among the better ones (even she had come to realize they weren't all fun), which the owners of the Gimbels department store—right across from Macy's and their fierce competitor—always attended as well. By June 27, Janet, on the one hand, would sigh, "Mrs. Blackwell's disgusting cocktail party this afternoon—I don't mean to be flip, but you wouldn't believe so many so famous people could be so dull." On the other, she was already regretting she had not pushed herself to live more in the moment, that she had failed to fully appreciate the rolled-out red carpets, the fashion shows, the lunches, the airplane ride to West Point for a photo shoot, and everything else that *Mademoiselle* had given her and which she suspected she would not see again for many years to come.

But in one way, Janet had in fact embraced what New York offered. On June 10, a third of the way into the guest editors' month, *Mademoiselle* threw its annual St. Regis ball—the crowning glory of the magazine's multiple parties. While Gael Greene would be sidelined during the College Clinic, she was very much at the center of things at the St. Regis hotel. She brought along her childhood friend Sidney, who was living in New York and selling scarves for his father; she had offered him up to the College Board editor, who was not only in search of men to attend the party, but in particular "a nice presentable Republican with a good address to put at Mrs. B's table." Fortunately, by the time Sidney was relating how he had campaigned for the left-wing Progressive Party's presidential candidate Henry Wallace, "Mrs. B. was slightly high and off dancing with a blue-eyed Scot in knee socks and formal kilt." The crème de la crème of Manhattan's bachelorhood, or some simulacrum of it, drank excessively, and openly discussed "the withers and flanks" of the GEs, speculating who would and wouldn't, eventually deciding they all would with the right alchemy of wining, dining, and foreplay. The ogling, poorly masquerading as flirtation, was led by *Life* magazine reporter Higgins Wintergreen Von Lemur, who swore his scar was not the result of a dueling match but of a lover's quarrel, at age seven, with his Hungarian governess, who bit him. Drunk, he rallied others in boisterous demands for cognac. Margaret Fechheimer, the college editor, intercepted the waiters and switched them to coffee, begging Gael Greene to do something because her table alone had already consumed two weeks of the College Board's contest budget.

Peggy thought the ball was fantastic; it was a real ball, and the party did not stop until well into the early morning. She had invited

Tom, the young man she'd met in Mexico the previous summer, the one who pushed her to apply to *Mademoiselle*'s contest: "You were the one who started it all," she told him. In the early morning hours, with the St. Regis party finally winding down, Tom suggested they go for a drive through Harlem in his MG. As dawn was breaking over Manhattan, Peggy climbed in, wearing her fancy dress, and they drove through every street in Harlem and the West Side, everything that Peggy had not seen, closeted as she was in the Barbizon up on the Upper East Side. They drove until six in the morning, when Tom finally dropped her back off at the Barbizon, and she giggled to herself as she climbed out of the MG in last night's clothes, raising eyebrows in the lobby.

Gael, in the meantime, found herself at the end of the night "crawling up the curb in front of the Barbizon and through a swinging door. A horde of hands swooped down at me and lifted me to unsteady feet." About to lose the top of her dress, she reached down to discover that in fact she'd lost her mother's stole, until what she thought was a pounding in her head turned out to be Oscar tapping her shoulder to let her know he'd found the stole draped around the fire hydrant. That night, Gael fell asleep under her narrow bed, the stole wrapped around her head, one end trailing out the open window. The next morning, the door opened suddenly and one of the Barbizon residents tossed a dozen Clark Bars at her, with the declaration, in lockjaw upper-class drawl, that "peanut buttah always shrinks mah head beautifully the mawnin' aftah."

Janet Burroway had had her own good time, although entirely sober. She was among the very youngest in guest editor history, and also a teetotaler. But instead of being embarrassed that she could not hold up to the likes of Gael Greene, Janet basked in the attention she received from being "eighteen, a virginal Methodist Phoenix freshman who had never had a cigarette or a drink." Early the next morning, around the time that Peggy was whizzing around town in the

MG, Janet returned to the Barbizon and wrote home: "If the Mlle. staff doesn't know how to write a magazine, they certainly know how to throw a dance." The evening had started right: she had done her hair as Enrico Caruso had advised after her session with him at the College Clinic ("a middle part, a deep wave on either side of it, and one side pulled farther back than the other"), and it behaved, much to her surprise. She was a hit as the only girl who didn't drink at a cocktail party. The decor for the St. Regis rooftop party reminded her of a Hollywood supper club with "pink quilted walls, 2 orchestras, a waiter for every 4 people." *Mademoiselle* "bless their hearts" had sat her next to "a very unpretty intellectual boy who talked fascinating serious politics and Europe and literature all the way through dinner." She danced with the pretty boys. Nevertheless, at the end of the evening, she held out for the "unpretty intellectual boy," a Fulbright scholar on his way to Oxford named Dick Aldridge, to offer to take her home. He did so, in a hansom cab through Central Park. "This," she wrote home, "is the New York I had in mind!"

Thereafter, the New York Janet had in mind became inextricable from Dick Aldridge, who, she noted, now seemed less unpretty (in the same way her Barbizon room now felt less small). She started to spend all her free time with him, often visiting with his family as well in their grand New York apartment. She promised her mother to find out his religion, and reported back the "violently important information; he is protestant." Assuring her parents further, she wrote: "I know that you think New York is a big, tough, frightening city, but even people who live all their lives in back-lawn-less apartments manage to raise kids who don't belong to street gangs and turn into second-story men." Dick Aldridge did not belong to a street gang, nor was he a burglar; he belonged to a very rich and respectable family—his father was a prominent New York gynecologist, and his mother was English, strict, brought up in India. Dick had, much to Janet's admiration as well as envy, already published his poetry in the *New Yorker*, and the *New York Times* had compared him to Robert Frost. Peggy would remember her rushing into the Barbizon one night: "I've got a date with an important poet!" This convinced Peggy even more that Janet was "never shy of blowing her own horn." But in fact nothing could have been further from the truth; just like the others, she was wracked with insecurity that would come to a head at the end of the month. (In 1968, the actress Cybill Shepherd too would sit in her room at the Barbizon "wondering how I would ever make it in this vast city just stockpiled with brilliant people.")

On top of the parties, the month of June 1955 had included a tour of the *New York Times* offices, a get-together with designers at the Empire State Building, lunch at Saks Fifth Avenue, and more. It was all rounded off with the traditional group photo for the August College Issue, everyone wearing the same mandatory outfit. For 1955, all twenty of the guest editors sat in stadium bleachers, grinning widely at the camera. This year's outfit was horrendous: a pin-tucked shirt buttoned to the very top with a heavy wool skirt. It made the 1955 GEs look like nineteenth-century governesses. Jane Truslow raved to the magazine's readers: "More N.Y. firms rolled out crimson carpets, entertaining us so royally that even the most calorie-conscious among us flung caution into the Hudson! Yet our impression of the city was also a collection of snapshots: Peggy La V. zipping down Park Avenue in a green MG . . . Joan's expression when she learned she'd won both U. of California short story contests . . . all twenty of us sleepily staggering out of taxis at Columbia's Baker Field at 6:45 A.M. (a unique experience—few of us had ever been photographed at dawn yelling 'Cheese!' to an echoing, empty stadium!)." Ultimately, what they had been, as Peggy perceptively noted, was "a traveling focus group," letting the editorial staff know what was on trend, the prettier among them working as free-of-charge models at the runway show at the Astor and on the pages of the August College Issue.

Behind the smiles of that final group photograph, however, there were the sorts of insecurities that only *Mademoiselle*'s guest editor program could stir up. The guest editorship had tested Sylvia Plath two years earlier; but in fact each June, college girls came to New York only to discover that there were others like them, but better versions—more talented, more ambitious, and in more emotional flux. And of course prettier. The yearly parade of overachievers, of well-dressed, well-maintained A students who planned on becoming writers and artists, were faced with tough realities when they switched from their college campuses to the bustle of Mad Ave and the likes of managing editor Cyrilly Abels scratching out their copy with her signature blue pencil.

When Janet Burroway had first stepped off the plane in New York, she was confronted by a billboard of "a gigantic VIVECA LINDFORS . . . in cerise neon." It seemed serendipitous: Janet had already picked Viveca, a Swedish-born actress currently performing on Broadway, to interview for the popular "We Hitch Our Wagons" feature in the magazine's College Issue. This interview was to be the highlight of Janet's month in New York. In the August 1955 issue, there is a photograph of Janet with Viveca Lindfors (a high-boned, dark-haired attractive woman in flamboyant bohemian layers) alongside the interview. Viveca has her hands placed in front of her, as if she had paused thoughtfully midsentence. Janet, sitting opposite, listens, her legs crossed, fully concentrating, it seems, and yet oddly self-conscious, as if she is concentrating on concentrating, on seeming to concentrate, her small hat perched on her head, her arms also crossed on top of her crossed legs. She holds a clipboard that looks much like the ones *Mademoiselle* gave out at its College Clinic.

Relaying the experience to her parents, Janet wrote that Viveca had said: "People all want to be happy nowadays. Why? You don't *learn* anything by being happy. Wisdom comes from unhappiness."

Janet puzzled over why during the interview she had insisted so much on contradicting this statement, even as it was something she had always believed as well.

In mid-June, she confessed in a letter home—on *Mademoiselle* pink letterhead—that much of her initial "violent unhappiness" in New York had been because of that interview with Viveca Lindfors. Janet had planned to impress the actress with her "flip sincerity," and the photographer was shouting "face the camera, baby," and someone else was taking efficient notes, and Janet had a lapful of typed questions that she couldn't care less about and a serious case of nerves: "I asked about schools, and she spoke about the beauty of her art, I asked about her life in Sweden, and she spoke about the wisdom in unhappiness." Janet fumbled to find the right words, and at one point, Viveca, the famous actress whose image had welcomed Janet to New York, turned to her and said: "You don't listen, do you?" and it was as if "she had slapped me in the face."

A couple of weeks later Janet finally saw *Anastasia*, the Broadway play in which Viveca was starring. "I was so ashamed because I hadn't known what an artist she was," Janet confided. She forced herself to go backstage after, even as there was nothing she wanted to do less; the "hard-faced, hoarse-voiced" woman guarding the stage door relented when Janet began to cry, begging to see Lindfors. It was a turning point: Viveca let her in and apologized immediately for being "short" during their interview, for failing to remember that Janet was young and nervous. Janet in turn confessed that *Mademoiselle* had wanted her to stress her interest in theater, yet what she really wanted to do was to become a writer. In a sense, by finding the courage to return to Viveca Lindfors, despite the debacle of an interview, Janet allowed herself to come into her own.

Soon after, it was time for them all to leave. The 1955 guest editor program ended at the end of June, as it did every year. But New York had left an indelible impression. Writing to her parents from her Barbizon room, Janet Burroway summed it up: "An Arizona girl sits in Arizona and New York is a distant gleaming—or, rather, glittering—place where all these things happen and if she could just get there she might find out that it *does* glitter all the time, and that she could be part of it, and that her life could be more important than PTA president and 3 kids and dishes. So—she *gets* to New York, and the really most amazing thing is that, unlike COLLEGE, THE THEATRE, MODELING, HAVING A POEM PUBLISHED IN SEVENTEEN, BEING A DESIGNER, and all the other things, it *does* glitter up close like it does from a distance, and the important people *are* real, and she *could* be part of it and *could* be one of them." New York had revealed the possibilities.

Peggy and Joan parted ways too. Joan—intentionally planning for an adventure on her way home—decided to take a circuitous trip back to California by train. She wrote to Peggy: "Brief rundown on activities since I left you at The Exclusive Barbizon yesterday morning; I arrived at Grand Central and couldn't get anyone to carry my bags, tell me where to go, or even look at me. As it neared 10 a.m., I got so upset and I just stood in the middle of the place with all these people rushing around me and unobtrusively crying." She eventually made it onto the train to Boston, from where she headed to Quebec, then Montreal, and eventually Chicago, where she boarded the sleek Zephyr to cross the country back west: "I didn't want to leave New York, but I certainly want to get home now. I'm certainly glad, however, that I'm taking this trip—what a lesson in clinical pathology."

For Peggy's amusement, Joan cataloged the groping, the unwanted passes, the perverted whispers on the lawn of the Boston Common, and the overconcerned fellow passengers shocked to see a young woman traveling the tracks alone. But once home: "Sacramento is killing me. I've never been in a place where everything moved so slowly and so aimlessly. Everyone seems to be frozen in exactly the same spot I left them in, 6 weeks ago." Her boyfriend,

Bob, the car salesman's son from nondescript Bakersfield, California, whom she was finding as tedious as ever, was not helping the situation: "I wish I were in New York," she declared. Joan knew what she wanted, even if she could not have it just yet. In the "Meet This Year's Millies" profiles for the August College Issue, Didion had written of herself: "Joan spends vacations river-rafting and small-boating in the picture-postcard atmosphere of the Sacramento Valley." Her interests included wanting to read "almost any book published" and also publishing one of her own. As Peggy recalled, in the following year as a senior at Berkeley, Joan took the prize money from her two most recent writing contest wins (as Jane Truslow had noted on *Mademoiselle*'s pages: "Joan's expression when she learned she'd won both U. of California short story contests . . .") and bought AT&T stock, starting her own investment fund before she had even finished college.

Peggy remained in Manhattan; she had written in her *Mademoiselle* profile that she had a "yen to stay in New York" and had brought along her senior lifeguard certificate "in case I can't find a job in my field." While Peggy was searching for a job, Joan suggested, with youthful insensitivity, that since Mr. Smith, the president of *Mademoiselle*'s publisher, Street & Smith, had just died while they were all in New York that June, she should present herself as a worthy candidate for a certain job that had recently opened up: "Think of the publicity for next year—in their column of ex-guest editors." Then, going in for a second dig, Joan added: "Is Burroway returning to Barnard, and to 'motor' through the Adironacks [*sic*] with that stuffy young man and his family?" Considering that Joan Didion was finding her boyfriend, Bob, "hopeless," she might well have preferred to have been at Barnard, in New York City, with a stuffy young man.

Editor-in-chief Betsy Talbot Blackwell helped Peggy get a job at *Living*, a magazine also owned by Street & Smith, but Peggy could no longer afford the Barbizon on her starting salary. Instead, she found a room at the less glamorous East End Hotel for Women. While she waited for the room to free up, Jane Truslow invited her to stay with her in an apartment on Fifth Avenue that belonged to an uncle and aunt. "If you don't mind we'll live in the servants' quarters," she explained. The apartment, with furniture covered in white cloths while Jane's aunt and uncle were at their summer residence, had its own elevator and, it seemed to Peggy, endless rooms. Two servant bedrooms and bathrooms had been left uncovered for Jane's use. The two former GEs made nightly dinners and went to the theater as much as they could, cheap standing-room tickets only.

✦

Less than two years later, Peggy LaViolette would return to California. Now it was Joan Didion's turn to head back to New York, in fact to *Vogue*, where this time she had parlayed another prestigious writing contest win into a job. She was once again in the same building as the *Mademoiselle* offices; it was 1958, and the future actress Ali MacGraw was one of the twenty guest editors. (The stunning MacGraw, chosen for her artwork, would, without previous precedent, feature on the front cover of that year's August College Issue.)

Joan sat in her *Vogue* office and wrote to Peggy, reminiscing about the day they had flown together on the Golden Gate in 1955, arriving at the Barbizon, where she thought she was seeing the Brooklyn Bridge from her room because it was "the only bridge I'd ever heard of." She had thought Peggy was "decidedly a femme du monde" because at least she had flown before. "Talk about innocents abroad."

While living in New York this second time, Joan Didion ventured up to Boston to visit Jane Truslow, the former guest editor-in-chief and Peggy's summer roommate in 1955. Jane's husband, Peter Davison, poetry editor at the *Atlantic* and a former lover of Plath, had been in England a year earlier looking for writers, and was told "about this marvelous American girl who was not only the center of a literary set but was a kind of mélange of Daisy Miller, the Girl of the Golden West, and Zuleika Dobson." This "marvelous American girl," a transatlantic femme fatale and renegade, turned out to be none other than Janet Burroway. Joan Didion, seemingly bristling with envy, even as Janet was no longer with the "stuffy" Dick Aldridge, offered up a quick slap: "About all Jane could find to say about [Janet's novel] was that Peter said it had its moments."

Joan, Peggy, Gael, Janet, and Jane would take markedly different paths in life. But they were all shaped by their time in New York. Janet had concluded that while she did "not always love this city," its "pull" on her was "fantastic; even apart, I think, from Dick, though he is all mixed up with it." New York had started to build her confidence but also poke holes in her previous beliefs. By the end of June, she had decided, with youthful élan, that she could, if she wanted, if she lost twenty pounds, be a model, or even "penthouse rich," but the world of fashion and merchandising was out for sure: "It's cheap and false and grabby and greasy, and I will design my own clothes, thank you, and have no part of it." At the same time, she was also seeing that all her prizes and awards in the past had "inflated my ego so high that I couldn't see over the top of it," and she was now "having a rough time because I've measured my worth by these prizes, and it shakes my foundations." The guest editor program was a testing ground from which even the very best emerged changed.

It was a singular and necessary environment. Within the pages of *Mademoiselle,* editor-in-chief Betsy Talbot Blackwell had manufactured and then tended to America's new cult of youth: a land of makeovers and bright, young things with perky smiles and unspoiled dreams. BTB realized it soon enough: "There are occasions when, on viewing the nation's long and heady love affair with Youth, I feel like the biter bitten." Her magazine peddled youth, and the guest editors were the saleswomen.

Nevertheless, the opportunities that *Mademoiselle* provided for young women were revolutionary. For its young women readers, the magazine unapologetically offered both visual and intellectual stimuli; for its guest editors, it offered a prestigious launching pad, a jumping-off point for each generation's most driven young women. This was especially valuable in the 1950s, a time when men—white men—ruled unchallenged, unopposed. Male dominance and female deference were entirely normalized. On-screen, formidable 1940s Joan Crawford and Katharine Hepburn had given way to bubbly 1950s Doris Day and Debbie Reynolds. This was a time when, as Chris Ladd points out, "higher education was a carefully groomed preserve of white men, insulating them not only from racial minorities, but competition from women. Virtually every administrator, professor and admissions officer was a white man."

These same privileges then carried over seamlessly into the workplace without so much as a raised eyebrow: "Every banker, attorney, accountant, realtor, doctor or bureaucrat . . . was a white man." It was against this background that BTB, her largely female staff, and her young guest editors created an alternate universe within the offices of *Mademoiselle* and, equally, within the hallways of the Barbizon: two places where women (although certainly white, middle-class women) were seen and heard, where, like BTB, they ruled, where they had beauty and brains as both producers and consumers. This was at a time when no one, as Janet Burroway recalled, had the word "feminism" in their vocabulary, but that didn't mean it didn't exist, even within the strict confines of the 1950s.

CHAPTER SEVEN

THE INVISIBLE

Gael Greene and "The Lone Women"

This photograph captures so many timeless elements of the Barbizon experience. A glamorous young woman dressed to the nines meets her date while her fellow residents look on. The younger set checks out her date from the mezzanine above while the older residents sit comfortably in the lobby, ready to remark on the goings-on.

In 1950, the *New York Sunday News* ran an illustrated feature about the Barbizon Hotel for Women with the heading: "No Men, but Who Needs Men?"

They had it so very wrong.

The decade ahead would in fact suggest the very opposite: any decent, self-respecting woman needed a man; a woman without a man was nothing. The days of independent Rosie the Riveter were long gone, as was the 1920s liberated flapper and the 1930s self-sufficient working girl. That is why Sylvia Plath and Joan Didion and all the others still found themselves oscillating—with all the angst and frustration that this elicited—between acting on their own dreams and following society's expectations for them.

Then, of course, there was needing a man, as in dating, going steady, marrying, and moving to the suburbs—and "needing a man" the way in which Grace Kelly reputedly did, and which was most certainly not discussed because it would have meant confronting the decade's glaring contradictions. After Grace was already married and crowned princess of Monaco, Malachy McCourt would hear of her coming to his bar around the corner from the Barbizon with "ugly, thuggish, beetle-browed types," and he could only square it with the rumors that "she had a fondness for men sharing a certain overstated attribute." Indeed, even prior to her marriage, she was known for a series of passionate love affairs, and also calculated ones; director Alfred Hitchcock, who would help make her famous in *Rear Window*, called her a "snow-covered volcano" but also, less subtly, the most promiscuous woman he had ever met.

The inconsistencies between women's desires and America's expectations of them wrought ire, anxiety, and moral contortions. The two essays in *Mademoiselle* magazine that provoked the most backlash among its young female readers were about sex. One was a 1958 short story about two college undergraduates in a hetero-sexual relationship; he is irritated by her, desiring her, repulsed that she puts out; she is cloying, quick to please him, emotionally overwrought. At the end, trying to release the tension between them, they hunt through the available cars behind the girls' dormitories—cars left intentionally unlocked, with boxes of tissues and clean seat covers. She settles on a station wagon, and before she knows it, his sexual desire has tipped over into assault. The other piece was a 1959 report on a frank discussion with college graduates about the role of premarital sex. The consensus was that men wanted virginal wives, but they also wanted to be experienced lovers, and they flocked to the girls who "put out," with whom they "practiced" in preparation for marriage with their bride. The magazine's readers might have been appalled but, as usual, *Mademoiselle* was ahead of its time: it discussed what plagued its audience; it didn't ignore these issues.

Just as female desire was not to be discussed openly, neither was female loneliness. If women were nothing without men, who then were the women who could not catch or keep them? Neither the lonesome woman nor the sexually active woman fit 1950s expec-tations for journeying the female path. (Nor, for that matter, the contentedly single woman or the gay woman.)

One of the key amenities that the Barbizon widely advertised was companionship. *Mademoiselle* regularly told its out-of-town readers that if they were to come to the big city, the Barbizon was the place for them to stay. In 1940, *Mademoiselle* called the hotel "a godsend," a place that was "cozy, unstarched," with "slews of young women interested in the same things you are." Living at the Barbizon, it promised, you would have new friends in less time than it took to say "How do you do." Within its walls there were more things to do than one had time for: the gymnasium, squash court, "a dandy swimming pool," the library with the newest bestsellers added each month, music and painting studios to be rented for an hour a day at $4 a month, monthly plays, concerts, and lectures. All for $12 a week for a room with running water and $15 for one with a bath. The views were unbeatable too. That message remained consistent for decades: a 1957 *Mademoiselle* piece, with a Barbizon advertisement running alongside it, promised, "If you're unescorted and the least bit apprehensive, stay at the Barbizon Hotel for Women, where you can join forces with others of your age and interest for an organized sally into the big city." What remained unsaid was that those easy friendships available at the Barbizon were to tide you over until you found your true love, your man.

Two years after Gael Greene had stayed at the Barbizon as a *Mademoiselle* guest editor, she checked herself back into the hotel. This time she came as an investigative reporter for the *New York Post*, assigned to write a multipart series titled "Lone Women." The newspaper promised its readers New York's untold story: "Our town—any big town—is full of them. They come—looking for careers, romance, adventure, an escape from boredom. What happens to them once they get here? What of their high hopes for spectacular success, their dreams of marriage to a handsome prince charming? Can they overcome the universal fears of metropolitan bachelor girls—fear of failure, fear of spinsterhood, fear of sexual assault?"

Gael was now twenty-three years old, and she booked herself into an L-shaped corner room on the tenth floor of the Barbizon, with "an ivory desk and dresser" "against the pale yellow walls. The print curtains matched the bed spread." She called it a cell. She didn't tell her readers that she had been there before, just two years earlier, in

June 1955, alongside Joan Didion, Peggy LaViolette, Janet Burroway, and Jane Truslow. For the readers of the *New York Post*, Gael posed as a newcomer, writing as if she had arrived at the hotel for the first time, as if she had never met Oscar before: "'Do you know Oscar, Miss?' the cab driver asked as a grinning jowly man in uniform threw open the cab door and peered inside. 'Oscar will take good care of you. He's famous. Everyone knows Oscar.'

"'I take care of all the girls,' the fat doorman cooed. 'Especially the pretty ones like you.'"

Of course Gael was not particularly pretty—there had been that dreadful trench coat she wore around the clock during her guest editorship. And she had also been left out of the *Mademoiselle* fashion show, relegated to watching.

Breakfast at the Barbizon the next morning must have nudged that memory awake because, as she told her *New York Post* readers: "It was at breakfast that I saw the Barbizon's two worlds on parade." There was the world that Grace Kelly and Carolyn Scott had inhabited—"Chattering quartets of trim young girls in hats and high-heeled opera pumps filled the center tables and booths of the hotel coffee shop. As one girl finished breakfast and trotted toward the door, another zoomed into the room, heels clicking, and took her place." The other world, however, was that of the "Lone Women": "Others breakfasted alone. They wore no hats. Uncomfortable, self-conscious, eyes averted, they sipped coffee and orange juice. One by one they slipped into the room, looked about eagerly seeking a familiar face and, finding no one, took stools at the counter. Other women alone sat at the tables for two which ring the room. With closed faces and arms held close to their sides they breakfasted—eyes darting to the door every few seconds, then dropping back to a book or newspaper. It was the same at dinner."

Gael took her place alongside the lonesome. With a book tucked securely under her arm, she proceeded to get to know this other half of the Barbizon. She first met Jenny, whom she joined for a plate of cold cuts and potato salad at one of the two-person tables. Jenny, "a young, flat-faced girl," was reading the novel *Compulsion*, the story of two smart, upper-class Jewish young men living in 1920s Chicago who randomly murder a boy to feel the thrill of existing above and beyond the law. It was a current bestseller. Jenny was twenty years old and had done two years at an East Coast women's college only to drop out, leaving behind her boyfriend, Reggie, at a neighboring men's college; she had abandoned the idealized life imagined for her at the prep school she'd attended—which had insisted on college, then marriage, then kids—because she wanted to do something she could get excited about. But instead she was spending her time waiting for the next weekend she would spend with Reggie. Being a girl of good stock, she had ended up at the Barbizon because of its reputation, its parent-approved status, and its safe neighborhood. She leaned conspiratorially toward Gael as she told her story.

Jenny was not, however, a huge fan of the Barbizon lobby, which she disapprovingly noted lots of men used as a place to "take a load off their feet and watch all the pretty girls go by." The trouble was that sometimes they also followed the girls out of the lobby and onto the street, where, as one young resident warned another, "It could happen on the street corner—any corner." She meant harassment, even assault. Jenny ditched Gael after dinner, and the *New York Post*'s young investigative journalist strolled around the lobby. She watched laughing couples leave for a night out and then a large group of girls heading off together for a movie, with Oscar making sure to pat their cheeks, smiling wide, as they departed. Gael listened around her:

"They're all the same. All trying to seduce you," one young woman instructed a friend as she eyed another's date from across the room.

"But, Mother, I want to come home—" another whispered from the phone booth.

"No mail for me?" said a plain-looking girl in bobby socks as the mail clerk passed a substantial pile of letters and hometown newspapers to another girl. Gael wandered off alone down Lexington Avenue, where it was starting to rain.

Gael Greene's assignment for the *New York Post* was to "live among them," the "young women alone," who "bravely concealed" the telltale marks of their predicament. The result was a serialized patchwork of impressions. Gael invited her readers to stand beside her in the Barbizon's hotel lobby and watch and listen: "A frozen smile of hopeful expectancy. / The foamy daiquiri glass on a tray outside her door. / An old biddy who scolds her for giggling during TV hours. / Cookies and banal conversation with her afternoon tea. / The glass of the phone booth as she presses her tear-streaked face against its soothing coolness. / A phone that does not ring. / Tears of homesickness. / Gentle smiles of recognition." Here was "New York's untold story," as the *New York Post* promised, which Gael Greene reported in 1957.

+

On a Saturday night the Barbizon's lucky ones (the Graces, so to speak) rode the elevator down to the lobby in velvets and furs, where their nervous dates were waiting for them. The petite female elevator operator shouted, "Up, up, up," as she headed off to pick up yet another batch of the lucky ones. The other half, the less lucky ones, had gathered in the lounge and were listening to Perry Como sing "You'll find that happiness lies, Right under your eyes, Back in your own backyard." No one, wrote Gael, seemed to get the irony that Perry Como was probably right and they might well be better off back in their hometowns than here. One dark-haired girl tugged at the wool in her hands (she was knitting a sweater) while just across from her two attractive girls fiddled with a jigsaw puzzle. They were all sitting on the floor of a tiny lounge on the Barbizon's topmost floor. It was only a matter of minutes before yet another girl jumped up with the battle cry: "I'm absolutely staaaaaaaaarved." Just like the others before her, and those soon after her, she fingered the change in her hand while she waited for the elevator that would take her to the lobby drugstore and, Gael thought, "a sweet, creamy, rich something to feed the void mistaken for an appetite."

The next day, however, there was a sense of excitement in the air: a wedding reception was planned for the wood-paneled recital room on the mezzanine, a place usually reserved for teas and girls in curlers watching *The Late Late Show* on the television set. It was a Barbizon resident who was getting married, in a church just down the street, after which she was returning "home" for the wedding reception. One of her Barbizon friends, Ellen, read this as a sign that there was hope for everyone. Her friend was twenty-eight (old!) and her husband-to-be was forty-five. "So now she's got a job, a home, a car and a husband—and she did it all in one year." (Later another Barbizon resident would wonder whether she did in fact win the coveted prize; it turned out the groom was shorter than the bride.) Ellen was a Katie Gibbs girl, living on one of the three floors reserved for them, where they were properly monitored by house mothers, early curfews, and a sign-out/sign-in book for after dark. She always wore the mandatory stockings, high-heeled shoes, and hat to class and, adding insult to injury, they weren't even allowed to wear sweaters. It would show their curves too much. Ellen was averaging one date a month.

Sometimes an evening's entertainment meant watching the people in the building across from the Barbizon: there was a woman in a red flannel nightgown and a man who walked around in his boxer shorts. Another ready form of entertainment was the television: there were two television sets in the whole of the hotel. Gael stopped by the television room on cowboy night. Girls were buried deep within the cushioned armchairs, their feet propped up on wooden benches. This was usually when rifts between the young women and the elderly longtime residents flared up—over program choices and manners. A sign at the entrance to the TV room said no smoking or eating, but everyone ignored it. Up on the eighteenth floor, in the only lounge where young ladies could bring their male guests after obtaining a pass from the front desk, there was silence. Gael walked through the empty room and onto the terrace, where she looked out onto the neon-lit city. Seeing both the Empire State and the Chrysler Buildings to the south, she was jolted by the reminder that she was smack in the middle of Manhattan.

Gael met Anna at one of the teas in the Barbizon recital/TV room. Unlike the other women, Anna took the initiative and introduced herself to Gael. She was the self-appointed "social director of this female fortress," and immediately wanted to know which floor Gael's room was on. She pulled out her notebook. Anna herself was on the fifth floor, where, she claimed, they had a "gay time." It was, in other words, a lark on the fifth, but Gael was on the tenth. Anna flipped through the book, noting they had not seen "774" in a while, and then lighting up when she remembered "1090"—a fellow tenth floorer that Gael simply had to meet. "1090" was called Sylvia. Sylvia, with "a colorless, puffy face," was not so pleased to see them, despite Anna's insistence: she blocked the door, as if she didn't want them coming in. Behind her Gael spied a half-unpacked suitcase, clothes in mounds, an empty wine bottle on its side, and on the dresser a Bloomingdale's cosmetics counter's worth of lotions and potions. Sylvia was from Philadelphia, a nurse: "Grace Kelly's mother said it was the best place to stay." Gael remembered a pair of sunglasses she'd seen in a shop window recently, with a sign beside them: "These are the exact replica of the pair worn by Her Highness, Princess Grace of Monaco."

Then there was Irene. She met her "beau" on a blind date (the first time that had ever worked out); he was a lawyer no less. But now he wanted to have an affair with her, meaning a sexual relationship, and Irene had said no but didn't know if she should feel flattered or insulted. Gael Greene, years more sophisticated even though she was only two years older than Irene, looked at her, and said: "Be flattered." These were also the realities of womanhood in the 1950s.

Even as Gael was surrounded by these Lone Women, she came upon someone she knew personally, and who did not fit the category at all. It wasn't her "low, sensual voice" but her "long-lashed green eyes" that roused Gael's memory: this young woman, Joan, had been at the University of Michigan with her. Joan was waiting for her placement agency to find her a job, which it hadn't yet done, and not working was getting exhausting: one day she even rode the Staten Island Ferry four times, and then walked from the dock to Fourteenth Street. When she wasn't riding the ferry, she washed her hair, shopped, and dated one young bachelor after another. Sometimes she helped the other girls out when her blind dates brought along a friend.

Joan did not belong to the Lone Women; she was among the lucky ones who tripped happily into the Barbizon coffee shop each morning and to an assortment of tables and friends to choose from. But she had seen things, she confided to Gael: she met most of her hallmates on the night a girl in the room next door "got roaring drunk and went psycho." She heard lots of noise and peeked in, where she saw a girl throwing things at the wall. When Joan inquired if she was okay, the girl hissed at her. Within minutes, with something *happening*, there were forty girls in Joan's room, and she'd even considered serving cocktails. When word came that the police had been summoned, the girls dashed back to their rooms, took out their pin curls, and put on sexy negligees. Joan, pretty Joan, just rolled her eyes as she told the story.

No less disturbing were the ones who were "neither young nor old and have peaked faces and the first hints of desperation in their eyes." But the worst, the very worst, said Joan, were the old ladies—"Barbizon's inner sanctum." Some had been here as long as twenty-seven years, having moved in only a couple of years after the hotel was built. They were still paying $8 a week for their rooms (or so she believed), while she and everyone else were paying $39. And their rooms were like museums; not only did their weekly rent hark back to another time but so too did their interiors.

Joan well knew that her way out of this life she was living at the Barbizon was a job, but she hadn't finished college, she didn't know how to type or take shorthand, and she'd been told she was too smart for the unskilled work for which she was qualified. While she chatted with Gael, the phone rang: it was her employment agency saying they'd set her up with an interview at a foreign film company. Joan rolled her eyes again: "Foreign films—that means dirty movies. I'd handle telephone contacts—that means answer the phone. There'd be some figurework—a little bookkeeping. Important records to file—translation: I should keep track of the boss's bets. Some job." She never went; she called her agency and told them that she'd come down with the Asian flu and headed off on a last date with Ted, whom she was planning to dump that night.

Jacqueline, another resident, was a nightclub singer from England who featured at a place called the Wonder Room. Small, slender, but with curves, her skin ivory and her platinum-blond hair in a neat French roll, she stared at herself in the mirror as she spoke to Gael, expertly smearing some sea green eye shadow across her lids while taking tweezers to her brows. She lived on the fifth floor—"the gay floor." She ate four candy bars a night for dinner and missed most of the TV room arguments because her work began at 11:00 p.m. and ended in the early morning hours. Although she was twenty-three, just like Gael, she looked thirty. She had a special bond with her next-room neighbor, Helen, eighteen years old, who looked to Jacqueline for mothering. Helen also lived Jacqueline's life vicariously, from the admiring men to the late dates and the numerous phone calls. She and Jacqueline routinely rapped on their shared wall to see if the other was in. Helen had a habit of throwing things at the wall light switch when she wanted to turn out the lights but was too tired to get out of bed. Recently, after a bottle of nose drops didn't do the trick, she'd picked up the room's heavy ashtray and thrown it; the crash sent Jacqueline rushing in. They both took care of each other, even as Jacqueline was the designated mother figure; when one of the elderly residents on their floor compared Jacqueline's singing to unwanted noise, Helen hung a wet paint sign on the old lady's door and squirted shaving cream along the threshold.

Billy Jo was a twenty-year-old college dropout, a fact that had infuriated her Southerner father, a respected dentist. As upset as he was, he was willing to pay her bills if she stayed at a women-only residence. So here she was at the Barbizon, "a tall, big-boned girl with mouse-colored hair, pale watery eyes and flawless skin." She left college because of a boy, a sophomore with a crew cut who didn't care for her. She got fed up trying to avoid him on campus; it was just easier to leave the college. She'd found a boyfriend again, this time in New York, and she would leave the Barbizon late, just before midnight, because he worked so late, and she liked to fix him some supper at his place. She'd hang a DO NOT DISTURB sign on her door when she left, and so far she seemed to have gotten away with it. "Sometimes I think there must be something the matter with me. I mean, I was brought up to be a nice girl—just like anyone else. Nice girl—whatever that is. . . . I'm a very nice girl. I never go to bed with two men in the same night. Principles." She had always believed that even nice girls could have sex as long as they weren't promiscuous, but even so there were obstacles of all kinds: "It always turns out they're married and have five children or suddenly get transferred to Seattle or—just disappear completely." She'd recently been seeing a lovely young man who bought her a bunch of violets as they were walking down the street together. But after that, he never called again.

Leaving Billy Jo, who had taken flight from her boy troubles under her bedcovers, Gael went to see if Lois wanted to have dinner in the coffee shop. Lois was a slender and attractive brunette with thick-lensed cat glasses behind which there were large hazel eyes. She carried herself well, her back straight, and her outfits always looked as if fresh from the dry cleaners: it was the very opposite of her room, which was "a rat's nest of empty cigaret [*sic*] packs, piles of newspapers and magazines and half-eaten food in delicatessen containers." She was twenty-eight, a college graduate, and was watching everyone around her get married: her younger sisters, her friends back home, her former apartment roommates in New York. She had found herself back at the Barbizon because she ran out of single roommates. As they stepped off the elevator along with a bevy of young girls whose dates were already waiting for them in the lobby, Lois grasped Gael's arm: "Look. It isn't fair. I'm not ugly. I'm not dumb. My clothes are as pretty as anyone else's. Prettier. What is it? . . . Perhaps if I were beautiful? When I was 18, I always told myself I'd be beautiful by the time I was 22. I would day-dream about what a pretty girl I'd be. When I reached 22, I promised myself I'd be beautiful for sure at 25. But when I got to be 25, I was too old to play the game. It's crazy. But I actually believed it." Lois changed her mind and headed back up the stairs to the TV room.

✦

Gael enjoyed the Barbizon's teatime, if not the TV room. From 5:00 to 6:00 p.m. every day, after a day of searching for a job, or taking classes, or withstanding the "aluminum and florescence [*sic*] of the commercial world," there was always tea. It took place in the mahogany-paneled room with burgundy velvet drapes up on the mezzanine, where a plump lady in a pastel knit dress played the organ. In between numbers, she would go sit with the other elderly residents huddled in one corner of the lounge. On this particular late afternoon, Halloween, it was cider and doughnuts instead of tea and cookies, and the lounge was bursting full. Eleanor, who worked for an advertising executive, was doing one of her impromptu marketing surveys. Today it was paper towels. Margaret noted that last night she'd opened too many drawers on her dresser and it all came tumbling down, including the glass top, which shattered at her feet. Linda wanted to know if anyone would go with her to the theater that night; she had a free ticket. She looked around and wistfully noted that she no longer enjoyed the theater now that she studied acting. Roberta, who had on a trench coat with just her swimsuit underneath, planned to head to the swimming pool down in the basement after she'd had her share of cider and doughnuts.

Gael went to wash her hair, but Anna, the Barbizon's unofficial social director with the notebook, tracked her down. She called to tell her that she was in Annette's room and Gael should join them. Annette was an art student, and she was handing out chocolates sent to her by an admirer gone overseas. Anna had just been to see a fortune-teller at "Bide a While Gypsy Tea Room," who told her "next year will be her lucky year: she will marry and have two children." Helen now insisted that they all go, especially with it being Halloween, and while Gael was none too happy, she tagged along, as did Jacqueline, the English club singer, and Helen, her "little sister" and neighbor. They arrived at a place that looked like "a thousand cheap diners in Manhattan," and were led into separate booths for their readings, where they were all told exactly what they wanted to hear. On their way out, three kids in monster masks passed by demanding pennies: *Trick or treat!*" Helen, Anna, and Gael walked

Jacqueline to her cocktail lounge, where she hurried in to get ready for her show, and then they returned to the Barbizon, outside of which Anna spotted three men in a parked car, and warned everyone to walk slowly but not turn their heads in the car's direction. When Anna's sister joined them in Gael's room, she said a strange man had put his hand on her knee that afternoon at the movies. Helen, still angry at the old resident who had called Jacqueline's singing noise, picked up the phone and asked the operator for room 582: "*Hello. Is this room 582? It is? Your broom is waiting downstairs.*" A pause. "*Your BROOM. Good night.*"

✛

In her series on the lone women of the Barbizon for the *New York Post*, Gael Greene did not broach the subject head-on, but the subtext was there: Lone Women could also turn into very unhappy, and even very desperate women. There had been suicides at the Barbizon over the years, but the hotel was good at keeping that quiet. Over the decades, only a few had been leaked to the press. In March 1934, a Mrs. Edith La Tour, thirty years old, came in from Bayside, Queens, registered at the hotel in the morning, and by evening had jumped, leaving behind a note: "I can't stand the pain any longer." In April 1935, Harriet Bean, a twenty-seven-year-old from Chicago who had been in the city for two years, died of an intentional overdose of sedatives. Only the *Chicago Daily Tribune* cryptically noted that, "about two months ago she had undergone an operation"—presumably an illegal abortion. In 1939, twenty-two-year-old Judith Ann Palmer, former University of Chicago coed, was found dead in her room at the Barbizon, a self-inflicted bullet to her head. She left two notes. One, "To Whom It May Concern," pointed out that there was $30 in the dresser drawer to pay for funeral expenses; the other was addressed to her mother, residing at a residential hotel in Chicago.

From the 1940s on, it seems the Barbizon Hotel for Women largely figured out how to keep its suicides out of the press.

The suicides continued nevertheless, even if the press coverage did not. Regina Reynolds arrived at the Barbizon very soon after the Unsinkable Molly Brown had sung her last aria there. Asked about the suicides, Ms. Reynolds guessed there had been about fifty-five over the years she lived at the Barbizon. On Sundays, one looked out the window to see if the coroner was there. It was always Sundays because Saturday was date night, and then came disappointment. Some women would hang themselves from the curtain rods. Malachy McCourt himself knew of at least three women who committed suicide at the Barbizon in the mid-1950s. "Two took an overdose and one threw herself out the window. That was kept hush-hush. Carol Andrews was her name? She was going out with a guy . . . and he dumped her."

The pressure to be a certain way, to look a certain way, to marry by a certain age, was intense. Malachy's first wife, a model, moved to the Barbizon to escape her parents, who lived nearby on Park Avenue. Most of the models suffered from bulimia, she discovered, with long lines in front of the bathrooms. Gloria Barnes Harper, with lagoon-blue eyes, left Wellesley College after freshman year because she had been signed as a Ford model, and like other young Ford models, she went to stay at the Barbizon. She witnessed a different kind of desperation among her hallmates—hunger, but not self-inflicted. They would come to her room each evening—she, the Ford model who had appeared on the cover of *Life* magazine before she had even graduated from high school—to see if she could get them a date that night. A date, a real date, meant a real dinner; no date meant saltine crackers.

It was the hypocrisy of the decade that struck Malachy McCourt the most. Particularly when it came to sex: "virginal" women were well versed in using "the French lever," and if that failed, as condoms do, there were illegal abortions in the places one would never want to go, that left you with infections, if you survived them at all. "The Barbizon had the aura of the Eisenhower era," he said. "Respectability was the order of the day. There was so much to be ashamed of as a woman. But you could redeem yourself by taking a job as a secretary or marrying." But sometimes you just couldn't redeem yourself.

There was so much that was hidden away in the 1950s. In those days, on the respectable Upper East Side of Manhattan, there were whispers of roommates who were "dykes, queers, fruits, and pansies," as Malachy recalled, and rumors that they had "Negro blood." Racial pejoratives were tossed about without a second thought. The Upper East Side was New York's whitest of white enclaves. Malachy would later write of New York at this time: "The summer of 1956 . . . blacks were invisible. Chinatown was an exotic venue for the tourists, with just a whiff of danger. Greenwich Village was a draw for the wide-eyed, with its bohemians and beats and the queers who shamelessly kissed and held hands out in the open." Malachy was both right and wrong: because it was precisely in the summer of 1956 that Barbara Chase arrived at the Barbizon.

✦

Women everywhere were defined by men. But women at the Barbizon were also defined by their whiteness, except that it was never spoken of because it was assumed. White Americans, regardless of their class, had always found common cause in their whiteness; it was the one sure thing they had. Even if you had no money or access, you still had your whiteness and the privilege that granted. The phrase "free, white, and twenty-one" became popular in the 1920s, and was used in the 1930s in a string of movies. For example, in the 1932 film *I Am a Fugitive from a Chain Gang*, a conversation between a socialite and a stranger takes place inside a speakeasy:

```
                    ENIGMATIC STRANGER
          You mind if we stay here a while, or
          must you go home?
```

The woman pulls back, eyes wide, insulted.

```
                    YOUNG SOCIETY WOMAN
          There are no musts in my life. I am
          free, white, and twenty-one.
```

The phrase persisted throughout the 1940s and 1950s: even Sylvia Plath had a character in *The Bell Jar* utter it. The racist saying had its roots in an 1828 law that stopped property ownership from being a prerequisite for suffrage. Voters merely needed to be free, white, and twenty-one (and of course men, but that was somehow overlooked when the phrase reemerged). Dorothy Dix, America's first advice columnist, was the one who recycled it during the 1920s and presented it on a platter to young white women as some sort of liberation slogan. Dix's real name was Elizabeth Meriwether Gilmer, but she had lifted her pen name from a slave who had saved the family silver during the Civil War. She would recklessly intertwine the 1828 phrase with white women's empowerment in the first half of the twentieth century.

Barbara Chase, however, while free and twenty-one, was not white. A student at Temple University, African American, and a reader of *Mademoiselle* magazine, she decided, like so many other college coeds that summer, to apply for the prestigious guest editor program. She thought nothing of it, which is the way she moved through life, whether truly unaware of the racism around her or willfully ignorant of it is hard to say. Moreover, as she saw it, she was already on a roll, and having other prizes improved one's odds—just as they had for Sylvia Plath and Joan Didion. Barbara Chase had recently won the *Seventeen* magazine illustration prize: the winning illustration was exhibited in the ACA Gallery in New York, where the curator for prints and drawings at New York's Museum of Modern Art happened to see it and purchased it for the museum.

Back in New York at the *Mademoiselle* offices, as deliberations began in the late spring about the finalists for summer 1956, Barbara Chase was a front-runner. But there were serious concerns voiced about choosing a young African American woman: as of yet, no fashion magazine had even published a photographic image of a black woman on its pages. As a guest editor, Barbara would have to be on the pages of the August College Issue, the most anticipated of the year. The *Mademoiselle* GE program was all about exposure, about bringing the readers and the GEs—the readers' peers, in essence—along for the ride as they told their story of their magical month in New York with breathless narration. There were also the GE biographies (with photo), their "We Hitch Our Wagons" celebrity interviews (with photo), everyday snapshots of their brief but glamorous lives at the Barbizon, and finally the traditional group photograph, in which they would all don the same outfit, the one that *Mademoiselle* had been paid to feature.

When the question of Barbara Chase's potential guest editorship came up, president of Street & Smith wrote to editor-in-chief Betsy Talbot Blackwell: "I will not take issue with anyone regarding their views on segregation. Personally I am sympathetic to the problem, however, it appears to me we have attempted to establish another 'first' when we weren't called upon to do so." He argued that people at the magazine had let "their liberalism" "dictate," and that, at best, they might gain "a few colored readers and possibly alienate—Southern stores—many white readers—possibly some advertising accounts." "Whose views prevailed here?" he demanded to know. Others were also concerned about the logistics. If they picked Barbara Chase—even as she was "attractive as all get-out" and "the most outstanding of the art contestants, by far"—it would be a logistical nightmare. There were questions, many, for which no one in the offices of *Mademoiselle* or Street & Smith Publishers could even find an answer: "Will she be allowed to stay at the Barbizon with the rest of the GEs!?" "What about dates for her when the big St. Regis do comes?; in restaurants when luncheon parties are given?; our Southern advertisers?" No one knew.

Yet anticipating this issue might eventually come up, a year earlier Street & Smith had in fact approached Betsy Talbot Blackwell, the staunch Republican Party member with a chauvinistic husband, about the possibility of an African American guest editor finalist. BTB had answered that she was not worried, and she held on to that view even now. Barbara Chase thus was chosen as one of the twenty 1956 guest editors. Barbara arrived in New York, where, as far as she could see, "the segregation was as rigid as in the South," even if others pretended otherwise. Barbara Chase was not light-skinned. She was used to being stared at, for various reasons, not just the color of her skin, but she also genuinely believed that no one at the Barbizon ever gave her "funny looks," or then again, perhaps she was choosing not to see it? When she walked into the hotel for the first time on June 1, 1956, she thought the place very glamorous, particularly the lobby. But that didn't mean she didn't think she belonged. Barbara always thought she belonged.

As one of the *Mademoiselle* internal memos had noted, Barbara was attractive, with a straight bob that curled up at the ends just above her shoulders (which sometimes she pulled back, adding white pearl earrings), almond eyes, and a dancer's body. In her *Mademoiselle* bio, Barbara Chase, guest promotion art director, was introduced to readers as a young woman who had "won scholarships to seven colleges, has a print included in the Museum of Modern Art's print collection. At Temple she directed the modern dance group and art-edited the annual while doing a six-foot clay composition and 20 art projects (she thrives on pressure). 'But the biggest event in my life,' she modestly insists, 'was acquiring a studio that's cold as a barn.' ... now she wants a 'one-man show and eventually one man.'" In a sense, with that last sentence, Barbara had announced that she was no different from the other girls, the white girls, at the Barbizon.

Even so, the other GEs did not quite know what to make of her, nor did the high-powered women of *Mademoiselle*. They had definite ideas about things, but then so did Barbara. Conflicts arose, but Barbara did not believe they were related to race but rather to class and age. Barbara guessed that the *Mademoiselle* editorial staff was surprised that she was sophisticated, educated, articulate. They seemed at a loss as to what to do with a self-described "girl who came from another planet, who doesn't know her place in life, who isn't aggressive, or angry, who is not particularly friendly, instead reserved, snooty and thinks she's the cat's meow." Barbara was there for the same reason as all the other GEs: "to have a good time, wear great clothes, and be an editor." Nor was she wrong in her evaluation of everyone's reactions. Fashion editor Edie Locke, who had arrived in New York during World War II as a teenage Jewish refugee from Vienna, understood that in many ways the decision to invite Barbara Chase to the guest editor program was part of the *Mademoiselle* staff's desire to be the "first," to always deliver "the first," and in this case to do so with a pat on their backs for their liberal impulses. And they expected gratitude in return, which Barbara had no interest in offering.

The 1956 *Mademoiselle* August College Issue is stamped with this same ambiguity; a clumsiness in presenting America's first-ever black woman on the pages of a mainstream ("white") fashion magazine, coupled with her invisibility. Barbara's presence is never remarked on in the August 1956 issue. She is simply there, often in badly overexposed snapshots that turn her blackness into smudged, indiscernible features. Yet there are articles that pepper the fat tome of a college issue that inadvertently speak to her presence (or was it intended as subtle provocation?). A multipage fashion pictorial is called "Forecast for Saturday night: **Black**," and features some of the white GEs, dressed in black, beside jazz musicians, most of them white but some black. Barbara remains out of sight. Another article is about integration and its problems at the University of Alabama following student demonstrations, and then mob violence, against its first "Negro student," at a time when "Southerners as conscientious as William Faulkner have urged that integration is morally right but emotionally unacceptable at the present time." Among the people the *Mademoiselle* staff writer for the article visits in Alabama is a group of college boys putting together a radio piece on the past week's events, which has to be vetted by the administration, which approves of everything except that the black student is referred to as "Miss Lucy": "Most white Southerners object to Negroes being called 'Miss' or 'Mrs.' or 'Mr.'" Many students at the University of Alabama had recoiled at the way in which Miss Lucy dared to arrive on campus: well-dressed and in a Cadillac. In a sense, Barbara Chase had dared to arrive the same way in New York.

Barbara breezed through the city, the Barbizon, and the *Mademoiselle* parties and luncheons as if she belonged. In part because she assumed all the parties, even the gala at the St. Regis (where she was coupled with "her type": blond and blue-eyed), were simply normal for New York. Betsy Talbot Blackwell's apartment, and the traditional June party there, did make an impression, however; Barbara remembered the beautiful art deco building on Park Avenue, and waiters with white gloves handing out champagne in wide coupe glasses, their shape designed to keep the bubbles bubbly longer. But Barbara did not seem particularly taken by the one gathering that made some of her cohorts swoon. One GE was instantly in awe as they entered Helena Rubinstein's three-floor apartment on Park Avenue, where the legend "was perched on a handsome sofa at one end of a long room, wearing an elaborate Chinese dress and exquisite, embroidered shoes." Small by birth but shrunken by age (she was in her eighties at this point), Rubinstein's "feet dangled, almost like a child's, barely touching the floor." She took the guest editors from room to room, showing off her art collection: "To my darling

Helena from Pablo" . . . "With affection, Salvador." Of course the previous year, in 1955, guest editor Janet Burroway had scoffed at the mediocrity of the collection, and perhaps Barbara, already a talented artist, did not think much of it either.

Even as Barbara's demeanor suggested insouciance to some, not everything went smoothly. She never spotted another African American anywhere near the Barbizon, let alone inside it, but she was treated civilly, the only telltale sign of segregation being that no one ever mentioned there was a swimming pool in the basement. Then again, she did not know how to swim and so she did not care that it was off-limits to her. In the *Mademoiselle* offices, Betsy Talbot Blackwell remained vigilant: "She would pull me behind a palm or run me out of the room for some sudden reason if there were Southern clients." But she never sat Barbara down to explain the realities of white Southern sensibilities because it was a given and needed little explanation. BTB and Barbara were both blunt and it became their mutual language. If BTB had a potential problem on her hands because of Barbara's race, she told her, and in turn, Barbara told BTB what she thought she should or should not do about it, depending also on what the other editors said or did.

But when it came time for the College Clinic, the extravagant fashion show in which the GEs paraded down the runway in the fashions scheduled to appear in the College Issue, and buyers watched and mingled, drinking liberally, BTB did not mince words: "Barbara, we can't put you in the fashion show because we have these people who are going to make a big fuss." They left it at that; Barbara did not argue. She spent the fashion show backstage, under the rafters: "They literally hid me." But it did not enrage Barbara. Her mother, a black Canadian Catholic brought up in a convent, had failed to convey the difficulty of being black in 1950s America. Or maybe it was all Barbara's doing. Years later her mother would note: "The problem with you, Barbara, is you don't know you're colored."

In the annual rite of passage in which the guest editor-in-chief breezily summarized the Millies' whirlwind month of June, Barbara's appearance in this list of girly delights is only one line: "There were afternoons at the Museum of Modern Art, afternoons lost on the subway, and the afternoon Barbara walked home alone in the rain 'to meditate' after Julie Harris's last matinee of *The Lark* . . ." Perhaps, like others at the Barbizon, Barbara was lonely. Yet as the guest editors of 1956 stand in an X formation around an outsize weathervane, looking up at the camera (the group shot was always aerial), dressed this year in matching red rain slickers, Barbara looks happy, a wide grin on her face.

Barbara Chase, quite possibly the first African American woman to ever reside at the Barbizon, posing with her fellow *Mademoiselle* guest editors in 1956.

It would be another five years before *Mademoiselle* had its next "first." In 1961, Willette Murphy, an African American college student, appeared on page 229, modeling a collegiate outfit—"Lamb, pied with stripes, with herringbone tweed—that's the scramble worn by senior class president Willette Murphy, '61. The cardigan is white pretend lamb lined in gray striped silk, the blouse matches lining, the shaped skirt is black and white tweed." Willette Murphy was the first black model to appear in an American fashion magazine; even the *New York Times* took note of this momentous stride in civil rights. But Barbara had already been there a full five years earlier, even if hidden under the rafters.

When the guest editor program was over, BTB secured a paid summer internship for Barbara at *Charm* magazine. She could not afford to stay on at the Barbizon; moreover, without her affiliation as a star guest editor at *Mademoiselle,* most likely she would not have been as welcome. She went home instead to Philadelphia, getting up at 6:00 a.m. daily to catch the Amtrak to Penn Station. She was "in seventh heaven" working in layout, pasting shoe illustrations by Andy Warhol (which is how he then paid the rent). Barbara would later regret discarding the Warhol illustrations they did not use. But it was Barbara's time at the Barbizon and *Mademoiselle* that proved to be life changing. In the "We Hitch Our Wagons" series, in which each GE picked one person they most wished to interview, Barbara had chosen Leo Lionni, *Fortune*'s art director. As she wrote in her "Hitch My Wagon" interview piece: "Born in Holland of Italian parents, Mr. Lionni's major criticism of America is that 'there's no room left for living because we spend so much of our lives being entertained.' In art as in life 'there are certain emotions involved. You can't be cute and decorative with everything.'" Leo Lionni saw something in Barbara, and he helped her secure a John Hay Whitney fellowship at the American Academy in Rome that same year.

Barbara would later write, "I was leaving to explore the world outside just as the United States was looking inwards and exploring its own Apartheid, which would leave it never the same again. I had no idea at the time that what was named the Civil Rights Movement was heading towards a summit point in the world which would render it unique. And I would experience it from an altogether different vantage point—a Yankee in Western Europe, a 'foreigner in a foreign land, and finally an American in Paris.' Philadelphia's Grace Kelly married European Prince Rainier, Marilyn Monroe married Jewish intellectual Arthur Miller, Jacqueline Bouvier married John F. Kennedy, James Baldwin published *The Fire Next Time*, Kenneth Galbraith wrote *The Affluent Society*. In Europe, I would meet them all in time." And Barbara, intentionally borrowing from Betsy Talbot Blackwell, would take on an extra name rather than discard her earlier one when she married. She became Barbara Chase-Riboud, renowned visual artist, bestselling novelist, and award-winning poet.

On the surface, Barbara Chase's unique experiences and successes suggest few parallels with the Barbizon's Lone Women. But their shared common denominator was visibility. Neither Barbara nor the Lone Women were visible, let alone represented, in popular images of the Barbizon. Nor, for that matter, on the pages of *Mademoiselle*. Both the Barbizon's residents and *Mademoiselle*'s readers were expected to be young white women, wives-in-waiting, fun, perky, and popular. And not everyone was.

If Barbara Chase and the Lone Women exposed the cracks in this 1950s false ideal, then Sylvia Plath cataloged the toll it took trying to achieve that ideal. It was a toll shared by many women, and it would eventually mobilize them to demand change.

CHAPTER EIGHT

"THE PROBLEM
THAT HAS NO NAME"

Sylvia Plath and the 1950s, In Memoriam

The famous 1953 *Mademoiselle* guest editors, with Sylvia Plath at
the very top of the star. Her legacy—and suicide—would continue
to haunt them, as would the Barbizon, to which they returned
several times over the years.

At first glance, Sylvia Plath betrayed little of her inner struggle. Laurie Totten, who had traveled with her from Wellesley, Massachusetts, to the Barbizon, found Sylvia to be "a typical coed" with "nothing remarkable about her." In some ways, Sylvia was very much of her time. Mary Cantwell, who would go on to write the Manhattan Memoir trilogy, was much like Sylvia: both were from East Coast women's colleges, thereby belonging (as a guest editor had sardonically noted about Sylvia) to the "East Coast intelligentsia." Mary Cantwell would arrive in New York in July 1953, just a month after Sylvia had left. That summer was hot, stifling, the humid air un-inhalable. Mary Cantwell, like Sylvia, craved New York at the same time that she feared it. She was "afraid to take the subway, afraid to get lost, afraid even to ask the women in the office where the ladies' room was," so afraid that instead she would leave her office and use the bathroom at the Bonwit Teller department store around the corner.

The Seven Sisters Placement agency, catering to graduates from the elite East Coast women's colleges, sent Mary out to interview with *Mademoiselle*'s managing editor, Cyrilly Abels: the very editor whom Sylvia had shadowed the previous month, whom Sylvia would rename Jay Cee in *The Bell Jar*, describing her as the woman with the great mind but the "plug-ugly" face. Mary Cantwell was less intimidated by Abels than Sylvia had been. In her view, Abels was basically "a slicked-up version of the ladies on the Connecticut College faculty," a "homely woman in her forties with a low smooth voice." Mary Cantwell, who did not consider herself glamorous, and being sure of rejection by the magazine and its fashionistas, decided she would reject them before they could reject her. To demonstrate she was above the frivolity of a women's magazine, she arrived for her interview in a plain pink Brooks Brothers shirt and a black-and-white gingham skirt. Her plan was to "shame" the Madison Avenue managing editor with her "chill." But Mary was exactly the type of young woman that Cyrilly Abels liked to hire: a simile of herself—a smart woman from a good women's college, and no slave to fashion. Abels proscribed to the rule that every autumn one buys no more than "two simple wool crepe dresses, princess-line to show off a bosom of which she was rumored to be very proud, and an absolutely correct coordinating coat from Trigère." During the interview, Mary made it clear she had read a lot, and Abels made it clear she was a close friend of all the writers that Mary read. With that out of the way, she hired Mary Cantwell. It was a lucky if "improbable" break considering Mary had no real skills, and some of her college classmates had already gone off to Katie Gibbs to acquire them.

The Street & Smith building on Madison between Fifty-Sixth and Fifty-Seventh Street contained not only *Mademoiselle* but also *Charm*, and with *Harper's Bazaar* across the street, Checker cabs "were forever unloading magazine editors, who were sometimes ugly but always chic." Mary soon learned to differentiate between the editors and the secretaries not only by the cabs but also by the fixedness of their hats: an editor never removed her hat, and Betsy Talbot Blackwell was the most hatted of them all. Lunch, much like hats, helped define the editorial pecking order: the editors-in-chief frequented L'Aiglon, where they ordered "biftek hache" and Bloody Marys. Cyrilly Abels was to be found more often than not in the Bayberry Room of the Drake Hotel lunching with the writer of the moment: "Dry Sack [sherry] for an aperitif and something wholesome, like calves' liver, for the entrée." The copywriters and other literary types nibbled on *saucisson* at the French Shack, or else knocked back martinis at a restaurant called Barney's. Even then, finding "the best" of anything was a badge of honor among the magazine women: those in the know would never buy a pair of gold earrings at Tiffany's but instead at a little place called Olga Tritt, on East Fifty-Seventh, where even the Duchess of Windsor shopped. Clothing, just like hats and food and jewelry, was hierarchical: "The younger fashion editors wore Seventh Avenue, the most powerful of the older editors wore whatever had debuted on the Paris runways a few weeks before, and the store buyers wore too much."

Mary Cantwell, who did not have nineteen other guest editors to keep her company, was forced to fend for herself in the lunch hierarchy in which she had no footing. Even as she had the fresh, young look of a girl in a Pepsi-Cola ad, she dined alone at Henry Halper's drugstore: it was where "all the young fashion editors went for a quick bite (they were always either going to or coming from 'the market')." The drugstore "employed a middle-aged black man just to push one's long-legged chair in to the counter. The egg salad sandwich, which was heaped with watercress, was 'the best in New York.'" There were also other "bests" that the magazine women had discovered: the devil's food cake at Hamburger Heaven; the coconut cake at the Women's Exchange; sundaes at Schrafft's on Fifty-Seventh Street. Hamburger Heaven, practically across the street from the Barbizon, was a staple, "where one slid into a wooden chair whose right arm curved around to form a little table" and "customers wore gold circle pins and spoke of Junior League dances and wedding receptions at the Georgian Suite." Sylvia Plath and Neva Nelson had often gone there for the fifty-five-cent burgers. In *The Bell Jar*: "...Heavenly Hamburger...where they serve giant hamburgers and soup-of-the-day and four kinds of fancy cake at a very clean counter facing a long glarey mirror."

On the one hand, postwar New York had the look of new beginnings, and young women like Sylvia Plath, Mary Cantwell, and others were anxious to start the lives they had dreamed about for so long. On the other hand, the all-female *Time-Life* magazine clippers were told they could never be reporters, and the women's fashion magazines paid a pittance because everyone assumed you'd soon be gone, wedded, pregnant; or else that you had what was called "mailbox" money coming in from parents and grandparents, with no worries as to your next paycheck. In 1951, a petition went around the offices of *Mademoiselle*, signed by all fifty-five employees (most of whom were women), asking that instead of a Christmas party they get a bonus. Several people, getting into the spirit of things, asked that the word "bonus" be substituted for "charity." Betsy Talbot Blackwell was not amused.

Mary Cantwell was placed in the promotions department as assistant to the press editor. One of her first tasks was to go through the newspapers and look for articles on Sylvia Plath's suicide attempt in the crawlspace of her mother's house. Sylvia's disappearance had turned into a national missing-person hunt—*Smith Girl Missing!*—until she was found, the worse for wear but alive. Two hundred national articles in total, and Mary's job was to cut and paste the clippings into her press editor's scrapbook for reasons she could not understand. She puzzled over whether this was good or bad publicity for the August College Issue, which was now on newsstands, and in which Sylvia Plath was prominently featured with the other GEs. Mary Cantwell asked her boss, Mr. Graham, what Sylvia had been like. "Like the others," he said, "Eager." Edie Locke, then assistant fashion editor, also remembered her as "just a very pretty blonde"— but then so many of them were. Many years later, Mary Cantwell would watch a documentary on Sylvia, thinking how indeed they were all the same then, even the ambitious ones who planned to resist, for however long, the suburbs, marriage, the white picket fence. The grainy images of Sylvia's graduation from Smith College suggested it was little different from her own: instead of the Smith

College daisy chain, Mary Cantwell had had a laurel chain, but it was also June, they also had the same pageboy hairdos, they also wore Arpège perfume.

Of course all the guest editors, by definition, were ambitious. That was why they were at *Mademoiselle* and the Barbizon. In 1956, Polly Weaver, *Mademoiselle*'s careers editor and later a women's rights activist, penned an article about the steady influx of young, single, ambitious women coming to New York since 1949 to find their place and make their mark. Weaver titled the article, "What's Wrong with Ambition?" Apparently lots, if you were to believe the responses the article elicited: one reader wrote in chastising ambitious women for having "forgotten the true functions, duties, and gracious living pleasures of the mature woman—creating for others, not for herself," and calling ambition "unnatural and frightening." Another reader went out on a limb: "I could shoot the first woman who went to work in a man's job."

+

If one's brewing ambition was not sufficiently anxiety-producing, something to feel ashamed about, then the other taboo—sex— certainly was. The consequences of premarital sex in an age without the pill or legal abortion could be devastating. In her journal Sylvia Plath spoke for her generation when she wrote, "I can only lean enviously against the boundary and hate, hate, hate the boys who can dispel sexual hunger freely," while her fate, as a young woman, was an unrelenting and unsatisfied "soggy desire."

These very anxieties of which Sylvia was so keenly aware enveloped the whole country that same summer with the publication of the scandalous Kinsey Report *Sexual Behavior in the Human Female*. Alfred Kinsey was a zoologist by training, whose research specialty had been gall wasps until he was asked to teach a course on marriage and discovered there was little to no research available. He changed his focus from wasps to human sexuality. Five years earlier he had published his findings on the human male, which had caused enough of a stir, but the 843-page book on women's sexuality that came out in the summer of 1953 led to a torrent of outrage. Even though it was a dry work of methodical research, based on thousands of interviews, it was utterly titillating and sold 270,000 copies in less than a month. More would have sold if people could get their hands on it. The book was banned in many places and some pastors forbade their flock from reading it. Not since Darwin's *On the Origin of Species* had there been such an uproar. Kinsey's methodology would be criticized (on campus at Indiana University, virgins were interviewed for one hour while nonvirgins were kept on for another hour; word got out and male students hung around to see who took two hours), but it was revolutionary to research women's sexuality, let alone take it seriously.

The findings were shocking too. The report included statistics on just how many women were engaging in same-sex relations, in adultery, in masturbation, and, of particular interest to the young women of the Barbizon, in premarital sex (half of all single women were having sex before marriage, it turned out). In June 1953, Cyrilly Abels toyed with the idea of publishing something in *Mademoiselle* about the Kinsey Report. She commissioned a long review piece that was to lay out the findings for the magazine's readers in a neutral but cautionary manner. Once ready, she sent it out to *Mademoiselle* staff for comment. In memo after memo, they responded: "Mothers and ministers will go up in arms, won't they? This is hot, sensational stuff"; "I must say this is far from what I expected, and consequently more interesting than I expected. For one example, his findings that college women from upper-middle-class, white collar families who marry late are better sexually adjusted certainly surprised me"; "should be read with interest and gratification by most women . . . the whole thing makes women seem very normal and very admirable as human beings. I'm inclined to be rather pleased—on the basis of the Kinsey Report—about being a woman"; "this certainly should hit our readers with a greater impact than any page of your nephew's top atomic secrets." But while the editorial staff was largely enthusiastic, there were concerns about the author's lack of analysis of the lengthy Kinsey Report, and the possible encouragement of premarital sex for the magazine's young readers. Betsy Talbot Blackwell decided they needed to solicit the opinions of their onsite guinea pigs—the guest editors who were right there in June 1953.

The debate around the Kinsey Report never shows up in *The Bell Jar*, nor in the later recollections of the guest editors from 1953, but on June 18, while at a showing of Mr. John's millinery, the GEs were suddenly told to return to the *Mademoiselle* offices at 5:00 p.m. instead of heading back to the Barbizon. Assembled in the mirrored conference room, BTB addressed them: "We are taking advantage of having a group of young college women here and asking you to report on a controversial article. . . . We are pledged to keep the contents of this article absolutely confidential, and may we count on you to keep *our* confidence?" To make it easier on those "more prudish," BTB decided to ask for a twofold response: for their personal opinion on the report and also its suitability for *Mademoiselle* publication. No discussion was permitted among the GEs until they had turned in their written reports that same evening to Cyrilly Abels's office. They were given a copy of the article each and sent off to read and write.

Neva Nelson offered some solid critical analysis, pointing out the report was based on Kinsey's statistics but that "statistics even from 9,460 people is not to be taken as the everlasting truth." Janet Wagner was game: she liked how it showed that "the facts disprove popular beliefs," and noted that while the finding that "girls with pre-marital experience were better prepared for marriage" might offend some, they were Mr. Kinsey's and not *Mademoiselle*'s, letting the magazine off the hook. Janet, although described by Sylvia as a country hick, was always partial to a little elitism and was pleased that Kinsey "studied women in different classes and the educated came out on top." Another GE smarted at precisely this, arguing that "many people are better off not knowing 'what it's all about.' . . . This would be true of the laborers and non-college women who already feel at a disadvantage without having sexual response added to their deficiencies" (this comment elicited an enormous exclamation point in the margin by Cyrilly Abels—an exclamation point that could just as easily have been an expression of the snobbish Radcliffe graduate as of the left-wing sympathizer in her). Of course this GE was perfectly right; one of the more serious criticisms later leveled at Kinsey was that his sample group was overwhelmingly made up of white middle-class college-educated women.

Laurie Glazer was perhaps the most direct about the effects of writing about sex: "It is extremely timely (and when is sex *not* timely? If people would *only* break down and admit that sex occupies a tremendous amount of society's time—via movies, advertising, even fashion: dressing to please a man's eye, etc.)" Indeed, the Kinsey Report would become crucial as the starter engine to the 1960s sexual revolution because it pointed out the hypocrisy of American society, which refused to discuss sex even as men and women were fully participating in its many variations behind closed doors. Carol LeVarn, Sylvia's best friend at the Barbizon and the inspiration for the morally loose and sexually charged Doreen in *The Bell Jar*, was glad to see that the Kinsey Report was doing away "with some old superstitions"—"high time" in fact—yet her "major criticism" suggested a character quite different from Doreen: "Is there no way to eliminate the implicit distinction between love and sex both on the part of Kinsey and the author?"

Sylvia Plath wrote the longest report, a full two pages, but for someone who was constantly balancing, and contemplating, the

1950s demands for women's chastity with her own sexual desires, and who strongly felt the sting of that double standard and its burden, she was surprisingly bland. Sylvia embarked on a point-by-point explanation of why and how the piece should appear in *Mademoiselle*. She wanted the writer of the review to leave all editorializing until the very end. As to the possibility that "some readers might take the statistics and implied go-ahead for experience seriously, as advisable, as well as pleasurable. And parents might resent the danger of this interpretation," Sylvia felt the writer had argued sufficiently that the statistics had to be placed "in relation to the moral philosophy of each of the readers." The kind of frankness Sylvia showed in her journals and letters was entirely gone here. It would be left to *The Bell Jar*'s protagonist, Esther Greenwood, to say what Sylvia Plath had really thought: "I couldn't stand the idea of a woman having to have a single pure life and a man being able to have a double life, one pure and one not."

That very night, when the guest editors were done reading the Kinsey piece and had submitted their reports, BTB sent the information on to the publisher, Gerald Smith, apologizing for intruding on his weekend although, as she wrote, she was glad he was not yet bored by "l'affaire *Kinsey*." But by the next day, those on the business side of *Mademoiselle*, having heard what was afoot, were apoplectic, writing to BTB that publishing this review of the Kinsey Report would mean "an avalanche of advertising and subscription cancellations. This kind of stuff is dynamite . . . and has no place in MADEMOISELLE." Revenue arguments won, and no mention of the Kinsey Report ever appeared.

This was *Mademoiselle* in a nutshell: full of contradictions, and in that sense entirely emblematic. Staffed by highly educated career women, the magazine brought similar young women to the Barbizon each June, to help mold a magazine catering to the very same kind of readership, who expected a mix of fashion and cutting-edge fiction, art, and commentary. At the same time, the magazine offered a prescription for womanhood that was its very opposite. Guest editor Dinny Lain (later Diane Johnson) noted that while *Vogue* was for sophisticated women, *Mademoiselle* was intended for a much younger female audience, and "yet how strict was the version of womanhood the . . . editors imposed on us." This was indeed the tightrope generation. As another 1953 GE explained, "We were the first generation after the war and the last generation before the Pill."

The rules were clear, and the expectations sky-high: women should be virgins, but not prudes; women should go to college, pursue a certain type of career, and then give it up to get married. And above all, living with these contradictions should not make them confused, angry, or worse, depressed. They should not take a bottle of pills and try to forget. Mary Cantwell witnessed many times over the consequences of failing to meet these expectations: sobs in the bathrooms, rumors of abortion, and hurried trips to Hoboken, New Jersey, to take care of it.

+

On Friday, June 26, most of the 1953 guest editors—including Sylvia—headed home. Sylvia was not the only one to leave feeling deflated by the experience. Only Janet Wagner seemed not to have had to contend with the jarring reentry into regular life after the excitement of Madison Avenue—she was now signed on as a Ford model. For Neva Nelson, it was probably the hardest return home. When she was submitting her thoughts on the Kinsey Report and premarital sex, she did not yet know. She did not know until she was back in California, standing at a bus stop, and felt sick. Neva was pregnant. The father was John Appleton, her date at the St. Regis rooftop ball. Sylvia and Carol had been right after all, and Neva's relationship with John Appleton had developed in the direction they suspected.

John Appleton had wanted Neva to stay in New York, and asked his grandfather at Street & Smith Publishers to help her find a job. The grandfather, horrified by Neva's lack of pedigree, pretended to call her in for an interview and then instead paid her off: he settled her Barbizon hotel bill, which was still due because of mix-ups with her plane ticket, and told her to return to California. She did as he said, although what he had offered was no fortune; she took the sleek, silver bullet of a train, the California Zephyr (the same that Joan Didion boarded two years later as she made her way home), famous for its "Vista-Dome Views" from the glassed-in top deck. She boarded with a shoebox of tinned Spam, hard-boiled eggs, bread, and shelf-stable mayonnaise. When she finally arrived in Oakland, California, penniless, needing to get to San Jose, she called up one of her mother's drinking buddies and asked for a bed for the night and a loan for the bus ticket. It was only later when she was standing at a bus stop in San Jose, and turned to be sick, that she knew. She spent the last couple of months of her pregnancy "in hiding" in a $12 attic room with only a bed, working in a hamburger joint to make ends meet. She met a couple who offered to help, eventually delivering the baby herself in their bathroom while they slept. Before they whisked the baby boy away, in what was almost certainly a baby racket they operated around Moffett Airfield, Neva gave him a name and wrote it inside his swaddling clothes: Michael Martin Murphey, Episcopalian. Neva would keep the secret for most of her life.

When the 1953 guest editors had introduced themselves to the magazine's readers in their bios, they all wrote that they aspired to become wives, mothers (preferably of three children), while keeping up a career. But privately they said otherwise. Toward the end of the month, Laurie Glazer and Sylvia finished off a bottle of white wine in Laurie's room, talking until the early morning hours. Conversation turned to the future, as it so often did in those days, and both swore they would not rush into marriage, perhaps not even get married, in fact anything to avoid ending up "in suburban boxes." In *The Bell Jar*, Sylvia wrote: "And I knew that in spite of all the roses and kisses and restaurant dinners a man showered on a woman before he married her, what he secretly wanted when the wedding service ended was for her to flatten out underneath his feet like Mrs. Willard's kitchen mat." It is hard to know if Sylvia already believed that as she sat in Laurie's Barbizon room in 1953, or if this feeling would come when she wrote the novel ten years later, having already experienced marriage.

Indeed, despite the promises to themselves and each other, they did all get married very soon after. Their stint in New York represented their ambition, which was now largely put aside because with marriage came babies, and fast. In 1956, Sylvia married the up-and-coming British poet Ted Hughes, whom she had met in Cambridge, England, where she was studying as a Fulbright scholar after graduating from Smith. They would become the darling couple of British literary circles, and she would have her first child in 1960. Diane Johnson returned home to marry the man to whom she had been engaged the summer of 1953. In a year she had a baby, and then within six years, she had another three. She was living the "1950s clichés, without believing in them, just stumbling in." Anne Shawber married Dick Stolley, to whom she had been "pinned" when she was a GE, and who would become a founding editor of *People* magazine. Janet Wagner would be married to an attorney within two years after that summer.

The pressures, the double standards, the desires and the prohibitions were just too much. Earlier in the summer of 1953, the handwriting expert hired by *Mademoiselle* to analyze the twenty guest editors informed BTB that one of the group was on the verge of a nervous breakdown. There were rumors immediately that it was Sylvia, but in fact it was her best friend Carol ("Doreen"), who had just lost her father, and to whom the editors had given a wide berth because of this. But what was telling was that more than a few of the GEs, upon hearing this news through the rumor mill, feared it was they who had set off the mental health alarm bells. All of them felt palpable relief after learning it was not them. The point is: perhaps it could have been any one of them.

But it was Sylvia Plath, aged thirty in 1963, in her flat in London, recently separated from her husband, poet Ted Hughes, who took her life early one morning, her head in the oven, the gas on, the kitchen door sealed with wet towels to protect her two small sleeping children nearby. It was her final, successful suicide attempt, with the first right after June 1953, and others most probably in between.

"Sylvia saved me over the years," Neva Nelson quietly confessed. "I didn't want to be known as the other one who killed herself."

+

Sylvia published *The Bell Jar* the year she died, the same year Betty Friedan was writing *The Feminine Mystique*. These publications marked the cusp of the women's movement, which would challenge the core values of the 1950s and the ways in which they besieged women. Friedan gave voice to America's white middle-class women in that tightrope generation. She said that, despite their privilege, they suffered from something she called "the problem that has no name." This "problem" played out in a Valium-soaked suburbia filled with college-educated women who had convinced themselves that a husband and six children was their ultimate dream. Only to discover it was not.

Years earlier, Betsy Talbot Blackwell had already noticed that upon arriving in the suburbs "a great sameness seemed to envelop most of them. The sameness of houses and cars and appliances began to erase the individual." Moreover, in the spirit of neighborliness, the idea was strong that one had to conform *together*; as *Fortune* magazine wrote, one suburban couple, too ashamed of their bare living room, smeared the windows with Bon Ami household cleaner until their dinette set arrived.

By the late 1950s, the average marrying age for a woman had dropped to twenty. One woman, presumably panicked by her twenty-five-years-of-age-and-still-single status, "took thirty-five jobs in six months in the futile hope of finding a husband." The number of women versus men going to college had dropped to 35 percent compared to 47 percent in the flapper decade of the 1920s. By the mid-1950s, 60 percent of women dropped out of college to marry, or to make themselves more marriageable by being less educated. Once married, they went to work only for the "PhT"—"putting husband through" college or graduate school. Girls were encouraged to go steady at twelve, and manufacturers made bras with foam rubber bosoms for girls of ten. Having two children was no longer enough; it was more impressive to have four, five, or better yet, six. Three out of ten women went blond and many more "ate a chalk called Metrecal, instead of food, to shrink to the size of the thin young models." Department stores reported that women were now three to four sizes smaller compared to 1939.

Phyllis Lee Schwalbe, *Mademoiselle*'s former College Board editor, the young woman who had mistaken George Davis for the porter, wrote a piece for the *New York Times* that Friedan would build on in her famous book. In summer 1960, as Plath was starting to work on *The Bell Jar*, Schwalbe wrote: "This June, while campus bells ring out . . . 100,000 women are graduating from colleges across the country. For the majority, in time, the satin-circled diplomas mark the descent from ivory towers to park playgrounds, push-button kitchens, supermarkets and finished basements. The road from Freud to Frigidaire, from Sophocles to Spock, has turned out to be a bumpy one." Presidents of women's colleges nationwide were scrambling to explain why women, if best suited to be wives and mothers, needed rigorous academic training: did that not set them up for depression, and rounds of Valium prescriptions to take the edge off? "The reason a college bred housewife often feels like a two-headed schizophrenic is this," wrote Phyllis. "She used to talk about whether music was frozen architecture; now she talks over frozen food plans. Once she wrote a paper on the Graveyard Poets; now she writes notes to the milkman. Once she determined the boiling point of sulphuric acid; now she determines her boiling point with the overdue repairman."

Nor could Sylvia Plath escape her generation's fate. The writer Janet Burroway, a 1955 GE with Joan Didion, developed an uncharacteristic case of jealousy toward Sylvia Plath, but when she finally met her at a British embassy reception, she declared her to be "just as nice as possible." After *Mademoiselle,* Janet would follow in Sylvia's footsteps in many ways: she too would win the Glascock Prize and then a Fulbright to Cambridge University in England. But it was at a party at Plath's London house, five weeks after Sylvia had given birth to her daughter Frieda in 1960, that Janet witnessed what she would later understand to be a revelatory moment: "What I remember in particular is this. I stood in the doorway of the narrow kitchen talking with Sylvia, who held Frieda in the crook of her left arm while she rattled pots with her right . . . you can't cook a meal one-handed while rocking an infant. . . . Finally, she took the baby into the living room and with some emphasis handed her to Ted—I want to say *shoved her at.*"

Later that year, Sylvia wrote a short story, "A Day of Success," which Ted Hughes would dismiss as "pastiche for a woman's magazine." It is the story of a writer and his wife. He sells a television play and heads off to a lunch with a "high-powered career woman while she nurses the baby and a daylong jealous fantasy." The late Sylvia Plath would go on to become a feminist icon, but she was no renegade in her time. At age seventeen, Sylvia wrote about her worries that marriage, children, and domestic life would take up precious space that she wished to reserve for her writing, but by twenty-two, she had come to terms with it. She wrote to the novelist and poet Olive Higgins Prouty that she no longer saw academia or a career as her destination but instead imagined a quiet amalgamation of the jobs of housewife, mother, and writer. She had accepted her prescribed lot in life even before she married Ted Hughes.

But while Sylvia had filled up pages wrestling with it, others did not even question it. Yet the fallout to come was felt across the board. Grace Kelly and her roommates at the Barbizon were of the same generation as Sylvia and her cohorts. Looking back, one former bridesmaid at Grace Kelly's grand royal wedding wrote: "The '50s romantic idea that there was just one Mr. Right and finding him would make life happy ever after were put to hard tests. All but one bridesmaid quit their careers to raise families. In the rough climate of the 1960s, with its intense questioning of values, there were some jarring breaks. All but one bridesmaid have been divorced. Two are twice divorced. Their '50s romantic ideas were strained in the '70s feminist movement." Sylvia Plath and her roommates were no different. Writer Diane Johnson's marriage lasted until 1965. Anne Shawber's marriage to *People* magazine founding editor Dick Stolley would dissolve in the face of his philandering, yet too late for Anne to restart her life. As their perfectly plotted lives started to show cracks, it was at first hard not to look toward Sylvia's seemingly perfect one. She had acquired a husband, children, and, it appeared, a career as a poet and writer.

For the women who spent the summer of 1953 with her at the Barbizon, she became their glue over the years, but also their albatross, their burden, a shadow that moved along with them through their lives even after she had ended hers. For Laurie Glazer, it started when Sylvia was still alive, and Laurie suddenly spied one of Sylvia's poems in a national magazine: "How annoying of her to haunt me from (glamorous) England, even as I sat reading her poems, my apartment overflowing with diapers and unfulfilled literary dreams." The haunting became more commonplace after Sylvia's suicide, and later the 1971 American publication of *The Bell Jar*. Laurie was standing in line at the grocery store when she picked up a magazine, flipped to yet "another nervous peon" of Plath, and was suddenly faced with their group photo in Central Park, star formation and tartan kilts. She thought: "I see that Sylvia Plath is still at the top of the star and I'm still at the bottom." Then, weighed down by her grocery bags, she walked to her car and wondered "if Sylvia is haunting the other eighteen ex-guest editors in the photo." It wasn't just the burden of everyday life that got to Laurie, it was also her "anonymity." Even in the pages of *The Bell Jar* she had been erased: "Here was Sylvia's disc jockey incident. (But, where was mine?) Here was Married Girl—we'd been so sorry for her—and here was Nice Girl. (Was Betsy me? No.) Nor the Towering Hayseed, lean and beige as a wheat stalk, who'd been transformed.... Twenty girls into a fictional [twelve] and no me in sight." As for Carol LeVarn, Sylvia's best friend and next-door neighbor at the Barbizon, she tossed away her copy of the novel, riled up by a "combination of pain and embarrassment."

Each generation has its couple, Janet Burroway speculated: the Victorians their Brownings, the flappers their Fitzgeralds. The 1950s generation had their Hugheses. Sylvia was the "trapped wife at the beginning of the woman's movement"; "she was not taken seriously"; she was "judged melodramatic, hysterical. She was not *heard*." Many guest editor "super achievers" who, like Sylvia, dreamed of greatness and worked hard for it, set it aside for marriage, husband, children, only to find themselves at the end of this haloed trajectory with divorce, depression, and, again like Sylvia, thoughts of suicide. This was really the long shadow of Plath for them: that she had avoided the missteps that the other women of the 1950s would have to endure.

Laurie Glazer, in 1973, would write to Neva: "I wonder how many of us went along with the '50s tide . . . being wife/mother/chief cook & bottle washer . . . and then, nodding vertically through The Feminine Mystique!"

The Barbizon Hotel, like Sylvia, would continue to haunt the 1953 guest editors: *The Bell Jar* had not only fictionalized and immortalized them but also the Barbizon ("the Amazon"). They were all now tied together inextricably. Some of the remaining guest editors would congregate at the Barbizon three more times in the coming decades. The first was in 1977 for the fortieth anniversary of *Mademoiselle*'s guest editor program. Neva Nelson, in a fit of patriotism, entered the Barbizon lobby wearing a polyester red, white, and blue striped dress. The magazine had hung portraits of its past famous GEs to view as you walked up the stairs to the mezzanine, where the now retired Betsy Talbot Blackwell held court on a settee. Neva's choice of polyester patriotism made her feel out of place until Edie Locke, the Jewish refugee and former fashion editor who was now the editor-in-chief of *Mademoiselle*, put her at ease, complimenting her on her small white purse, a fashion note Neva had at least hit on key. Once everyone had a drink in their hand, the 1977 crop of guest editors was introduced one by one in the main lobby of the Barbizon as everyone peered down at them from the mezzanine, applauding loudly.

The new GEs bore little resemblance to Sylvia, Neva, Janet, Laurie, and the others from 1953. There were now fourteen again, instead of twenty, and three of them were men. In 1972, under pressure to bring equality to the workplace, Edie Locke had agreed to open up the guest editor contest to men (although finding men who wanted to participate was another matter altogether). Nor were the female GEs enthusiastic about this nod to equality, ironically powered by the burgeoning women's movement. One 1972 GE, a student at Radcliffe, asked, "Why give men places on the board of a women's magazine? Consider the difficulty women have in landing high-placed jobs on men's magazines." The eleven female guest editors were still staying at the Barbizon, while the three male GEs, barred from the women-only hotel, had rooms at the Tudor Hotel on Forty-Second Street. In the *Mademoiselle* offices, they no longer reported to Cyrilly Abels but to the new managing editor—Mary Cantwell. The 1953 guest editor Laurie Glazer, just glad to get out of the house, booked a room at the Barbizon, and partied all night.

In 1979, Neva and the others once again walked into the Barbizon, this time for the promotion of a new film about Sylvia Plath. A young woman who was welcoming everyone exclaimed: "You're the '53 editors!" It made them feel like survivors of the *Titanic*. They took the thick folders offered to them: press releases and a paperback edition each of *The Bell Jar*, as if they didn't already own one. Roses were everywhere—a nod to the rose that Sylvia famously held in her hand for her "Jobiographies" photograph, taken right after she had been crying from being called out by BTB. The former GEs chatted among themselves, and at least two of them admitted they still had the god-awful kilt they wore for the group star-formation photo shoot. The Sylvia Plath film being promoted had left a bad taste in their mouths, and they were reluctant to discuss it. Already *The Bell Jar* had sullied their memories of their summer together, and now this—a film in which they all came off as closeted lesbians, or at least that's how they saw it. Anne Shawber was used to the sort of speculation that unfurled around Sylvia; she and her husband had been living in England just when "the great Sylvia Plath fad was beginning." Looking back, Anne blamed much of Sylvia's breakdown on *Mademoiselle* and the way in which they had bungled the editor matchups. Anne had graduated with a journalism degree and would have jumped at the chance to be guest managing editor, but instead they had had her shadowing the shopping editor, a role for which she could not care less, while Sylvia was forced to do the kind of detailed-oriented work for which her artistic temperament was unprepared, let alone her typing skills.

The 1953 guest editors' last Barbizon reunion was in 2003—this time to celebrate them, rather than the *Mademoiselle* GE contest or Sylvia. Eight showed up at the hotel, now called the Melrose. Some of the former editors were there too. Gigi Marion, who had worked in the College Board editorial department, recalled how she went up to Smith College to chat with Sylvia to see if she was suitable. Sylvia had written to her mother after that day's afternoon tea that she was no longer sure she would get a spot; the other contestants had been more qualified than she had imagined they might be. Marion had seen their meeting differently: she could tell Sylvia would be good but she was "on the cusp a little on how she might fit in. Her behavior was almost a performance, which I found a bit of a problem. You might be there another day and find an entirely different personality." Marybeth Little, the pregnant College Board editor at the time, remembered only "a nice effervescent way about her," but then so many of the others had that too, she added. It was what Edie Locke had said too: they were all the same. One generation, one type of girl, in many ways.

But while Sylvia had been frozen in time, immortal blond hair and bright red lipstick, the others had not. When Laurie Glazer expressed regret over not yet having written a novel, another of the group tried to comfort her. She said: "There's still time." "It passes, darling," Laurie replied. After the reunion, one GE wrote to the others: "Do you find it as unpleasant as I that the reunion would not have taken place had Sylvia not stuck her head in the oven?" Dinny Lain/Diane Johnson noted that the nineteen who remained from that summer were called "survivors," "implying, perhaps, a faintly suspect, overbearing, and slightly inappropriate tenacity to life."

This would be the last time they gathered at the Barbizon. The eight "survivors" sat out on the hotel terrace where once Sylvia had laid out after a dip in the Barbizon pool when she had been feeling particularly low. They blinked into the setting sun as they reminisced about a time and a New York that, for both better and worse, was long gone.

CHAPTER NINE

THE END OF AN ERA

From Women's Hotel to Millionaires' Apartments

The Barbizon coffee shop figured in many stories of the hotel. It is where the writer J. D. Salinger hung around, picking up the hotel's young residents. It is where Sylvia Plath sat drinking coffee on the morning of the Rosenbergs' execution, angry at the world's indifference. Here, model Astrid Heeren poses with coffee and cigarettes, a model's staple, in 1964.

I ronically, it would be the onset of the 1960s women's movement that would sound the death knell for the Barbizon. The residential hotel built in the 1920s on the promise of women's independence and the nurturing of their artistic talents and all-around ambition would become a casualty of that very same goal. The movement would call into question the need for sequestering women: What was the line between aiding women's growth and independence in a no-man environment, protecting them in a man-free zone, and cloistering them from the world and its gendered realities?

Change was in the air. In September 1959, *Mademoiselle* contacted beatnik poet Allen Ginsberg at 170 East Second Street, in New York's Alphabet City. As a "gesture at the beginning of a new decade," the editors were reaching out to a number of "young creators" who over the past several years had "voiced significant protests against entrenched attitudes." They wanted a piece from Ginsberg and others for the January 1960 issue. The result was "Seven Young Voices Speak Up to the Sixties," and it began with an editorial note: "Whatever one may think of them, certainly if more voices like these speak up, lively and idiosyncratic, we may look forward to the decade with cheerful curiosity." The January 1960 issue created tremendous buzz, with Joyce Johnson, girlfriend of Jack Kerouac, claiming that *Mademoiselle* had just given "several thousand young women between fourteen and twenty-five" a "map to a revolution." The magazine was as forward-thinking as ever, anticipating change that was only just on the horizon.

The following month, in February, four African American college students famously sat down at a Woolworth's lunch counter reserved for whites in Greensboro, North Carolina, and refused to leave. In November, a young John F. Kennedy was elected president, taking office in 1961 with a challenge to Americans to "ask not what your country can do for you," but "what you can do for your country." Women flocked to the civil rights and anti-war movements, yet, more often than not, they found their job was to make coffee while men "made politics." A women's movement slowly began to percolate alongside those countless cups of coffee.

In 1961, the birth control pill was introduced. It would prove to be revolutionary for sexual relations and gender equality, but the effect was not immediate by any means. To get a prescription for the pill, you still had to be married, or pretend to be married. Judith Innes, Radcliffe College graduate and Barbizon resident, managed to get hold of the pill under false pretenses but that was hardly enough protection. The ideas by which Sylvia Plath and her cohorts' sexual desires had been directed and controlled remained firmly in place: the assumption was that men were sexual and therefore blameless. Blame, in all sorts of ways, lay with women. Men got excited, and either women had to put in their best effort to prevent that from happening or else, if they failed, take care of his "pain." Stories of classmates and friends caught in a dark room alone with a man, who would push her down on a table, were commonplace. Tippi Hedren, the dazzling blond star of Hitchcock's thriller *The Birds*, was discovered at age fourteen by Minnesota's Donaldson's department store. On her twentieth birthday, she flew out to New York, checked into the Barbizon, and signed with Eileen Ford. While peddling Sego, a diet drink, the one-hundred-pound Tippi was discovered by Hitchcock, who liked to bring in relative unknowns to play lead roles, in part because they were easier to prey upon. Tippi understood this unequivocally once the first live shoot was over and she looked at herself in the mirror: the ravens and magpies, ordered by Hitchcock for the film, had gouged her cheek, just missing her eye. But one didn't even need to be a Hitchcock to have that kind of power over women.

The Barbizon, therefore, was still a safe place, and a necessary one, even as optically the world was starting to change. Joan Gage, a budding writer, arrived there in 1961 looking gray and emaciated; she had just about survived her college final exams with the help of cigarettes, coffee, Mars bars, and Dexedrine, the popular diet-pill that was in fact over-the-counter speed. But the toxins were worth it. She had made it to New York, and the city would prove to be trans-formative. Joan, who was from the Midwest, mistakenly drank the shrimp cocktail at La Fonda del Sol, but was also introduced to her first communist at the White Horse Tavern, Dylan Thomas's favorite haunt, and even learned how to eat an artichoke. She liked to wear "slacks," which was hardly an issue anymore for most young women, but the Barbizon fashion police at the front desk were having none of it, and when she tried to stride briskly across the lobby in them, from the elevator and out the front door, they ordered her right back before she could sully the hotel's reputation.

The year 1962 saw the publication of the notorious *Sex and the Single Girl*, which, like the January 1960 *Mademoiselle* issue, was channeling the zeitgeist. Before ascending to editor-in-chief of *Cosmopolitan* magazine, copywriter Helen Gurley Brown became famous for her outlandish self-help book, in which she called for a sexual revolution of sorts. She advised women to make the radical decision to marry much later in life (as she herself had). "I think marriage is insurance for the *worst* years of your life," Brown wrote. "During your best years you don't need a husband. You do need a man of course . . . but they are often cheaper emotionally and a lot more fun by the dozen." Referencing the outcome of far too many women who had married in the 1950s, she added: "Isn't it silly? A man can leave a woman at fifty (though it may cost him some dough) as surely as you can leave dishes in the sink." The book, endorsed by the somewhat unlikely duo of Hollywood star Joan Crawford and burlesque entertainer Gypsy Lee Rose, changed the conversation or, certainly, forced one onto America—much like the 1953 Kinsey Report on female sexuality had done.

That said, Helen Gurley Brown was still seeped in the value system of the 1950s. A woman should do anything to look good, she berated: a high-protein diet, dress purchases over food purchases, nose jobs, wigs, artful makeup. Your surroundings too were an important extension of your image and not to be overlooked. An effective mantrap of a single gal's apartment required a good TV for *him* (although not so big that it would take time away from you), a brandy snifter whimsically filled with cigarettes, sexy cushions, a well-stocked liquor cabinet. But it was also a tight ship: any liquor downed by your prince was to be replaced by him, and twenty restaurant dinners on him equaled one home-cooked meal from you. Within this morass of questionable advice, there was a message that young women at the Barbizon had long known: a single woman had to be able to provide for herself. Sexual freedom only came with economic freedom. The flappers knew that; the Gibbs girls knew that; the Powers models knew that.

What Helen Gurley Brown was advising—such as that a sleepover date might enjoy breakfast in bed the following morning, preferably a glass of half clam and half tomato juice with a wedge of lemon, an omelet surprise, toast, and coffee—was not exactly new. It just hadn't been said so publicly for decades now. The novelist Mary McCarthy, writing in the 1930s, referenced the "perennial spinster" ("the single gal"—in Brown's parlance) "whose bed the morning after a sexual adventure will always be made up . . . while coffee for two drips in the Silex and toast pops out of the electrical toaster." Just as much of a throwback was Brown's rediscovery of female ambition. Brown told her young readers to wear clean lingerie every day, to mix up various styles and periods of furniture for flare and sophistication, to stop "being a slug" and get out there. Joan Didion followed Brown on her Los Angeles book tour for an article in the *Saturday Evening Post*, where she pointed out that Brown's battle cry was "old-fashioned ambition so increasingly uncommon that her young readers will recognize it only from early Joan Crawford movies." In other words, the repression of female sexuality and ambition during the 1950s had been such that Helen Gurley Brown was being revolutionary by being retrograde.

In 1963, one year after *Sex and the Single Girl* hit the bookstores, Betty Friedan published *The Feminine Mystique*. While the two authors would disagree on what constituted women's liberation, both understood that a woman without an independent life would suffer in a variety of ways. Betty Friedan wrote that women were being advised "how to catch a man and keep him," while simultane-ously taught "to pity the neurotic, unfeminine, unhappy women who wanted to be poets or physicists or presidents." Friedan was right. In one of Betsy Talbot Blackwell's many marketing surveys, a student at Radcliffe in 1956 repeated the mantra she had fully absorbed: "Our dedication is to marriage and the family—the roots from which are nurtured stable individuals and a stable society." This declaration by a young woman at one of the country's most competitive universities was coming almost twenty years after *Mademoiselle*'s first Careers Issue in 1938, aimed at all the new women in the workforce. It was as if there had been a nationwide brainwashing that had lasted two decades plus.

While Helen Gurley Brown made a name for herself by advocat-ing late marriage and fun sex, Friedan caused a stir by pointing out that the most pressing question women were now asking themselves was also the most censured: "Is this all?" It was the verbal articula-tion of the physical gesture that Janet Burroway had witnessed, and understood, in Plath's London house just three years earlier, in 1960, when Sylvia had "shoved" their newborn at her husband, Ted Hughes. It was not a statement about motherhood; it was a statement about the raw deal, the dashed hopes, the quashed dreams.

For decades, the Barbizon had been the place to go if you were a woman like Sylvia and so many others asking yourself this very question: "Is this all?" By the mid-1960s, over 350,000 women had stayed at the Barbizon since the hotel had first opened its doors in 1928. More than 50 percent arrived because of word of mouth back home in small-town USA, while the rest were compelled by the hotel's print advertisements that presented a world in which everyone was forever young and surrounded by friends in a city that could look terrifying from afar. Actress and Charlie's Angel Jaclyn Smith, then known as Ellen Smith, arrived at the Barbizon in 1966 from Texas to study at Ballet Arts in Studio 61 at Carnegie Hall. Like so many Barbizon residents, Jaclyn had worked on her parents for months before they let her go, making her promise she would never use the subway (she never did). Five years after Joan Gage had been turned back in her slacks, the Barbizon remained "very proper"—heels expected, slacks still forbidden. There were still the same tiny beds "like cribs," the same flowered blue bedcovers and matching curtains. But Jaclyn was a small-town girl, like so many residents at the hotel, and she did not mind the old-fashioned ways that continued to be promoted as suitable for the hotel's residents: as far as she was concerned, the Barbizon coffee shop was good and friends were plentiful. She spent time with the model Dayle Haddon and the dancer Margo Sappington. In the summer they would all go up to the rooftop to sunbathe. For Jaclyn, the hotel represented "a time of rules and anticipation," which suited her just fine. But in the two years she spent there, the hotel and New York would also teach her an "emotional independence" that she would rely on for years to come; the ability to fend for herself, not only financially but emotionally. In many ways, it's what Helen Gurley Brown and Betty Friedan were trying to teach to their millions of readers too.

Indeed, even as there was change afoot, and some began to balk at the outmoded notion of a women-only anything, the Barbizon was still the catalyst for the kind of transformative coming-to-New-York story that the hotel prided itself on and was not shy about publicizing through advertisements and magazine puff pieces. There was the case, for example, of Dana from Michigan, a dancer with "luminous eyes" who returned to the Barbizon, stopping off at the coffee shop after her dance rehearsal at the Juilliard School, still dressed in tights. The composer Gian Carlo Menotti, whose studio was two blocks away, and who liked to take his coffee breaks at the Barbizon coffee shop, called over the waiter, who knew every resident's vocation as well as her aspirations, and asked about Dana. Menotti then scribbled a note on a paper napkin and had the waiter bring it over to her: "If you're interested in participating in the Spoleto Festival in Italy, call this number." She did—once she had told a better-informed friend about the note, who marched her right over to the nearest telephone. Betty Buckley, later the stepmother on the classic television show *Eight Is Enough*, arrived at Grand Central Terminal from Texas, registered at the Barbizon, and was out the door in fifteen minutes exploring the city. That very day, she happened to walk into a rehearsal hall for the final auditions for the Broadway musical *1776*. She waited her turn, figuring that since she was used to singing fourteen shows a day for $75 a week at a Texas amusement park, she could manage this. She got the job, and in one day had basically gone from Grand Central to the Barbizon to Broadway. The same year, a seventeen-year-old high-school dropout, Lorna Luft, Liza Minnelli's half sister, was also at the Barbizon, just as her older sister had been years before at their mother, Judy Garland's, insistence. A few weeks later, she too landed a role on Broadway, in the musical version of *Lolita*.

+

Young women continued to check into the Barbizon, but they weren't the only residents to call it home. By the 1960s, the hotel harbored a more eclectic mix of women. A 1963 *Saturday Evening Post* article noted, "Tenants this year include a sizable band of aristocratic 70 year olds and one aged 80; a Playboy bunny; a perennial candidate for New York state office; a stunt girl; a model who sells Hong Kong junks on the side; a grande dame who has been playing the Barbizon pipe organ on the mezzanine every evening since 1935; and one fashionable merchandising student who shall be memorable for her name alone—Lady Greenslit." The perennial candidate for New York state office was Alice Sachs, a book editor. She was in fact the hotel's longest-residing guest, having moved to the Barbizon when they still dressed in evening gowns for dinner on the terrace. A staunch Democrat in the heavily Republican stronghold of the Upper East Side, she nonetheless persevered in her candidacy, once getting local Chinese restaurants to pass out special fortune cookies urging customers to vote for her.

Betsey Johnson, the future fashion designer famous for costume-like wearable fantasies, was at the Barbizon in 1964 as a *Mademoiselle* guest editor. She was assigned to their fabric library, which was something all fashion magazines had at the time: a cataloging room for thousands of pieces of fabric. D. J. White, its director, left on maternity leave, and Betsey Johnson was asked to stay on. She took the fabrics that no one was using and started to design her own clothes—T-shirts, T-shirt dresses, hand-crocheted fabrics, and velvets—which she sold out of the Condé Nast bathrooms, figuring that everyone who worked at *Mademoiselle, Glamour, Vogue,* and *Brides* eventually had to go to the bathroom, which is where she cleverly left a little catalog of her clothes.

One of Jaclyn Smith's friends, who would often visit her on the sixth floor, was Melodee. Melodee was the kind of young woman in which the Barbizon specialized: small-town girls who had asked themselves Friedan's key question: "Is this all?" Young women like Melodee, if they could not sing, dance, act, or model their way out, would type their way out of small-town America. Melodee left behind her fiancé in Florida to attend secretarial school in New York. Her mother had accompanied her to the hotel, which was helpful because in the early fall especially, the Barbizon would receive about a thousand applications, and at best only half the applicants would get rooms. As her mother was registering her at the hotel, Melodee hatched a plan with two other young women who had just gotten there too: the Beatles were arriving at the Hotel Astor that very day, and they were going to catch a glimpse of them. Once their mothers had all left, and the three young women had quickly unpacked, they ran over to the Astor to join thousands of other screaming fans. While the Beatles never showed up, it did make their first day in New York memorable. (On that very same day, *Mademoiselle*'s flamboyant Leo Lerman, who had replaced George Davis, and who always had his finger on the cultural pulse, announced to his assistant, Amy Gross—years later tapped by Oprah to be editor-in-chief of *O Magazine*—"For the April issue, we're going to be doing a boys band from England called the Beatles." Amy looked at Leo, "a cross between a rabbi and Oscar Wilde," whom she adored and whose cultural compass she usually trusted, and thought to herself that with a name like "the Beatles," the band was doomed to fail.)

Days after moving into the Barbizon, Melodee discovered Malachy's. It was certainly no-frills, she told her new friends back at the hotel, but it was a real singles bar. With so many possibilities on offer in New York, Melodee soon broke off her engagement back in Florida and began to date, quickly learning how best to hedge her bets. She had a system: she would get ready, wait for her date to call up from the Barbizon lobby, have a friend pick up the phone and say she had stepped out for a moment while Melodee dashed to the mezzanine to see who was on the lobby phone. If she liked what she saw, she would run back to get her bag. If she did not, she either hid in her room or sneaked out of the Barbizon through its coffee shop exit.

After the secretarial course was over, Melodee found work at an advertising agency, where she would arrive each morning in full sixties fashion: miniskirt, poor-boy sweater, Mary Jane shoes, and false eyelashes. But while fashions had changed radically from the 1950s cinched waists and swinging petticoated skirts, that did not mean everything else had. On her first day at the Ted Bates advertising agency, two account executives tossed money on her desk and told her to go buy them cigarettes. The first time they did it, she went; the second time, she refused. Her refusal was the kind of small gesture that, accumulatively, would lead to the change that the January 1960 issue of *Mademoiselle* had laid out to its readers as a possible road map. The personal was becoming political, and for Melodee, having money tossed at her was very personal.

Change, however, moved at different speeds depending on the color of one's skin. Artist and *Mademoiselle* guest editor Barbara Chase had been a pioneer when she stayed at the Barbizon in 1956, most likely the first black woman to have done so, but over ten years later, things had barely changed. Phylicia Rashad, the actress who would play Mrs. Huxtable in *The Cosby Show*, arrived at the Barbizon in 1968 as a sixteen-year-old for a summer stint with the prestigious Negro Ensemble Company. One of the hotel's few African American residents, her first room, blue, was unnecessarily large and expensive, and so she switched to a yellow room, the kind that Sylvia Plath had, with the signature floral bedspread and matching curtains and a shared bathroom. New York had an active art scene, which thrilled Phylicia, but as to race, "it felt like you were living in America," which meant she was surrounded by segregation and white people wherever she went, especially at the Barbizon on New

York's Upper East Side. While the 1960s was a decade of questions and slowly shifting values, it would be the disco decade of the 1970s when real change would start to become visible. Ironically, it did not bode well for the Barbizon.

✦

On August 26, 1970, Helen Gurley Brown marched down Fifth Avenue with Betty Friedan. They were joined by the photogenic Gloria Steinem, cofounder of *Ms.* magazine, who in 1963 had gone undercover as a Playboy bunny, exposing the sexism and racism in that organization, and arguing that in fact all women were routinely treated as Playboy bunnies. Ten thousand women, the younger ones in jeans and T-shirts, the older ones in summer floral dresses, marched with these three feminist icons. It was the Women's Strike for Equality, celebrating the fiftieth anniversary of the Nineteenth Amendment, passed in 1920, which granted women the right to vote: it had also been the impetus for the construction of women's hotels in the 1920s. Brown, Friedan, and Steinem linked arms with a group of veteran suffragettes, and the march swelled as bystanders joined them, some marchers hoisting signs that read: "Don't iron while the strike is hot!" and "I am not a Barbie Doll!" Men stood on New York's sidewalks and watched; some heckled, one wearing a brassiere on Forty-Fifth Street, others shouting "Bra-less traitors!" at them as they made their way down Fiftieth Street.

It was the beginning of a new era, and it was marked at *Mademoiselle* by the end of the old one. Editor-in-chief Betsy Talbot Blackwell was stepping down from her post. A lifetime smoker, her coughing fits were now ear-shattering. Incoming guest editors were told to pretend they could not hear what sounded like a freight train passing through, although BTB liked to say this was her way of announcing her entry. She was now called "Mother" by much of the staff, but she had continued to move along with the times, to insist on *Mademoi-selle*'s trailblazing "firsts." Just the previous year she had "O.K.'d my first four-letter word in copy." In her parting "Editor's Memo" to the magazine's readers, she cataloged her journey from 1935 to the present: "The birth and growth of nylon and TV, of zippers and jets and no-iron fabrics and the big wig habit . . . of 'Black is Beauti-ful,' revolution on campus, and Women's Lib. The era has brought us a whole new vocabulary: the UN and A.A., freeways and hippies, ballpoints and Beatles, consumerism and communes, rock 'n' roll, smog, test-tube babies, ethnic everything. In fashion, pantsuits have become staple wear for women—unforeseeable as late as the 1940s, as have micro-miniskirts, bikinis, bodystockings, hotpants."

Her send-off was drawn out, with honorary dinners and person-alized gifts, including spring flowers from actress and former guest editor Ali MacGraw (also a onetime roommate of Gloria Steinem's), who thanked Betsy for igniting her career by putting her on the front cover of the 1958 August College Issue. The cherry on the cake (which was pink, of course) was a party thrown in her honor by Condé Nast, the magazine's publisher after Street & Smith, on the rooftop of the St. Regis hotel, everything adorned with pink roses. Even with all the well-wishers around her, BTB must have paused to remember the guest editor balls that had taken place on that same rooftop every June from 1937 on. But she understood this was a new era: Edie Locke was going to be the new editor-in-chief of *Mademoiselle*, for-going BTB's trademark hats, cigarettes, and Scotch.

But it was not new beginnings for everyone. The Barbizon began to falter. A residential hotel built for the New Woman of the 1920s was now less alluring. For those looking for a husband, it was a place bereft of men. As one former resident complained: "I don't know why girls interested in meeting men and having a life of their own would ever choose to live in a place like that. When they date, they can't have people up—they drop the boys at the door." For those looking for the quintessential New York experience, as countless young women before them had, there was now something stodgy about the Barbizon, embodied by its older residents, "the Women" (as they had always been called by the hotel's young residents). The Barbizon's cultural programs, which had once included concerts, recitals, and plays, were now reduced to a television set on the mezzanine floor. Free afternoon tea continued in the "dark Tudor cavern above the lobby," but hardly anyone bothered to show up these days. Those who did were mostly the elderly ladies gathered around one of their own, Mrs. Anne Gillen, who played the hotel organ from 5:00 to 6:00 p.m. dressed in pearls and a pillbox hat, while the younger ones who had nowhere else to go gathered around the hotel's social director, who thought it was fun to play a game coming up with categories of horses. Just as this was a time of confusion for many, so was it for the Barbizon. By the 1970s, the hotel's luster had finally and truly vanished. Helen Gurley Brown's single girls were at Studio 54, not the Barbizon.

Marching down Fifth Avenue, Betty Friedan, Helen Gurley Brown, and Gloria Steinem had linked arms in sisterhood and a demand for gender equality. But for the Barbizon, sex discrimination was in fact central to its mission. It was a strictly women-only hotel residence, from which men were intentionally excluded. The Barbizon thus found itself joining forces with two unlikely partners, the New York Mets and a chain of Bowery hotels, to appeal to the Commission on Human Rights and request an exemption from new mandatory requirements for gender-based equality. The Mets wanted to continue to host ladies' night eight Saturdays a year; the single-room occupancy dormitory hotels on the Bowery were deemed too dangerous for women; and the Barbizon wanted to continue to be "a home for women."

That the Barbizon needed to be women-only to continue to function as a sanctuary was a valid claim—and the Barbizon won its appeal. It would be permitted to continue in its mission as a women's residential hotel. But that victory was soon overshadowed by a different kind of reality: plummeting occupancy rates. The 1969–1970 economic recession had not helped matters, but the real nail in the coffin was the departure of Katie Gibbs in 1972, which translated into the emptying out of two hundred rooms across three full floors. Yet even as the hotel's occupancy fell to 40 to 50 percent, the front desk staff refused to change their old ways: they were quite willing to turn away Gucci-clad women who had dared to arrive without the required references. That Gucci-clad women were even bothering to show up was itself surprising: the hotel, increasingly run-down, was showing its age.

To add to all of this, New York in the 1970s was a city on the brink of bankruptcy. President Gerald Ford, with Donald Rumsfeld and Alan Greenspan whispering in his ear, had declared there would be no government bailout and that New York City should just drop dead—as the *Daily News* famously announced on its front page. Even the city's police force was handing out tourist pamphlets titled "Welcome to Fear City," illustrated with a hooded skeleton head, and with pointers on how to make it out of the city alive. When Joan Faier encountered the Barbizon at this time, she was confronted by some miserable visuals that mimicked New York city in general: "dimly lit hallways, heavy mahogany furniture, and a gaping hole in the sky-blue paint near the mezzanine's elaborate crystal chandelier." She had a one-windowed room, and the now outdated radio speaker fixed above the bed had been painted a horrible "Pepto-Bismol pink." Another resident declared that the hotel reminded her of Miss Havisham, the spinster recluse in her run-down mansion from Charles Dickens's *Great Expectations*. Moreover, the Barbizon could do just so much to shield its residents from the harsh realities of 1970s New York: in 1975, seventy-nine-year-old Ruth Harding, a lonely resident who liked to hang out in the lobby and talk to anyone willing to listen, was strangled to death in her eleventh-floor room. Her murder went unsolved.

✦

The same year that Ruth Harding was murdered in her room, a trendy and controversial hotelier, David Teitelbaum, was brought in to try to save the hotel. The Barbizon's owners, exasperated with the falling occupancy rates, turned to Teitelbaum, known for choosing jeans and gold chains over pinstripe suits, flexibility over intransigence, Hollywood glam over East Coast conservatism. It was 1975, deep into the disco era. Standing in his snakeskin cowboy boots, Teitelbaum looked around the lobby and took particular note of "the Women," the Barbizon's eldest residents, the wrinkled ladies like the late Ruth Harding, who served as a daily warning to the younger guests to move on while they still could. They were Gael Greene's Lone Women but now a couple of decades down the road. Lori Nathanson, just graduated from Vassar College in 1979, was making conversation with one of them in the elevator when she was asked how long she'd be staying: "Not long," she replied. "Yes," said the elderly woman, "that's what I thought too." Lori went straight to her room and cried.

The Women had become a serious eyesore, Teitelbaum decided. It was clear to see, if you observed a full twenty-four-hour cycle of the hotel's life, that they were "lobby sitters in curlers and slippers," who clustered in groups gossiping and chiding the younger residents. One Barbizon resident recalled the benches by the two elevator banks where the Women positioned themselves strategically to offer unsolicited advice to younger hotel guests heading out for the evening:

"Now where are you going?"

"Now I'm not sure you have on the right clothes."

"Now are you sure about those shoes?"

With the new manager, Barry Mann, whom he had brought over from the St. Regis, Teitelbaum started to make changes. First, they cleared the furniture out of the lobby, which made the Women none too happy, with one hollering: "Where is my seat?!" Next, they moved out the "dour desk clerks" who had continued to rate guests A, B, and C and demanded to see their reference letters, even as there were no longer enough guests to go around. Out too went the pink and lime furniture, the cabbage-rose wallpaper, and the pictures of weeping clowns; in came chocolate and vanilla hues, *Vogue* posters, and green plants galore. The restaurant and the famed coffee shop received a sprucing up as well.

Teitelbaum tried to resurrect the Barbizon's halcyon days, or at least honor them, hoping that would be enough to save the hotel. The few remaining New York City women's hotels still in operation at this point were the Allerton House, the Evangeline, and the Martha Washington. Yet Teitelbaum believed he could make a newly dusted-off Barbizon (with a half million dollar's worth of dusting) profitable. He wanted to continue to offer longer-term residencies to the "new girl in town," as well as overnight stays for the businesswoman on the go who would be grateful for a man-free night. He turned the oak-paneled recital room into a meeting room. The Barbizon library was closed and added on as rental space for the health club that had taken over the basement swimming pool, where Rita Hayworth had once posed for *Life* magazine. The library books were moved to the "date rooms" on the mezzanine. As a nod to the old days of white gloves, teas, and formal dances, and to the nineteenth-century Barbizon art movement after which the hotel was named, Teitelbaum hung a framed Impressionist print of a young girl wearing a flowered bonnet in each room.

With that done, he organized a fiftieth anniversary party for the hotel, and while Princess Grace Kelly of Monaco did not attend, she did send a letter confirming that she had "wonderful memories of the three years I spent at the Barbizon." But do what he might, it was clear that those were bygone days. The hotel had changed from "a fresh-faced starlet to a withered spinster." The only former-resident-turned-celebrity to show up for the party was 1950s actress Phyllis Kirk, who appeared with Vincent Price in the 3D horror *House of Wax*. Phyllis reminisced about Oscar the doorman and the afternoon teas on the mezzanine. The hotel's manager from 1944 until 1972, Hugh J. Connor, also at the party, recalled how Judy Garland would call him obsessively to check on the whereabouts of her daughter, Liza Minnelli.

In some ways, the only thing the Barbizon still had going for it was its idiosyncrasies. Kim Neblett, once checked into the Barbizon, learned to love its quirkiness. She was a fashion model and while she had just made $1,000 for the week, the previous year, her first in the New York, she had made only $1,062 in total. There was one month when she was so broke she could not afford her room and instead slept on the floor of a friend's room. Yet the hotel said nothing even as it forwarded her calls to her friend's room where she "secretly" lived until she was able to earn enough to book a room again. She embraced the diverse age range of residents, "even the crazy old ones," that helped fuel "weird scenes" day and night such as "screaming at six o'clock in the morning." She had found that if you started laughing at all the various incidents, then the crazy ones began to laugh too, and, she insisted, in this way everyone found some equilibrium. She saw a certain heroism in the Women, the ladies who had stuck it out all these years: "They are still in New York. They may be hiding at the Barbizon in their little cubbyholes, but they are still here in New York. That's something."

Writer Meg Wolitzer did not see it quite so generously. Her hair fragrant with Gee, Your Hair Smells Terrific shampoo, that "1970s beauty mainstay," Wolitzer arrived in 1979 with the very last set of guest editors at *Mademoiselle*. Even though BTB was no longer at the helm, the GE program had continued. Wolitzer wryly observed that the *Mademoiselle* offices mirrored the Barbizon hotel perfectly, both "wanting to be current and to compete, yet clinging to the wholesome collegiate sensibility that we, the guest editors, were meant to embody." But of course the 1979 college editors did not embody these bygone sensibilities.

The hotel's decline, its wear and tear in both appearance and service, manifested in various ways: on her first morning, Wolitzer was awoken by the hotel maid "slamming her fist against my door like a D.E.A. agent." She opened her eyes, pulled back the orange-and-yellow bedspread (one of Teitelbaum's improvements) and took in her grim, narrow room. She was not impressed. The hotel's only saving grace for her was its legacy. Wolitzer had Sylvia Plath on her mind. In fact, Wolitzer was very much sharing the same space that Sylvia had occupied twenty-six years earlier for the simple reason that nothing had changed since: there were still only 130 rooms that came with a private bathroom; 94 with a shared bathroom; and 431 rooms—the cheapest kind, the kind in which the guest editors lived, described to Nanette Emery in 1945 by Phyllis Lee Schwalbe as a "dormitory-hotel life"—with access to hallway bathrooms.

But this was 1979 New York, not 1953 New York, and the bankrupt city reminded Wolitzer of "an episode of *Kojak*." Two years earlier, New York had been terrorized by the Son of Sam killing sprees that left six dead and seven wounded, Times Square was one of the most crime-ridden areas of the city, and the only reason to go to Bryant Park was to buy drugs or sex. Gone were New York's glory days, or so it seemed in that grim decade. As if to match the city's mood, Meg Wolitzer and her fellow GEs brought an irreverence to the same *Mademoiselle* magazine assignments that had once thrilled Sylvia Plath, Joan Didion, Gael Greene, and so many others. At a Scent Seminar at Revlon, they were asked to sniff various perfumes and describe what the scent conjured up for them; one GE pretended to be deep in thought while she rattled off the tagline for Revlon's competing Charlie perfume—"I would say it's kinda free, kinda wow!" she declared to those gathered around the table. At a Milliken Textiles breakfast at the Waldorf Astoria, they giggled when Ginger Rogers was, literally, wheeled out. For the annual GE makeover event, Meg and her friends were brought to Saks Fifth Avenue in their "rumpled, Barbizonian, sleep-encrusted worst." A male GE had his beard replaced with a "'70s gaystache," that was quite becoming, while Wolitzer, post-makeover, cried out, "I look like a prostitute!" On the last night, they all trailed up to the Barbizon roof, just as Sylvia Plath had done on her last night, and held an impromptu ceremony in her honor. They would be the very last group of *Mademoiselle* guest editors. After them, the contest was disbanded. It would be another twenty-two years, in 2001, before *Mademoiselle* ceased publication, by then a shell of its former self, at best.

The 1980s vision for a solvent New York radically changed the face of the city. A New York in which the working class lived side by side with the rich (the New York the CEO of Neiman Marcus tried to show Neva Nelson in 1953 when he had the cabdriver take a circuitous route through Manhattan) would cease to exist. New York would be saved, but in the process, old New York would be lost. The city would find salvation not through federal funding, which President Gerald Ford had made eminently clear, but by catering to private developers and conglomerates promised tax breaks, incentives, and favors. It would be the making of the Trumps and others like them. The 1980s foreshadowed everything that New York would come to represent: money, excess, artifice, and indulgence. It was now Yuppies and Madonna. It was the Odeon, cocaine, Danceteria, and ecstasy.

The Barbizon needed to catch up, because New York would no longer pivot around rent control, the system that had allowed the working and middle classes to live centrally and permanently in

Manhattan. When David Teitelbaum was first hired as a consultant for the Barbizon in 1975, he had discovered that well over a hundred of the hotel's residents were covered under rent-control protection laws: their monthly rents could be raised only by infinitesimal amounts, and their rights as permanent tenants were guaranteed. In 1979 the hotel again changed hands, but Teitelbaum was kept on. The new owners, an Indian hotel chain, wanted exactly what New York was starting to embody. That meant turning the Barbizon into a luxury hotel for women . . . and men.

The news was not well-received by the Women. A "bejeweled" elderly resident "who identified herself only as 'a famous theater actress'" claimed that "a lot of the nicer women" were against the plan, and she herself was convinced that the addition of men would "encourage a great deal of prostitution." The Women momentarily put aside their various differences to create a tenants' association, and hired Leonard Lerner, a successful tenant rights lawyer. Alice Sachs, the persistent Democratic candidate who had lived at the Barbizon since 1935, was in no mood to move. She and the others were paying an average of $275 a month for their rooms, which included daily maid service, a front desk that took messages, and a fantastic location. In contrast, rents for small-size apartments on the Upper East Side were starting to creep up in the range of a thousand dollars a month. Men or no men, she was staying put. Alice Delman, another longtime resident, was none too happy at the thought of seeing men "in the halls at all hours of the night in various stages of dress." But with the hotel continuing to lose money, Barry Mann, the Barbizon's manager hired by Teitelbaum, had the most convincing argument for the change: "there's only one sex left."

At first, Teitelbaum offered $1 million to clear the place of the Women. Their attorney flat-out rejected it and countered with $10 million or, he suggested (with more than a little sarcasm), there was always the option of building an apartment building for 114 women on a vacant Manhattan lot. Under New York rental laws, their Barbizon rooms were untouchable, categorized as SROs, single-room occupancy units in multi-tenant buildings with shared bathrooms. Unable to convince the Women to move, Teitelbaum and the new owners had no option but to let them stay; so they decided to carve out a special wing of reconditioned rooms for them instead. With that hurdle out of the way, Teitelbaum had effectively cleared the way for men to enter the hallowed halls of the Barbizon while maintaining the older female residents' rights.

The Barbizon Hotel in 1980, having seen better days, shortly before it would go unisex.

The closing bell for the Barbizon Hotel's fifty-four years of single-sex living was strategically set to ring on Valentine's Day 1981. The

titillation of being the first man ever to spend the night at the Barbizon (if you didn't count Malachy McCourt and a handful of others
who'd claimed to have made it up the stairs) brought such an influx of
phone calls that the hotel decided on a well-publicized raffle drawing
on February 12 to determine who would be the first man—as well as
the first couple—to officially make it past the lobby. The male raffle
winner turned out to be a thirty-nine-year-old homeopathic doctor
from Cambridge, Massachusetts, who looked a lot like Captain Stub-
ing on *The Love Boat*. Dr. David Cleveland got the call two days before
Valentine's that he had won, and that a limousine would be meeting
him at JFK airport in New York to whisk him to the grand opening.
For weeks, the doctor had been trying to ask out a waitress at the
Parrot Café in Cambridge, around the corner from Harvard University. He had even bought two tickets to the island of Curaçao for a
weekend getaway, which she had refused. The Barbizon win—with
limousine service, free meals, and Broadway shows included—also
did not shift her position. Thus Dr. Cleveland, balding, with tufts of
white curly hair on either side of his head, bought a wide-lapeled
tuxedo with a ruffled shirt and an oversize bow tie, and headed off
to New York alone.

On Saturday, February 14, at 11:30 a.m., a one-hundred-by-forty-
five-foot, ten-story-size Valentine banner fluttered on the outside of
the Barbizon Hotel. Sammy Cahn, the lyricist for a string of romantic
hits, crooned into the microphone set up in the lobby, singing some
of his best-known songs, including "Love and Marriage," "It's Been
a Long, Long Time," and "All the Way." He even incorporated the
doctor's name into a special song for the occasion. Photographers
were on hand as Dr. Cleveland was kissed on the cheek by Wendi
Teitelbaum (David Teitelbaum's daughter), dressed in a tight-fitting
bellhop outfit. Waiters and waitresses in white hardhats (to match
the decor of the scaffolding-covered hotel) walked around with trays
of champagne and served slices from an enormous, perfect cake

replica of the Barbizon. Dr. Cleveland, perhaps revealing why he could not get the Parrot Café waitress to go on a date with him, pulled out a can of "aphrodisiac" smoked oysters he had brought along as a lark and posed for the flashing cameras.

William Nicholas of Long Island, a wholesale fabric showroom manager, and his wife, Catherine, won as the first couple, and together with Dr. Cleveland, they were introduced to the crowd that had gathered, and then ceremoniously handed their room keys to much applause. Dr. Cleveland (and Mr. Nicholas) were thus the first men to walk the forbidden bedroom floors; or certainly the first to do so officially, without attempting to bribe the hotel employees, or scale the fire escape, or dress up in a surgical suit. Seventy other men had also booked rooms at the Barbizon for that first memorable weekend.

The splashy event had made an impression, and longtime resident, Democratic candidate, and key member of the Women, Alice Sachs, was feeling optimistic, telling a television crew, "I'm excited. I'm interested. I hope everything works out well." Another of the Women went further and admitted, "I've come to the conclusion only today because I really didn't know and it was a concept, an idea whose time has come." David Teitelbaum, unable to purge the Women, was now advertising them as part of the mythological history of the hotel.

Nine months later, however, Teitelbaum temporarily closed the hotel for a full multimillion-dollar facelift. He continued to insist that while now unisex, his vision for the refurbished hotel remained a women-centered space, even if men were permitted in. "Just because you put a skirt hanger in a room doesn't mean you're catering to women," he said. While the hotel manager was male, the marketing director, interior designer, design coordinator, and chef he had hired were all young and female. There would be a full spa experience available, and pink marble walls in the lobby and the lobby bar. Rooms would have makeup lights, French hand soap from Le Gallet, bath foam, and hand lotion.

Teitelbaum, a college dropout who had grown up on a date farm in California, was an outlier among the other New York developers. He did not believe in rebuilding but rather in redoing a place, in restoring old buildings—not to their original glory but by rethinking their insides. He had publicly criticized fellow developer Donald Trump for destroying the art deco Bonwit Teller friezes of dancing women that he had provisionally promised to the Metropolitan Museum of Art. Trump's promise gave way to the ease of a jackhammer; it was, after all, so much more simple to destroy them than to take the time and expense to remove them intact. In contrast, Teitelbaum wanted to preserve old New York while making it profitable again. He envisioned the new Barbizon as a European spa hotel, offering a visual nod to its French Barbizon arts roots. But his vision was expensive and soon ran over budget to the tune of millions. He had to seek a deal with the Royal Dutch Airlines KLM's Tulip Hotel Management Division. While the deal meant that the Barbizon would now be renamed the Golden Tulip Barbizon Hotel, it also meant Teitelbaum's renovation could be done, with a final budget of $60 million.

In 1984, the hotel's reincarnation finally complete, KLM Tulip celebrated with a Dutch festival that included herrings, tulips, Dutch gin, and New York mayor Ed Koch. The hotel conversion had included a serious restructuring: the former Barbizon Hotel for Women with almost seven hundred tiny rooms was now the Golden Tulip Barbizon with 368 spacious rooms with private bathrooms. Artist Richard Haas was commissioned to paint a leafy and somewhat tacky trompe l'oeil on the recessed ceiling above the lobby and the mezzanine. Interior walls were painted pink with ochre sandstone details; the intention was to play off the rosy colors of the Moorish brick on the outside of the Barbizon, and also to echo the early morning light over the forest of Fontainebleau that had inspired the Barbizon artists. A restaurant was now on the mezzanine where before nervous young ladies had peered over to check out their dates.

In 1985, Peggy LaViolette, Joan Didion's best friend and fellow *Mademoiselle* guest editor from the summer of 1955, came to stay at the Golden Tulip Barbizon with her husband, Don. They were heading east for Christmas: a daughter was working at *Elle* magazine and a son at the *New Yorker*. Peggy had read in the *New York Times* that the Barbizon had been recently converted to a regular hotel from the women-only residential hotel where she and Joan had stayed next door to each other. Feeling nostalgic, Peggy booked a room. When she walked in, she was struck by how dramatically the hotel had changed. Gutted of its original interior, it now showcased 1980s decor—heavy drapes, soft couches, everywhere deep cream paint with touches of gold trim. The menu at the Café Barbizon, up on the mezzanine, was the typical 1980s "international cuisine" fare, such as avocado stuffed with Norwegian shrimp, chicken salad with curry and celery, potato salad with bacon bits and scallions, Barbizon rice pudding, and brownie à la mode. Their hotel room was constructed out of a cluster of the type of tiny rooms in which she and Joan had stayed exactly thirty years earlier.

As Peggy made her way down the hall of their floor that same evening, an elderly woman suddenly brushed past her in a rush to get to the end of the hall, where she paused and then pulled open an unmarked door. She turned and looked Peggy over before stepping inside. In that moment, as the old lady held the door open, Peggy glimpsed the all too familiar green paint and the same doors she remembered as leading into the Barbizon's tiny rooms, each just large enough for a single bed, a sink, a minuscule desk and chair. The old woman glanced back again at Peggy, said nothing, and then closed the door behind her. Peggy shivered as if she had seen a ghost. She had, of course, seen one of the Women.

She returned to Don and her room. All night it was snowing, the wind cold and howling. The heat came on and blasted their room until Peggy and Don were sure it was a hundred degrees in there:

just as Joan Didion had suffered from an overenthusiastic air conditioner at the start of her stay at the Barbizon in 1955, so now, in 1985, Peggy suffered from an out-of-control radiator. She and Don unsuccessfully tried to wrench open the window. Hotel personnel came but they were no less able to stop the radiator, nor open the window. The next morning, with breakfast done, they threw their suitcases into a taxi as fast as they could and were gone. It was the last time Peggy stepped foot into the Golden Tulip Barbizon. For all of Teitelbaum's promise, there remained something dowdy and difficult about the hotel.

But a new wave of hope, mixed with some trepidation, arrived when Steve Rubell and Ian Schrager, owners of the famous nightclub Studio 54, the enfants terrible who had been sent to prison for tax evasion at the very height of their nightclub's popularity, now bought the hotel from KLM's Tulip. Rubell and Schrager had emerged from prison, following a year's incarceration, with fresh bold plans to shake up the hotel business. They believed the industry had languished and now hotels offered little more than a bed for the night, maybe with some added luxuries. Their plan was to take hotel living from drab to club, and they began growing a hotel portfolio, in 1988 adding the Barbizon to it. But bad luck, mixed with the crack cocaine epidemic of the 1980s, turned those plans sour. Police were called to a room at the Barbizon in which Craig Spence, a former television correspondent and once powerful Washington lobbyist, was staying with another man. As they arrived, he came rushing out of the room screaming that the other guy had a gun. They found cocaine and a crack pipe inside. Spence, it turned out, was a major client of a gay escort service to which various key members of the Reagan and George H. W. Bush administrations also belonged. Soon after, Georgette Mosbacher, socialite, owner of La Prairie cosmetics, and wife of the secretary of commerce in the Bush administration, was mugged in the hallway just outside her Barbizon room door by a well-dressed, Uzi-toting thief. Mosbacher, known as the most glamorous member of the Bush White House, managed to resist his attempts to force her into the room and instead stripped herself of her own jewelry and handed everything over. These kinds of incidents were difficult to recover from. Guests stayed away. Sure enough, in 1994, Ian Schrager (Steve Rubell had died of hepatitis shortly after the purchase of the Barbizon) was forced to foreclose on the hotel.

But Schrager was not yet ready to let go of the Barbizon, and in 1998, he bought it back (it was exactly what the hotel's original owners had also done during the Great Depression). With the buy-back came yet another renovation. This time, to lower costs and raise funds, the Barbizon's pool and former coffee shop were leased out to the Equinox fitness chain, which turned the space into a full three-floor workout experience for any New Yorker able to pay the monthly gym fees. There was also a plastic surgeon on-site two days a week to administer Botox shots, collagen injections, and chemical peels—right down the hall from the yoga room.

Yet through all this, the Women had never budged. They had hung on through David Teitelbaum's and Ian Schrager's various tenures and renovations. One could still find the secret door on eight different floors of the hotel, from the fourth to the eleventh: at the very end of the floral-carpeted hallway, there was a door and behind that door, a time machine, with narrow halls, shared bathrooms, and tiny rooms.

By the late 1990s, however, the Women were down to twenty-nine. The staff now called them "the perms." They haunted the hotel, and even for those who spent their working shifts opening doors, they remained a mystery; the bellhop would nod to them, greet them, knowing they lived in the hotel, and yet it was as if they had appeared out of nowhere. But the Women were more than a ghostly presence; they were living reminders of what this hotel had been and meant before its rooms were gutted, one renovation after another throughout the 1980s and 1990s.

✦

On September 12, 2001, the day after the attack on the Twin Towers of the World Trade Center, the city stood still. In New York, from Fourteenth Street down, you could smell something burning. Lines of people stood outside St. Vincent's Hospital ready to give blood to those who were wounded. But no one was wounded; everyone was dead. The Twin Towers had collapsed with almost three thousand people in them.

Everywhere there were remainder signs of a normality that had just disappeared; on newsstands you could find *New York* magazine's Fall Fashion issue, although now it made your stomach turn to think that anyone cared what the season's "it coat" would be. It seemed like New York was lost again. What no one could have predicted at that moment was that instead it was the beginning of New York's ultimate gentrification and corporatization, of the remaking of Times Square into a shopping mall, of tourists in "I ♥ New York" T-shirts, of stunningly low crime rates, of uninhabited mega-apartments for the world's super-rich that sheltered their taxes but nothing else.

Shortly before the Twin Towers came down, the Berwind Property Group out of Philadelphia, looking to build an upscale hotel chain, had bought up the Barbizon for an estimated $69 million. They renamed it the Melrose Hotel at the Barbizon. Berwind thus also became the new caretakers of the Women; the company's CEO occasionally brought them home-baked cookies. While the Women had managed to hold on to their rooms, everything else that had constituted the Barbizon Hotel for Women had slowly disappeared: gone were the music rooms, the library, and the outdoor terraces (now attached to $1,200-a-night suites that the rapper and music producer P. Diddy liked to reserve). The Melrose, aiming for a high-end crowd, also featured the Landmark Restaurant and lobby Library Bar. Every day an elderly woman came in, sat down, and ordered a cup of tea with a $375 shot of Louis XIII 220-year-old cognac.

A year later, in 2002, dark-haired Tony Monaco arrived at the Melrose as assistant general manager. The back of the building, where the Women lived behind the secret doors, was still largely untouched. Twenty-one elderly ladies remained, scattered in the back, in the only part of the hotel that was still authentically original, on the fourth, seventh, eighth, ninth, and eleventh floors. The Equinox gym now took over a fourth floor of the hotel, and Tony watched as they yanked out the Barbizon's original pool, poured concrete over the hotel's famous second-floor mezzanine from which its young women would look down into the lobby, and then, with electric saws revving, cut out the recital room's organ pipes that Mrs. Anne Gillen, in pearls and pillbox hat, had played every day during tea hour from 5:00 to 6:00 p.m.

Everything for the Women was about to change once again. The influx of tourists that followed 9/11, in part responding to the patriotic appeal by New York's mayor Rudy Giuliani to come visit, did not want to dish out hundreds of dollars for their rooms. They were looking for bargain rooms, and the Melrose was not that place. Berwind pivoted. In 2005, the company announced that it was turning the Barbizon into condominiums. New York's real estate market was booming, and hotels uptown, downtown, east and west were capitalizing on it: the famous Plaza Hotel announced it was doing the same that very year. Once the very last hotel guest reservation had been honored, the only residents left were Tony Monaco and the Women. The Barbizon's final incarnation as a condominium building was about to begin.

Berwind relocated Tony and the Women temporarily to the nearby Affenia Garden Suites Hotel on Sixty-Third Street between

Second and Third Avenues but, more often than not, Tony would spend the night at the Barbizon, amid the gut renovation that he was now overseeing. By then, despite all the renovations, despite the Barbizon going from rethought, to redone, to renovated, it looked outdated, with pitted brass and stained upholstery. It would have been given a "C" by the Barbizon's former front-desk monitor Mrs. Mae Sibley. Tony Monaco, of a conservationist mindset, salvaged the small metal gold sign that read THE BARBIZON, still hanging on the side of the front door entrance on Sixty-Third Street. It would later become part of his haphazard office decor as manager of the new condominiums.

The gutting that would turn the Barbizon from a hotel to a collection of luxury apartments was all-encompassing. Its insides were pulled out; all the floors were stripped down. The third floor was converted into a shared space for the building's new tenants, and includes a lounge, a screening room, and a catering kitchen. The challenge of the condominium project was to try to create lush grandeur from the bones of a former women's hotel with low ceilings, in a section of the city that, while technically on the Upper East Side, was now on a "traffic-choked intersection, on the edge of Midtown." The building was covered over in scaffolding. The original windows were replaced with French casement windows more than six feet high. Foyers, long galleries, and French doors were integrated into the seventy apartments to give a sense of height, light, and grandeur. Details were carefully chosen, from rosewood parquet, to limestone kitchen flooring, to marble bathroom floors, and sophisticated touchpads to control heat, light, and sound. The name of the condominiums would be Barbizon/63.

Among those who first bought into the Barbizon/63 was Nicola Bulgari, of the Italian jewelry company, who snapped up a $12.75 million duplex penthouse on the seventeenth and eighteenth floors. British actor and comedian Ricky Gervais settled, at first, on a more humble one-bedroom on the ninth floor, buying a second and larger apartment with two balconies on the twelfth floor three years later, in 2011. The former chairman of Meow Mix cat food bought three separate two-bedroom apartments for his children, for a combined total of $12 million. His wife spent less than ten minutes choosing from the available floor plans. The building's new tenants could not have been more different from the young women for whom the Barbizon had been a soft landing upon their arrival in New York, with only the hotel's address, which they had read about in the magazines, carefully written out on a piece of paper.

The Barbizon/63 condominium renovation did not leave out the Women. It legally could not do so. Berwind decided to make the fourth floor exclusively theirs. Those who could be persuaded to move to that floor received one-bedroom units and large studio apartments. There were some holdouts, however, such as Regina Reynolds, who had arrived in 1936, and lived on the eleventh floor, the very same floor where *Titanic*'s Molly Brown stayed. A couple of others also dug in their heels and insisted on staying put in what were legally their single-occupancy rooms (SROs) under rent control. But they too got a redo, if only to eliminate the Women as eyesores for the rich and famous who were about to arrive.

The fourth floor of Barbizon/63 where the Women live looks much like a luxury hotel, with cream-colored wallpapered hallways, large white doors, and bright sleek sconces lighting the way on the softly carpeted corridors. Framed black-and-white stylized photographs of an old Manhattan that the Women still remember hang on the walls. There is also a large bricked terrace with wrought iron furniture, the kind of outdoor space that makes regular New Yorkers living in minuscule apartments green with envy. If you step outside onto the terrace, Tony instructs, turn to face the Barbizon, and throw back your head and look up as far as possible, you see dizzying, glorious art deco layer upon layer of rose bricks and staggered edges that seem to lead far up into the sky. No one but Tony ever goes out there.

The large outdoor terrace on the fourth floor of Barbizon/63, available to the Women, but which they seldom use.

Today there are only five of the Women left. They are not a tight group, as one would like to imagine, growing old together amid a daily diet of afternoon teas and reminiscences. They barely greet one another, if at all, and it is only Tony whom they recognize as worthy of their interaction. "They are all hoarders, not just of stuff but information, memories." As required by law, they have a house-keeper who comes in every day, Monday through Friday. They pay monthly rates dating back to when they arrived; in the case of Alice Delman, it is the 1950s. Alice, the lead information hoarder, is writing her own memoir. Somewhere, one imagines, she has a box full of old brochures and newspaper clippings and jotted private notes of the scandals that got out from under the hotel management's tight control, as well as those that did not.

In 2011, the Friends of the Upper East Side Historic Districts applied for landmark status for Barbizon/63, formerly the Barbizon Club-Residence for Women. The building stands outside of the boundaries of the Upper East Side historic district, even after those boundaries were further extended. But the organization argued that it was not about geography in the case of the Barbizon, it was about legacy: the building had to be landmarked because of its social importance. At the same time, Berwind, which had ripped out the insides but left the outside largely intact, understood how to monetize the Barbizon's social importance. The condominiums sold remarkably well, despite many a New York real estate agent's raised eyebrows and snide remarks about low ceilings and so-so location. Advertisements for the Barbizon/63 tapped into the building's glorious past and the famous women who had passed through its doors. The walls of the building's shared space on the third floor are decorated with black-and-white photographs of the glamorous movie stars and models who once lived there.

But there were also the thousands of others, unnamed, who passed through those doors: young, ambitious, full of anticipation, tasting their first freedoms. They might not have become famous, even as they had hoped, but they were all courageous—even Gael Greene's Lone Women. Whether aspiring actresses, dancers, fashion models, nightclub singers, seamstresses, secretaries in training, nurses, or entrepreneurs, they all embodied both the possibilities and contradictions of what the twentieth century offered American women. In the 1920s, they had headed for work in Manhattan's skyscrapers as New Women, unbound from nineteenth-century restrictions by World War I and the women's vote. The youngest among them expressed their newfound liberties with painted lips, blunt cuts, flapper dresses, long pearls, and speakeasy martinis. The 1930s Great Depression cast censure on these workingwomen, but that did not stop them. Many now worked to make ends meet, and just as many to keep their families back home afloat. Typing and modeling, those uniquely "feminine" professions, which the Barbizon's young women could not be accused of taking away from men, became their go-to jobs. But this decade also produced the first wave of power career women, like *Mademoiselle*'s editor-in-chief Betsy Talbot Blackwell, who created a program for young women much like herself, brimming with talent and ambition, even as they were increasingly being told, especially after World War II, that they should be mothers and wives to the exclusion of all else. For these guest editors, the month of June at the Barbizon was a time of both opportunity and reckoning that could either buoy you for the years ahead or slide you ever closer to depression. And even in the 1960s and 1970s, while some women felt they no longer needed the protection of the Barbizon's salmon-colored walls, there were still others who understood that their escape from small-town USA necessitated a soft landing, especially if they were to find the courage within themselves to make their escape.

The Barbizon, through much of the twentieth century, had been a place where women felt safe, where they had a room of their own to plot and plan the rest of their lives. The hotel set them free. It freed up their ambition, tapping into desires deemed off-limits elsewhere, but imaginable, realizable, doable, in the City of Dreams.

ACKNOWLEDGMENTS

This book was hatched in November 2014 in the lobby bar of a Marriott conference hotel in San Antonio with my Oxford University Press editor, Susan Ferber. I have her to thank for starting me on this path, and also fellow historian Marci Shore for putting me in touch with Gillian MacKenzie, who became my extraordinary agent. A year into the research, I stumbled across Susan Camp, who had turned an interest in the models of her youth into a vocation and an archive. Always generous, Susan has been both cheerleader and vital source.

I interviewed countless women (and a few men) along the way, and I want to thank you all, even if you do not find your story here (apologies especially to the 1968 *Mademoiselle* guest editors!). I learned from each of you, was inspired by all of you. For those whose stories shaped this book, I thank you for your openness. Neva Nelson, whose herculean efforts to reunite the 1953 class of *Mademoiselle* guest editors turned her into an archivist and truth-teller. Peggy LaViolette Powell, whom I have only met over the telephone, although many times, and who is as fun as can be, and with a memory that puts the rest of us to shame. I flew to California to meet former *Mademoiselle* editor-in-chief, the late Edie Raymond Locke, then ninety-seven years old, spending two delightful afternoons with her and her husband. My conversations with Phyllis Lee Levin, who is still publishing books in her nineties, are something I cherish. Malachy McCourt, the Irish writer and bon vivant, was as charming as expected at the Upper West Side restaurant where we met, but I also thank him for his sincerity and insight. Barbara Chase-Riboud, who agreed to meet while she was in New York at the Yale Club, visiting from her home bases and studio in Milan and Paris, was a phenomenon, still electrifying. Barbizon/63 manager Tony Monaco's appreciation of the hotel's history made for good conversation. Others I would like to thank for sharing their time and memories are Gayle Baizer, Lanie Bernhard, Joan Gage, Gael Greene, Amy Gross, the late Gloria Harper, Diane Johnson, Lorraine Davies Knopf, Laurie Glazer Levy, Ali MacGraw, Dolores Phelps, Jane Phipps, Janet Wagner Rafferty (and her daughter Christina Sciammas), Phylicia Rashad, Sue Ann Robinson, Patty Sicular, Jaclyn Smith, Nena Thurman, and Judi Wax.

Researching the Barbizon also confirmed my faith in the generosity of those who teach, write, and create. Janet Burroway, writer and professor, shared her remarkable cache of personal letters home from June 1955. Melodie Bryant, who started on a documentary about the Barbizon about a year before I began my research, abandoned it after significant work but shared her video interviews with me. Others responded to my queries with equal generosity of spirit: Heather Clark, Miriam Cohen, Tracy Daugherty, Rose A. Doherty, Nyna Giles, Teresa Griffiths, Halley K. Harrisburg, Kristen Iversen, Mark Weston, and Timothy White. For archival access, I thank the American Heritage Center at the University of Wyoming, Laramie; the New-York Historical Society Archives; and the Condé Nast Archives. Many thanks to University of Wyoming students Skye Terra Cranney and Baylee Staufenbiel, who photographed copious *Mademoiselle* memos on my behalf, and to Leah Cates, Vassar graduate who tackled the endnotes. I am grateful for funding from Vassar College's Emily Floyd Fund and the Lucy Maynard Salmon Research Fund. Vassar College not only offered financial support but my Vassar colleagues and friends cheered me on throughout.

I feel so fortunate to have Emily Graff as my editor; she has a rare talent for seeing the entirety of a book before it is there, and her editorial wisdom spurred me on throughout. Tremendous thanks also to Morgan Hart, the most patient production editor, and to editorial assistant Lashanda Anakwah. Deepfelt thanks to my far-flung academic friends who continue to provide intellectual sustenance; to my dear Wesleyan friends with whom both banalities and milestones are unfailingly celebrated (and especially to Anne Dunham, Vivian Trakinski, and Adrienne FitzGerald, who lent help at various times); to my friends in numerous locales and countries who are always there for a dinner date; and to the novelist Daphne Uviller, my café writing partner. A special thanks for the love and support from my parents in New York, my sister and her family in San Francisco, and my in-laws in Hungary. This book is dedicated to my lovely husband, Zoltán, and our daughter, Zsofi.

Notes

INTRODUCTION

7   *They felt empowered*: Ali MacGraw, telephone interview with the author, April 5, 2016.

CHAPTER ONE

14   *It was not until James McGough*: Kristen Iversen, *Molly Brown: Unraveling the Myth* (Boulder, CO: Johnson Books, 2010), 13–29, 169.

15   *She wired her Denver attorney*: "Mrs Margaret Brown," Encyclopedia Titanic, updated August 22, 2017, https://www.encyclopedia-titanica.org/titanic -survivor/molly-brown.html.

16   *She had both wit and spirit*: Iversen, *Molly Brown*, 233.

16   *She once wrote of herself*: Iversen, *Molly Brown*, 236.

18   *Humble as it might be*: Letters between Margaret Tobin Brown and Estelle Ballow, 1931, Molly Brown Collection, Denver Public Library Digital Collection.

18   *She most likely participated in meetings of the Pegasus Group*: "Books and Authors," *New York Times*, March 5, 1933.

18   *The front entrance of the club-hotel*: Gale Harris, "Barbizon Hotel for Women," Landmarks Preservation Commission, Designation List 454 LP-2495, April 17, 2012, 4, http://npclibrary.org/db/bb_files/2012-BarbizonHotelforWomen.pdf.

19   *Critics of nineteenth-century New York*: "Color Splashes in the City's Drabness," *New York Times*, October 9, 1927.

19   *In the midst of this building boom*: "Temple Rodeph Sholom Sells 63d St. Site," *New York Times*, January 31, 1926.

19   *The temple ended its half-century-long residency*: "Prepares to Quit Temple," *New York Times*, September 26, 1926.

20   *The new secretaries of this new world*: Sara M. Evans, *Born for Liberty: A History of Women in America* (New York: Free Press, 1997), 183.

20   *The old-fashioned women's boarding houses*: "New Club for Women Rivals Any for Men," *New York Times*, February 24, 1929.

21 *"In town it is no longer quite"*: Laura Pedersen, "Home Sweet Hotel," *New York Times*, August 6, 2000.

22 *For some suites, Mrs. Sabis*: Walter Rendell Storey, "Making the Hotel Room More Homelike," *New York Times*, December 14, 1930.

22 *In 1903, New York hotelier Simeon Ford*: Paul Groth, *Living Downtown: The History of Residential Hotels in the United States* (Berkeley: University of California, 1999), 20.

23 *The situation could be so embarrassing*: Nikki Mandell, "A Hotel of Her Own: Building by and for the New Woman, 1900–1930," *Journal of Urban History* 45, no. 3 (March 19, 2018): 521, https://journals.sagepub.com/doi/abs/10.1177/0096144218762631.

23 *Those better off and creative in spirit*: Mandell, "A Hotel of Her Own," 519.

23 *At her wedding she refused*: "New Club for Women," *New York Times*.

23 *"Observation automobiles" full of gawkers*: "New Club for Women," *New York Times*.

23 *The* New York Herald *jeered*: Christopher Gray, "For Career Women, a Hassle-Free Haven," *New York Times*, July 1, 2012.

23 *An early brochure for the Martha Washington*: Virginia Kurshan, "Martha Washington Hotel," Landmarks Preservation Commission, Designation List 456a LP-2428, amended June 19, 2012, 4, http://s-media.nyc.gov/agencies/lpc/lp/2428.pdf.

24 *The kind of women who came to stay*: Kurshan, "Martha Washington Hotel," 4.

24 *In 1914, New York saw a second residential hotel*: Mandell, "A Hotel of Her Own," 526.

24 *He and his partner, James S. Cushman*: Mandell, "A Hotel of Her Own," 531.

25 *Silk wanted to offer rooms*: Christopher Gray, "It Looks as if It's One Building but It's Really Two," *New York Times*, December 8, 2002.

25 *Heralded by the* New York Times: "New Club for Women," *New York Times*.

25 *These women's club-hotels*: Mandell, "A Hotel of Her Own," 526.

26 *Over champagne and canapés*: Mandell, "A Hotel of Her Own," 532.

26 *The AWA hotel found*: "New Club for Women," *New York Times*.

27 *William H. Silk, with the*: "Reflects Modern Woman," *New York Times*, September 25, 1927. No original documents from the Barbizon exist today and therefore the number of rooms I cite are always based on articles written at various points in the hotel's history. In this case here, the architect planned on 720 rooms. Later, it seems the number of rooms dipped under 700, presumably because some rooms were reconfigured.

27 *Rates started at $10*: Advertisement, *New York Times*, September 11, 1927.

28 *Entering the Barbizon, a guest encountered*: Many thanks to architectural historians Diane Al Shihabi and Kimberly Elman Zarecor for their input and expertise.

29 Architectural Forum *declared*: Matlack Price, "The Barbizon," *Architectural Forum* 48 (May 1928), http://s-media.nyc.gov/agencies/lpc/lp/2495.pdf.

29 *Accommodating owners offered painters*: "Fontainebleau Forest," *Los Angeles Times*, May 31, 2009, https://www.latimes.com/archives/la-xpm-2009-may-31-tr-barbizon31-story.html.

29 *At New York's Barbizon Hotel*: "City's First Club Home for Women to Open in Fall," *Daily Star* (Queens Borough), June 25, 1927.

29 *The largest was fifty by seventeen feet*: Harris, "Barbizon Hotel for Women," 4.

29 *In the first-floor lounge*: Harris, "Barbizon Hotel for Women," 3.

30 *With a strangely erotic choice of words*: "New Club for Women," *New York Times*.

30 *When asked by a reporter*: Iversen, *Molly Brown*, 237.

31 *jazz came from the black ghetto*: Evans, *Born for Liberty*, 176.

32 *One bootlegger, barely thirty*: Louis Sobol, "Speakeasy" (Part 3), *Hearst's International—Cosmopolitan*, May 1934.

33 *"Fine," she said, and proposed*: "Belle Livingstone, 'Salon' Hostess of Prohibition Era, Is Dead Here," *New York Times*, February 8, 1957.

33 *One of her speakeasies*: Louis Sobol, "Speakeasy" (Part 2), *Hearst's International—Cosmopolitan*, April 1934.

33 *Then there was Janet*: Sobol, "Speakeasy" (Part 3).

34 *A muraled sign*: Sobol, "Speakeasy" (Part 3).

34 *The swankiest speakeasy:* Sobol, "Speakeasy" (Part 2).

35 *Roger Wolfe Kahn*: Sobol, "Speakeasy" (Part 2).

35 *New York's Broadway*: Louis Sobol, "Speakeasy" (Part 1), *Hearst's International—Cosmopolitan*, March 1934.

36 *At King's Terrace*: Eric Garber, "A Spectacle in Color: The Lesbian and Gay Subculture of Jazz Age Harlem," http://xroads.virginia.edu/~ug97/blues/garber.html. I would like to thank my Vassar College colleagues Professors Hiram Perez and Quincy Mills for their input here.

36 *She'd been "discovered"*: Sobol, "Speakeasy" (Part 2).

37 *The baby lamb*: Sobol, "Speakeasy" (Part 1).

37 *Before World War I, a single woman at a bar*: Joshua Zeitz, *Flapper: A Madcap Story of Sex, Style, Celebrity, and the Women Who Made America Modern* (New York: Broadway Books, 2006), 6.

38 *It is what sixteen-year-old Lillian Clark Red*: "Plays Cinderella with a Check Book," *New York Times*, January 18, 1926.

38 *A Monsieur Cestre*: "Frenchman Calls Our Girls 'a Bit Fast,'" *New York Times*, January 11, 1926.

38 *Of the women born before 1900*: Zeitz, *Flapper*, 21.

39 *New York's Rabbi Krass*: "Criticizes Modern Woman," *New York Times*, April 19, 1926.

39 *With much greater originality*: "Warns of Chewing Gum," *New York Times*, July 31, 1926.

39 *When dress manufacturers*: "Sizes Askew on Women's Clothing," *New York Times*, January 17, 1926.

39 *Between 1920 and 1926*: "Woman's Dainty Footprint Has Grown Larger," *New York Times*, February 21, 1926.

39 *"You'll get the shock of your life"*: "Lady Astor Here; Lauds Modern Girl, Chides Mothers," *New York Times*, August 3, 1926.

39 *A month later into her trip back home*: "Lady Astor Flashes Wit in Speech Here," *New York Times*, September 10, 1926.

40 *The room, featured in* Vogue: Helen Appleton Read, "Features: Opposite Aspects of Twentieth-Century Decoration," *Vogue* 72, no. 13 (December 22, 1928).

40 *Even as the Barbizon*: "Wellesley Club Rooms: New York Members Take Floor in the Barbizon," *New York Times*, August 7, 1927.

41 *"The Barbizon has become"*: Advertisement, *New Yorker*, October 4, 1930.

41 *In the January 1928*: *Junior League Magazine*, January 1928: 9.

42 *According to the 1930*: Qianye Yu, "A Room of Her Own. Housing for New York's Working Women, 1875–1930" (M.A. thesis, Graduate School of Architecture, Planning and Preservation, Columbia University, May 2019), 77, https://academiccommons.columbia.edu/doi/10.7916/d8-c1qq-em47.

42 *Her death certificate*: Evans, *Born for Liberty*, 176.

42 *"Seriously, have you seen a Flapper"*: "Has the Flapper Disappeared?" *Junior League Magazine*, January 1928: 16–17.

43 *Hotel owners stormed city hall*: Laura Pedersen, "Home Sweet Hotel," *New York Times*, August 6, 2000.

CHAPTER TWO

47 *In 1909, already forty-six years old*: Rose A. Doherty, *Katharine Gibbs: Beyond White Gloves* (self-pub., CreateSpace, 2014), 24.

47 *Borrowing money from friends at Brown University*: Doherty, *Katharine Gibbs*, 34–35.

48 *Her advertising suggested*: Doherty, *Katharine Gibbs*, 26.

48 *The school's 1920 tagline*: Doherty, *Katharine Gibbs*, 36.

48 *In fact, these provocative words*: Doherty, *Katharine Gibbs*, 39.

48 *The product fit the very image*: Doherty, *Katharine Gibbs*, 63.

48 *In 1933, she would marry*: James A. Welu, "Obituaries: Helen Estabrook Stoddard," American Antiquarian Society, https://www.americanantiquarian.org/proceedings/44525161.pdf.

49 *The young women studying*: Doherty, *Katharine Gibbs*, 49.

49 *The future British prime minister*: Bennett Lowenthal, "The Jumpers of '29," *Washington Post*, October 25, 1987.

50 *On Tuesday, December 5, 1933*: Louis Sobol, "Speakeasy" (Part 1), *Hearst's International—Cosmopolitan*, March 1934.

51 *The Barbizon Hotel had not been cheap*: "New York. The Wonder City. Intimate Inside Life in the Year 1932," Hotel Files: Barbizon, New-York Historical Society Archives, New York, New York [hereafter cited as N-YHS].

52 *With the Great Depression fully under way*: "Barbizon Default," *New York Sun*, April 20, 1931.

52 *Chase National Bank stepped in*: "Takes Over the Barbizon," *New York Times*, April 18, 1931.

52 *The following year, Chase*: Untitled short report, *Sun*, June 2, 1932, Hotel Files: Barbizon, N-YHS.

52 *Then just a month later*: "Bondholders Buy Barbizon Hotel," *Sun*, July 5, 1932, Hotel Files: Barbizon, N-YHS.

52 *The lucky bidder*: "Recorded Mortgages," *Sun*, July 28, 1932, Hotel Files: Barbizon, N-YHS.

52 *By 1934, there would be*: Sara M. Evans, *Born for Liberty: A History of Women in America* (New York: Free Press, 1997), 203.

52 *Black women looking for domestic work*: Evans, *Born for Liberty*, 215.

53 *More than 80 percent*: Evans, *Born for Liberty*, 202.

53 *There was also widespread belief*: Nancy Woloch, *Women and the American Experience*, 3rd ed. (New York: McGraw-Hill, 2000), 457.

53 *"To a Young Woman Who Is a Poet"*: Advertisement, *New Yorker*, September 24, 1932, 58.

54 *"Intelligent Young Women LIVE Intelligently!"*: Advertisement, *New Yorker*, October 21, 1933, 91.

54 *"You Woman What Now?"*: Advertisement, *New Yorker*, September 15, 1934, 106.

55 *By 1932, twenty-six states*: Betsy Israel, *Bachelor Girl: The Secret History of Single Women in the Twentieth Century* (New York: William Morrow, 2002), 150.

55 *As FDR was being inaugurated*: Woloch, *Women and the American Experience*, 438–39.

55 *The stock market crash had exposed*: Woloch, *Women and the American Experience*, 439.

55 *only one-third of Barnard College's class*: Israel, *Bachelor Girl*, 152.

56 *To accommodate the flood of students*: 1937 Katharine Gibbs Manual of Style. From the personal archives of Susan Camp [hereafter cited as SC], generously shared with the author.

57 *In 1934, Katharine's elder son*: Doherty, *Katharine Gibbs*, 70.

57 *Its location was touted*: Katharine Gibbs New York Catalog, 1939–40, 21, SC.

57 *Their meals (breakfast and dinner)*: Katharine Gibbs New York Catalog, 1939–40, 21–22, SC.

57   *They also had their own*: Nan Robertson, "Where the Boys Are Not," *Saturday Evening Post*, October 19, 1963, 29.

57   *The back pages of the Gibbs yearbook*: 1943 *Platen*, Gibbs School Yearbook, SC.

58   *Never mind that many Depression-era students*: Doherty, *Katharine Gibbs*, 76–77.

58   *Frances Fonda, the future mother*: Doherty, *Katharine Gibbs*, 86.

59   *This recognition was often reinforced*: "Woman's Work to Be Discussed," *New York Times*, January 6, 1935.

59   *The 1930s on-screen heroine*: Woloch, *Women and the American Experience*, 468.

59   *A 1935 handbook* So You Want to Be a Reporter: Israel, *Bachelor Girl*, 153.

60   *Elizabeth Curtis, social director*: "Girls Capable of Better Work in Offices or Professions If They Leave Family Home," *Washington Post*, December 7, 1935.

61   *As Powers boasted*: John Robert Powers, *The Powers Girls* (New York: E. P. Dutton, 1941).

61   *Elsa Maxwell, the Waldorf Astoria in-house party hostess*: Powers, *Powers Girls*.

61   *Because blond and cute*: E. J. Kahn, "Profiles: Powers Model," *New Yorker*, September 14, 1940, 24.

61   *These models were not supermodels*: Nicole Levy, "This NYC Modeling Agency Shaped the Fashion World as We Know It," *This Is New York: A Blog About New York Neighborhoods*, September 7, 2016.

62   *Evelyn had always dreamed of New York*: Evelyn B. Echols, *They Said I Couldn't Do It, but I Did!* (Chicago: Ampersand, Inc., 2008), 29.

62   *The hospital was owned*: Echols, *They Said I Couldn't Do It, but I Did!*, 29.

63   *While Evelyn was waiting*: Echols, *They Said I Couldn't Do It, but I Did!*, 29–30.

63   *Not for nothing had she won*: Kahn, "Profiles: Powers Model."

66   *In 1938, Kathryn Scola*: Alice Hughes, "A Woman's New York: Hollywood Is Making Movie on New York's 'Women-Only' Hotel," *Washington Post*, July 12, 1939.

67   *Her parties for the rich and famous*: Frank S. Nugent, "THE SCREEN; A True-Confessional Romance," *New York Times*, August 26, 1939.

67   *The movie's heroine, Marcia Bromely*: Nugent, "THE SCREEN."

68   *So it was that Phyllis McCarthy*: St. Clair McKelway to Bruno R. Wiedermann, September 28, 1939, accessed November 20, 2018, https://microship.com/st-clair-mckelway-recommends-phyllis-mccarthy-to-barbizon/. Blog by Ms. McCarthy's son, Steve K. Roberts, based on the letter and newspaper clipping he found; excerpted on NPR's *All Things Considered* on October 21, 2014. I would like to thank Mr. Roberts for generously sharing this memorabilia.

69 *That this was indeed Phyllis McCarthy's approach*: George I. Bushfield, "Just for the fun of it!" accessed November 20, 2018, https://microship.com/st-clair-mckelway-recommends-phyllis-mccarthy-to-barbizon/.

70 *Robin Chandler Duke, later a Wall Street pioneer*: William Norwich, "The Trailblazer," *Vogue*, August 2006.

71 *But the economic climate*: "New Plan in Effect on the Ritz Tower; Mortgage Is Paid Off on Barbizon Hotel," *New York Times*, February 2, 1940.

72 *As if to mark this moment*: "New Marquee Erected at the Hotel Barbizon," *Gazette*, June 1, 1940.

72 *Evelyn Echols, whom Mr. Powers*: Echols, *They Said I Couldn't Do It, but I Did!*, 35.

73 *When General "Wild Bill" Donovan*: Doherty, *Katharine Gibbs*, 82.

CHAPTER THREE

77 *Betsy Talbot Blackwell was never willing*: Angela Taylor, "At *Mademoiselle*, Changing of the Guard," *New York Times*, April 4, 1971.

77 *Fifty years later she would fondly recall that same hat*: Betsy Talbot Blackwell to Dr. Susan Spencer, December 2, 1965, box 7 correspondence, 1965, the Betsy Talbot Blackwell Collection, American Heritage Center, University of Wyoming, Laramie [hereafter cited as BTBC].

78 *BTB's father, Hayden Talbot*: As quoted in Cathy Ciccolella's college essay, November 11, 1963, box 7 correspondence, 1963, BTBC.

78 *She spied them in a shop window*: Taylor, "At *Mademoiselle*." *Charm* magazine of the 1920s was different from the one started in the 1940s.

78 *The daughter of the vice president of Street & Smith*: "Memo from the Editor" (column), box 7 correspondence, 1965, BTBC.

79 *On a miserable February morning*: "Memo from the Editor," BTBC.

79 *The salaries on offer were low*: "Memo from the Editor," BTBC.

79 *She changed around the entire magazine*: "A Short History of *Mademoiselle*," 1945, online, BTBC.

79 *Blackwell directed her staff*: "A Short History of *Mademoiselle*," 1965, draft version, online, BTBC.

80 *In fact, she seemed to be perpetually*: Neva Nelson's recollection. As quoted in Elizabeth Winder, *Pain, Parties, Work: Sylvia Plath in New York, Summer 1953* (New York: HarperCollins, 2013), 34.

80 *Her love of shoes*: Taylor, "At *Mademoiselle*."

80 *Her golden rule was*: "Betsy Talbot Blackwell. Editor-in-Chief of Mademoiselle," box 7 correspondence, 1965, BTBC.

81 *What BTB had effectively done*: The Writers' Institute: A Monthly Special Report for Writers, Literary Agents, Publicists, Artists, Cartoonists and Photographers: "*Mademoiselle*: A Publication Portrait" (no date)—online, BTBC.

81 *The College Board editor, just three years out of Vassar*: "Memo from the Editor," BTBC.

81 *Later, the* Los Angeles Times: "Betsy Blackwell, Former Magazine Editor, Dies," *Los Angeles Times*, February 18, 1985.

82 *Advertisers went crazy for the College Issue idea*: "Memo from the Editor," BTBC.

82 ABC *news reporter Lynn Sherr*: Julia Keller, "To a Generation, *Mademoiselle* Was Stuff of Literary Dreams," *Chicago Tribune*, October 5, 2001.

82 *The February 1954* Mademoiselle *issue*: Meg Wolitzer, "My *Mademoiselle* Summer," *New York Times*, July 19, 2013.

82 *The publishers originally refused*: Taylor, "At *Mademoiselle*."

83 Mademoiselle *became a prolific publisher*: Writers' Institute, "Mademoiselle: A Publication Portrait," BTBC.

83 *she did not have the budget*: "A Short History of Mademoiselle," 1965, BTBC.

85 *A flyer for College Board membership announced*: From the personal archive of Phyllis Lee Levin, generously shared with the author.

85 *Just out of college*: Phyllis Lee Levin, *The Wheels of Fashion* (New York: Doubleday, 1965), xvi.

85 *BTB had not been exaggerating*: BTB, "The Dollars and Cents of Fashion Magazines," speech to the Chicago Fashion Group, September 26, 1951, BTBC.

86 *Eight hundred and fifty young women*: BTB, "Dollars and Cents."

88 *The very next day the most anticipated of telegrams*: Telegram to Nanette Emery, May 8, 1945. All of the following references to Nanette Emery, unless otherwise noted, are from her diary and memorabilia, courtesy of the Nanette Emery Mason Private Collection.

88 *Lanie Diamond, a 1947 GE winner*: Lanie Bernhard, telephone interview with the author, April 12, 2016.

89 *Nanette would miss out on seeing*: Gale Harris, "Barbizon Hotel for Women," Landmarks Preservation Commission, Designation List 454 LP-2495, April 17, 2012, 7, http://npclibrary.org/db/bb_files/2012-BarbizonHotelforWomen.pdf.

89 *When Cloris Leachman arrived*: Michael Callahan, "Sorority on E. 63rd St.," *Vanity Fair*, April 2010, 169.

89 *Her 1945 collection*: "McCardell 'Newies,'" courtesy of the Nanette Emery Mason Private Collection.

89 *At first, American women*: Sara M. Evans, *Born for Liberty: A History of Women in America* (New York: Free Press, 1997), 243.

91 *The writer Diane Johnson, author of a string*: Diane Johnson, "Nostalgia," *Vogue*, September 2003, 208.

91 *The sum of $150*: Marybeth Little, College Board editor, memo to BTB, November 16, 1953, box 3 correspondence, 1946–1955, BTBC.

92 *It was she who pulled aside*: Harmon and Elsie Tupper, "The Barbizon—For Women Only," *Collier's*, December 25, 1948, 21.

93 *When men would drive by the hotel*: Nan Robertson, "Where the Boys Are Not," *Saturday Evening Post*, October 19, 1963, 29.

93 *One Ohio resident explained*: Tupper, "The Barbizon," 21.

94 *Miss Peck, who would end up being*: Taylor, "At *Mademoiselle*."

95 *After dinner, Nanette and her new friends*: Jan Whitaker, "When Ladies Lunched: Schrafft's," *Restaurant-ing Through History*, August 27, 2008, https://restaurant-ingthroughhistory.com/2008/08/27/when-ladies-lunched-schraffts/.

96 *When General Ike Eisenhower*: "Memo from the Guest Editor," *Mademoiselle*, College Issue, August 1945, 10–11.

96 *Nanette's workload was not demanding*: *Mademoiselle* College Board to Nanette Emery, April 10, 1945, courtesy of the Nanette Emery Mason Private Collection.

96 *Consulting with an expert*: Nanette Emery and Bernice Peck, "Young Fat," *Mademoiselle*, August 1945, 213.

97 *Manhattan of the 1940s*: John Cheever, "Preface," in *The Stories of John Cheever* (New York: Vintage, 2000).

98 *Phyllis Lee Schwalbe, when she arrived*: Levin, *Wheels of Fashion*, xvii.

99 *George's three-story brownstone*: Phyllis Lee Levin, interview with the author, New York City, August 17, 2016.

99 *George Davis rented rooms*: Rachel Shteir, "Everybody Slept Here," *New York Times*, November 10, 1996.

101 *Abels was supposedly an unattractive woman*: Edie Raymond Locke, interview with the author, Thousand Oaks, CA, October 25–26, 2018.

101 *George was unwilling to sacrifice form*: Elizabeth Moulton, "Remembering George Davis," *VQR Online: A National Journal of Literature & Discussion* 55, no. 2 (Spring 1979).

102 *A review by Richard Wright*: Richard Wright review of Carson McCullers's *The Heart Is a Lonely Hunter* in the *New Republic*, August 5, 1940, 195.

102 *She was a "plump woman with sad brown eyes"*: Mary Cantwell, "Manhattan, When I Was Young," in *Manhattan Memoir* (New York: Penguin, 2000), 159.

103 *Just a year after Rita*: George Davis to BTB, November 13, 1948, box 5 correspondence, 1942–1953, BTBC.

103 *And then there were the tears*: Davis to BTB, November 13, 1948.

104 *He wrote: "Understand, I am sure"*: George Davis to BTB, January 14, 1949, box 5 correspondence, 1942–1953, BTBC.

105 *But as soon as he had given*: George Davis to BTB, January 14, 1949.

105 *BTB's husband, James Madison Blackwell*: Locke, interview.

106 *One Columbia University professor theorized*: Evans, *Born for Liberty*, 244.

106 *In* Counterattack: The Newsletter of Facts on Communism: Counterattack, Letter No. 118, August 26, 1949, box 3 correspondence, 1949, BTBC.

106 *Another Red-seeing newspaper*: "'Mademoiselle' Forum Found Red," *The Tablet*, September 1949, box 3 correspondence, 1949, BTBC.

107 *Truman Capote, in his unfinished novel* Answered Prayers: Moulton, "Remembering George Davis."

107 *In 1951, Davis suddenly married*: Moulton, "Remembering George Davis."

107 *Again he could not hold back*: George Davis to BTB, July 14, 1953, box 5 correspondence, 1942–1953, BTBC.

108 *She contacted Street & Smith's legal team*: Street & Smith to BTB, July 30, 1953, box 5 correspondence, 1942–1957, BTBC.

108 *She was no stranger*: "A Short History of *Mademoiselle*," 1965, BTBC.

109 *What bothered her most*: BTB to Gerald Smith of Smith & Street, March 17, 1952, box 3 correspondence, 1946–1955, BTBC.

CHAPTER FOUR

113 *Meche Azcarate from Mexico*: Laura Brown, "Barbizon Hotel," *New York Sunday News*, March 5, 1950.

113 *Phyllis Kirk, lead actress*: Buddy Basch, "Courage Brings Actress Success in New Field," *Tarrytown Daily News* (New York), January 25, 1978.

113 *Shirley Jones, later to star*: Joyce Haber, "Shirley Jones Find Success, As Usual, with the Partridges," *Los Angeles Times*, November 29, 1970.

113 *Judy Garland insisted her daughter, Liza Minnelli*: Basch, "Courage Brings Actress Success."

114 *Even J. D. Salinger*: Philip Marchand, "Open Book: *Salinger*, by David Shields and Shane Salerno," *National Post*, September 6, 2013.

114 *Mae Sibley was used to being called*: Harmon and Elsie Tupper, "The Barbizon—For Women Only," *Collier's*, December 25, 1948, 82.

114 *She wanted one thing*: Nyna Giles and Eve Claxton, *The Bridesmaid's Daughter: From Grace Kelly's Wedding to a Women's Shelter—Searching for the Truth About My Mother* (New York: St. Martin's, 2018), 9–12.

116 *In 1945, Lorraine Davies*: Lorraine Davies to family, letters from the personal archives of Lorraine Davies Knopf, generously shared with the author.

117 *A former front-desk employee*: Nan Robertson, "Where the Boys Are Not," *Saturday Evening Post*, October 19, 1963, 29.

117 *Fire-hazard cooking appliances*: Tupper, "The Barbizon—For Women Only," 82.

117 *The extent of Mae Sibley's power*: Robertson, "Where the Boys Are Not," 29.

117 *In the afternoons, free tea was served*: Giles and Claxton, *Bridesmaid's Daughter*, 14.

118 *She lived there from 1947*: "About Little Edie," Grey Gardens Online, accessed May 30, 2017, http://greygardensonline.com/about-little-edie/.

118 *Years later, she would write to a friend*: Walter Newkirk, *Letters of Little Edie Beale: Grey Gardens and Beyond* (Bloomington, IN: AuthorHouse, 2009), 52.

119 *It was only a week after arriving*: Giles and Claxton, *Bridesmaid's Daughter*, 16.

121 *Much like his former boss*: "Harry S. Conover, 53, Is Dead; Ran Model Agency 20 Years," *New York Times*, July 25, 1965.

122 *Her first serious job*: Giles and Claxton, *Bridesmaid's Daughter*, 23.

122 *When she again encountered the photographer*: Giles and Claxton, *Bridesmaid's Daughter*, 32.

124 *Residents' frequent budgetary self-reprimands*: Tupper, "The Barbizon—For Women Only," 82.

124 *Many residents were putting money*: Tupper, "The Barbizon—For Women Only," 82.

125 *Barbizon manager Hugh J. Connor*: Tupper, "The Barbizon—For Women Only," 20.

125 *She had left for New York*: Tupper, "The Barbizon—For Women Only," 82.

126 *Natálie had started out in New York*: Robert Lacey, *Model Woman: Eileen Ford and the Business of Beauty* (New York: Harper, 2015), 84.

126 *And just as Natálie*: Lacey, *Model Woman*, 83–84.

127 *While the ideal Ford model*: Lacey, *Model Woman*, 105.

127 *Eileen took matters into her own hands*: Giles and Claxton, *Bridesmaid's Daughter*, 46–48.

129 *When he said girls, he meant it too*: Suzanna Andrews, "Hostage to Fortune," *Vanity Fair*, December 2004.

129 *The agency also caught the eye of Sherman Billingsley*: Lacey, *Model Woman*, 109.

130 *The Fords supplied their models*: Phyllis Lee Levin, "A Fashion Model's Face Is Still Her Fortune," *New York Times*, February 10, 1958.

130 *The blonde said her name*: Janet Wagner Rafferty, *A Model Life: Life Stories from My Youth* (self-pub., CreateSpace, 2009), 50–55.

131 *Betsy Talbot Blackwell was now*: Neva Nelson, interview with the author, Cape May, NJ, May 21, 2016.

131 *So there was Janet*: Janet Wagner Rafferty, video interview with Melodie Bryant, October 14, 2012, generously shared with the author.

131 *Eileen handed her a map*: Lorraine Davies Knopf, telephone interview with the author, March 3, 2016.

132 *Eileen thought there was*: Giles and Claxton, *Bridesmaid's Daughter*, 51.

132 *As Eileen Ford would later pretend*: Lacey, *Model Woman*, 106.

133 *But in fact these were among Grace's first*: Giles and Claxton, *Bridesmaid's Daughter*, 52.

133 *She didn't like that, and she rejected Dolores*: Dolores Phelps, telephone interview with the author, March 22, 2019.

133 *At five eleven and of Swedish stock*: Douglas Martin, "Lily Carlson Is Dead at 85; One of First Models for Ford," *New York Times*, December 24, 2000.

134 *What Gita—whom Janet would soon refer*: Janet Wagner Rafferty, telephone interview with the author, April 6, 2016.

134 *Yet Grace Kelly*: Michael Kilian, "Grace: The Steamy Sex Life of the 'Ice Princess,'" *Sun-Sentinel* (Fort Lauderdale, FL), May 11, 1987.

135 *Formerly called O'Rourke's*: Malachy McCourt, interview with the author, New York City, April 15, 2016.

135 *One final touch*: Malachy McCourt, *A Monk Swimming: A Memoir* (Rockland, MA: Wheeler, 1998), 76.

135 *In every bar in New York*: McCourt, *Monk Swimming*, 75.

135 *Soon after opening night*: Malachy McCourt, video interview with Melodie Bryant, June 15, 2012, generously shared with the author.

136 *At first, Malachy had thought*: McCourt, interview with the author.

136 *Even the Gibbs girls*: McCourt, video interview with Bryant.

137 *Sometimes, Malachy noted*: McCourt, video interview with Bryant.

137 *He was "on the booze then"*: McCourt, interview with the author.

137 *If they were telling the truth*: Callahan, "Sorority on E. 63rd St.," 172.

137 *As for inviting them in*: Callahan, "Sorority on E. 63rd St." 172.

138 *In 1958, the future actress*: Colette Hoppman, "Who's Game?" *Mademoiselle*, College Issue, August 1958.

139 *Thinking back on the 1950s*: Lisa Anderson, "In Happily Ever After? It Never Happened, Says a Bridesmaid of Princess Grace," *Chicago Tribune*, June 15, 1989.

140 *Lorraine Davies, Tangerine Queen and model*: Lorraine Davies Knopf, *A Good Name* (self-pub., CreateSpace, 2014).

CHAPTER FIVE

145 *"So I began to think"*: Sylvia Plath, *The Bell Jar* (New York: Harper Perennial, 2005), 85.

145 *In April, the College Board editor*: Sylvia Plath to Aurelia Schober Plath, April 24, 1953, in *The Letters of Sylvia Plath, Volume I, 1940–56*, eds. Peter K. Steinberg and Karen V. Kukil (New York: HarperCollins, 2017), 596.

146 *"I now have a white bag"*: Sylvia Plath to Aurelia Schober Plath, April 30 to May 1, 1953, in *Letters of Sylvia Plath*, 606.

146 *Sylvia arrived at Grand Central Terminal*: Sylvia Plath to Aurelia Schober Plath, May 5, 1953, in *Letters of Sylvia Plath*, 609.

147 *She wrote to her mother after receiving*: Sylvia Plath to Aurelia Schober Plath, May 8, 1953, in *Letters of Sylvia Plath*, 613.

147 *they warned (as if they already knew)*: Marybeth Little to Neva Nelson, May 5, 1953. From the personal archives of Neva Nelson [hereafter cited as NN], generously shared with the author.

147 *Sylvia was twenty years old*: Elizabeth Winder, *Pain, Parties, Work: Sylvia Plath in New York, Summer 1953* (New York: Harper, 2013), 81.

148 *The clothing expenses were justifiable*: Sylvia Plath to Aurelia Schober Plath, May 13, 1953, in *Letters of Sylvia Plath*, 617.

148 *Sylvia, excited for her brother*: Sylvia Plath to Warren Plath, May 13, 1953, in *Letters of Sylvia Plath*, 621.

148 She *was helped off the train*: Sylvia Plath to Aurelia Schober Plath, June 3, 1953, in *Letters of Sylvia Plath*, 630.

148 *Sylvia was delighted by her "darlingest single"*: Sylvia Plath to Aurelia Schober Plath, June 3, 1953, in *Letters of Sylvia Plath*, 630.

149 *In the center of the fifteenth floor*: Neva Nelson, letter and sketched plan, May 24, 2016, NN.

150 *There were twenty GEs in total*: Diane Johnson, telephone interview with the author, November 27, 2018.

150 *A young woman who had abandoned Wellesley College*: Nan Robertson, "Where the Boys Are Not," *Saturday Evening Post*, October 19, 1963, 30.

151 *On the plane, during the last leg of the trip*: Neva Nelson, interview with the author, Cape May, NJ, May 21, 2016.

154 *In* The Bell Jar*, Sylvia would remake*: Plath, *Bell Jar*, 6.

154 *But Sylvia seemed more fascinated by rural Iowa*: Laurie Levy, "Outside the Bell Jar," in *Sylvia Plath: The Woman & the Work*, ed. Edward Butscher (New York: Dodd, Mead & Company, 1985), 43.

155 *When the "guest eds"*: Levy, "Outside the Bell Jar," 43.

155 *Betsy Talbot Blackwell was in a black-and-white*: Nelson, interview with the author.

156 *Sylvia and Neva were waiting*: Nelson, interview with the author.

156 *"At last, obediently"*: Plath, *Bell Jar*, 102.

157 *"Write us a note* in your own handwriting"*: Polly Weaver to guest editors, May 1, 1953, NN.

157 *Sylvia's was the downturned rose*: Andrew Wilson, *Mad Girl's Love Song: Sylvia Plath and Life Before Ted* (New York: Scribner, 2013), 200.

157 *She pulled it close toward her*: Plath, *Bell Jar*, 27.

158 *Neva Nelson, like the others, would pass by*: Neva Nelson, email to Heather Clark, November 13, 2014, NN.

158 *Dinny Lain and a giddy Laurie Glazer*: Johnson, telephone interview.

158 *Everyone tried to offset the oppressive summer heat*: Levy, "Outside the Bell Jar," 43.

158 *Neva would sit down beside her*: Winder, *Pain, Parties, Work*, 98.

159 *Sylvia, as always, gave a positive spin*: Sylvia Plath to Aurelia Schober Plath, June 3, 1953, in *Letters of Sylvia Plath*, 632.

159 *The girls were herded to the park*: Levy, "Outside the Bell Jar," 44.

159 *Laurie Totten, Sylvia's neighbor*: Winder, *Pain, Parties, Work*, 51.

159 *Another five days later*: Winder, *Pain, Parties, Work*, 85.

160 *"All the other girls"*: Sylvia Plath to Aurelia Schober Plath, June 13, 1953, in *Letters of Sylvia Plath*, 637.

160 *And while Plath continued to insist*: Plath, *Bell Jar*, 5–6.

160 *Carol too had submitted a short story*: Winder, *Pain, Parties, Work*, 86.

160 *She was very blond*: Plath, *Bell Jar*, 4.

160 *Instead of congratulating Carol*: Winder, *Pain, Parties, Work*, 113.

160 *One time, unable to cross a congested street*: Winder, *Pain, Parties, Work*, 114.

161 *She had set her sights*: Sylvia Plath to Aurelia Schober Plath, June 8, 1953, in *Letters of Sylvia Plath*, 633–34.

161 *There is a photograph in the August issue*: Anne Shawber to Neva Nelson, 1980, NN.

161 *"And when my picture came out"*: Plath, *Bell Jar*, 2.

162 *Sylvia was irked*: Sylvia Plath to Aurelia Schober Plath, June 13, 1953, in *Letters of Sylvia Plath*, 635.

162 *After finishing off a third*: Winder, *Pain, Parties, Work*, 117–19.

162 *The next day an enormous bouquet*: Winder, *Pain, Parties, Work*, 123.

162 *To add insult to injury*: Winder, *Pain, Parties, Work*, 124–25.

163 *Days later, Sylvia was still*: Sylvia Plath to Aurelia Schober Plath, June 13, 1953, in *Letters of Sylvia Plath*, 635.

163 *In* The Bell Jar, *Sylvia, as Esther, recounted*: Plath, *Bell Jar*, 9.

164 *In her journal, Sylvia wrote*: "Appendix 4: Journal Fragment 19 June 1953," in *The Unabridged Journals of Sylvia Plath 1950–1962*, ed. Karen V. Kukil (New York: Anchor Books, 2000), 541–42.

164 *But Neva was clueless*: Nelson, interview, and Winder, *Pain, Parties, Work*, 146.

165 *"It was a queer, sultry summer"*: Plath, *Bell Jar*, 1.

165 *"Only I wasn't steering anything"*: Plath, *Bell Jar*, 3.

165 *On June 8, she wrote*: Sylvia Plath to Aurelia Schober Plath, June 8, 1953, in *Letters of Sylvia Plath*, 633.

166 *and then again she repeats*: Sylvia Plath to Aurelia Schober Plath, June 8, 1953, in *Letters of Sylvia Plath*, 634.

166 *"I was supposed to be"*: Plath, *Bell Jar*, 2.

166 *Writing to her brother*: Sylvia Plath to Warren Plath, June 21, 1953, in *Letters of Sylvia Plath*, 641.

166 *Just the day before*: Wilson, *Mad Girl's Love Song*, 208.

166 *Janet Wagner, who was at the country club*: Winder, *Pain, Parties, Work*, 176–78. Yet the veracity of this account is questionable for various reasons.

167 *Sylvia summed up her month*: Sylvia Plath to Warren Plath, June 21, 1953, in *Letters of Sylvia Plath*, 642.

168 *Sylvia would return to her mother's house*: Winder, *Pain, Parties, Work*, 200.

168 *In her suitcase, instead of clothes*: Winder, *Pain, Parties, Work*, 204.

168 *She understood that exposure*: Sylvia Plath to Aurelia Schober Plath, May 18, 1953, in *Letters of Sylvia Plath*, 628.

169 *Two weeks after leaving the Barbizon*: Wilson, *Mad Girl's Love Song*, 214.

169 *In the days that followed*: Johnson, telephone interview.

CHAPTER SIX

173 *It was unusual*: Peggy LaViolette Powell, correspondence with author, 2016.

174 *The stewardesses, as they were called then*: Joan Didion, "California Notes," *New York Review of Books*, May 26, 2016.

174 *Peggy's mother had insisted*: Peggy LaViolette Powell, correspondence with author, 2018.

175 *The Golden Gate stopped twice*: Elizabeth Rainey, "Education of Joan Didion: Her Uncollected Works and What They Tell Us," Charlene Conrad Liebau Library Prize for Undergraduate Research, Spring 2010, 16. And Powell, correspondence, 2018.

175 *New York beckoned as California receded*: Joan Didion to Peggy LaViolette, July 1955, Joan Didion Letters, BANC MSS 84/180 c v. 1, Bancroft Library, University of California, Berkeley [hereafter cited as BLUC].

175 *As a college senior*: Rainey, "Education of Joan Didion," 10.

176 *(Even so, one day)*: Powell, correspondence, 2016.

176 *When Peggy graduated*: Powell, correspondence, 2016. Joan Didion would write to Peggy a couple of months later, congratulating her on having purchased an Olivetti: "Glad you're getting an Olivetti—you'll love it. (As the girl who owns one-) Even after 2 years, I still feel kind of good everytime I look at mine." (Letter from Joan Didion to Peggy LaViolette, August 9, 1955.)

176 *The feminist Betty Friedan*: Sara M. Evans, *Born for Liberty: A History of Women in America* (New York: Free Press, 1997), 237.

177 *Both wore nylon hose*: Powell, correspondence, 2018.

177 *Nevertheless, when Joan*: Joan Didion, "Goodbye to All That," in *Slouching Towards Bethlehem: Essays* (New York: Farrar, Straus and Giroux, 2008).

177 *Joan opened the window wide*: Didion, "Goodbye to All That," 226.

177 *Their first sighting of the towering skyscrapers*: Didion, "Goodbye to All That," 229.

178 *Joan had caught a cold*: Didion, "Goodbye to All That," 226–27.

178 *Instead, she called her on-again off-again boyfriend*: Joan Didion to Peggy LaViolette Powell, 1955–2004 (bulk 1955–1960), BLUC. And "To Peggy from Joan," *Vogue*, November 9, 1958.

178 *She called herself Jan*: Frank Tempone, "Janet Burroway Carries On, Reinvents Self," *Chicago Tribune*, March 21, 2014.

178 *She was a self-described "Arizona greenhorn"*: Janet Burroway's letters home, letter from May 31, 1955, from the personal archive of Janet Burroway [hereafter cited as JB], generously shared with the author.

179 *Finally, she spied a young woman*: Janet Burroway, video interview with Melodie Bryant, May 30, 2013, generously shared with the author.

179 *The bus eventually emerged*: Janet Burroway's letters home, letter, no date, 3, JB.

179   *Once checked in at the Barbizon*: Janet Burroway's letters home, postcard, no date, JB.

179   *The next day she elaborated*: Janet Burroway's letters home, letter from May 30, 1955, 1, JB.

179   *She called it brother's size*: Burroway, video interview with Bryant.

180   *Still, she had to admit*: Janet Burroway's letters home, letter from May 30, 1955, 1, JB.

180   *Janet had arrived wearing Indian moccasins*: Peggy LaViolette Powell, telephone interview with the author, October 16, 2018.

180   *She wrote home*: Janet Burroway's letters home, letter from May 31, 1955, 2, JB.

180   *She worked on her application*: Gael Greene, "Aimez-Vous Trilobites?" in *Don't Come Back Without It* (New York: Simon & Schuster, 1960), 50.

181   *When she received the telegram*: Gael Greene, interview with the author, New York City, April 15, 2016.

181   *Gael, on the other hand*: Greene, interview.

182   *It was Jane's job*: Jan Truslow, "Memo from the Guest Editor," *Mademoiselle*, August 1955, 238–40.

182   *She wanted to "bomb the Eastman Kodak people"*: Greene, "Aimez-Vous Trilobites?," 52–53.

182   *Gael was subjected*: Greene, "Aimez-Vous Trilobites?," 54.

182   *Gael Greene found it ironic*: Greene, "Aimez-Vous Trilobites?," 53.

182   *"sailed between the mirrors"*: Janet Burroway, "I Didn't Know Sylvia Plath," in *Embalming Mom: Essays in Life* (Iowa City: University of Iowa Press, 2004), 3.

183   *"in black sheath"*: Nina Renata Aron, "A women's magazine that treated its readers like they had brains, hearts, and style? *Mademoiselle* was it," *Timeline*, https://timeline.com/mademoiselle-smart-women-magazine-1870bf328ba1.

183   *"'Believe in Pink!'"*: Burroway, "I Didn't Know Sylvia Plath," 3.

183   *Janet's automatic distaste*: Burroway, video interview with Bryant.

183   *Unlike the others*: Powell, telephone interview, October 16, 2018.

183   *During the interviews, Janet Burroway*: Janet Burroway's letters home, letter from May 31, 1955, 1, JB.

183   *New York, however*: Janet Burroway's letters home, letter from June 5, 1955, 1, JB.

183   *A few days later*: Janet Burroway's letters home, letter from May 31, 1955, 2, JB.

183   *She had even more to say*: Janet Burroway's letters home, letter from June 5, 1955, 2, JB.

184   *Peggy LaViolette liked to head off early*: "Owner of the Tailored Woman Looks Back on Store's 45 Years," *New York Times*, September 29, 1964.

184   *The floor of the main lobby*: Peggy LaViolette Powell, telephone interview with the author, November 1, 2018.

185   *By June 7, Janet Burroway wrote home*: Janet Burroway's letters home, letter
        from June 7, 1955, 1, JB.

185   *It turned out that "Mr. Perfect"*: Powell, correspondence, 2016.

186   *One night, later during Joan's second stint*: Didion, "Goodbye to All That," 228.

188   *As the guest editor in the merchandising department*: Janet Burroway's letters
        home, letter postmarked June 16, 1955, JB.

188   *She had also discovered*: Janet Burroway's letters home, letter from June 9,
        1955, 2–3, JB.

189   *It certainly rated better than*: Janet Burroway's letters home, letter from "Sat
        nite" (June 14?), 1955, JB.

189   *Midway through the month*: Powell, telephone interview, October 16, 2018.

189   *The hushed talk*: Powell, telephone interview, October 16, 2018.

189   *The day Plath came*: Powell, correspondence, 2018. While Janet Burroway
        does not recall Plath visiting (and makes no mention of it in her letters home),
        in a letter to Lynne Lawner on June 8, 1955, Sylvia Plath writes that she was
        in New York and "lunched with cyrilly abels of *mlle*."

189   *Janet, who did not get to meet her*: Burroway, video interview with Bryant.

190   *But while a guest editor*: Greene, "Aimez-Vous Trilobites?," 55.

190   *Guest editor-in-chief Jane Truslow*: Tracy Daugherty, *The Last Love Song: A
        Biography of Joan Didion* (New York: St. Martin's Griffin, 2016), 72.

190   *All the merchandise*: Janet Burroway's letters home, letter from June 7, 1955,
        3, JB.

191   *There was the annual June gathering*: Powell, telephone interview, October
        16, 2018.

191   *While Peggy delighted*: Burroway, video interview with Bryant.

191   *Betsy Talbot Blackwell also hosted a party*: Powell, telephone interview, Octo-
        ber 16, 2018.

191   *By June 27, Janet*: Janet Burroway's letters home, letter from June 27, 1955,
        3, JB.

192   *While Gael Greene would be sidelined*: Greene, "Aimez-Vous Trilobites?,"
        56–57.

192   *She had invited Tom*: Powell, telephone interview, October 16, 2018.

193   *Gael, in the meantime*: Greene, "Aimez-Vous Trilobites?," 58–59.

193   *She was among the very youngest*: Burroway, "I Didn't Know Sylvia Plath," 4.

193   *Early the next morning*: Janet Burroway's letters home, letter from June 11,
        1955, 3, JB.

194   *She promised her mother*: Janet Burroway's letters home, letter from June
        16, 1955, 2, JB.

195   *In 1968, the actress Cybill Shepherd*: Michael Callahan, "Sorority on E. 63rd
        St.," *Vanity Fair*, April 2010, 172.

195   *Jane Truslow raved to the magazine's readers*: "Memo from the Guest Editor,"
        Mademoiselle, College Issue, August 1955, 242.

195 *Ultimately, what they had been*: Rainey, "The Education of Joan Didion," 10.

196 *When Janet Burroway*: Janet Burroway's letters home, letter from May 30, 1955, 2, JB.

197 *In mid-June, she confessed*: Janet Burroway's letters home, letter from June 13, 1955, 1, JB.

197 *Writing to her parents*: Janet Burroway's letters home, letter from June 7, 1955, 3–4, JB.

198 *"Brief rundown on activities"*: Joan Didion to Peggy LaViolette, postmark July 17, 1955, Joan Didion Letters, BANC MSS 84/180 c v. 1, BLUC.

198 *"Sacramento is killing me"*: "To Peggy from Joan," July 5, 1955, BLUC.

199 *In the "Meet This Year's Millies" profiles*: "Meet Mlle's Winning Team!," *Mademoiselle*, August 1955, 249.

199 *As Peggy recalled*: Powell, telephone interview, November 1, 2018.

199 *Peggy remained in Manhattan*: "Meet Mlle's Winning Team!," *Mademoiselle*.

199 *While Peggy was searching for a job*: "To Peggy from Joan, Sacramento, CA," July 1955, BLUC.

199 *Considering that Joan Didion*: While at *Mademoiselle*, Janet Burroway interviewed with admissions at Barnard and received a scholarship to continue her studies there, thereby leaving the University of Arizona.

200 *Joan sat in her* Vogue *office*: "To Peggy from Joan," November 9, 1958, BLUC.

200 *Jane's husband, Peter Davison:* "To Peggy from Joan," BLUC.

201 *Janet had concluded*: Janet Burroway's letters home, letter from June 25, 1955, 1–2, JB.

201 *At the same time, she was also*: Janet Burroway's letters home, letter from June 25, 1955, 3, JB.

201 *BTB realized it soon enough*: Random excerpt from a draft of a speech—online, BTBC.

202 *This was a time when*: Chris Ladd, "The Last Jim Crow Generation," *Forbes*, September 27, 2016.

202 *This was at a time*: Tempone, "Janet Burroway Carries On."

CHAPTER SEVEN

205 *After Grace was already married*: Malachy McCourt, *A Monk Swimming: A Memoir* (Rockland, MA: Wheeler, 1998), 79.

205 *Indeed, even prior to her marriage*: Tim Donnelly, "The Lady Is a Vamp," *New York Post*, April 7, 2013.

206 *In 1940,* Mademoiselle *called the hotel*: "Added Attractions," *Mademoiselle*, August 1940.

207 *That message remained consistent*: "New York," *Mademoiselle*, July 1957.

207 *The newspaper promised*: Gael Greene, "Lone Women," Series, *New York Post*, November 25, 1957. I would like to thank Gael Greene for allowing me to photograph these articles from her own private archive.

209 *She first met Jenny*: Greene, "Lone Women," November 18, 1957.

210 *Gael invited her readers*: Greene, "Lone Women," November 18, 1957.

211 *Gael stopped by the television room*: Greene, "Lone Women," November 19, 1957.

212 *She was the self-appointed*: Greene, "Lone Women," November 20, 1957.

213 *Even as Gael was surrounded*: Greene, "Lone Women," November 21, 1957.

214 *Jacqueline, another resident, was a nightclub singer*: Greene, "Lone Women," November 22, 1957.

215 *Billy Jo was a twenty-year-old college dropout*: Greene, "Lone Women," November 24, 1957.

216 *From 5:00 to 6:00 p.m.*: Greene, "Lone Women," November 25, 1957.

217 *On this particular late afternoon*: Greene, "Lone Women," November 25, 1957.

218 *In March 1934, a Mrs. Edith La Tour*: "Wife of Merchant Plunges to Death," *New York Times*, March 2, 1934.

218 *Only the* Chicago Daily Tribune: "Chicago Girl a Suicide," *Chicago Daily Tribune*, April 3, 1935.

218 *In 1939, twenty-two-year-old Judith Ann Palmer*: "Girl Ends Her Life in Hotel Room Here," *New York Times*, July 9, 1939. And "Ends Life in New York," *Chicago Daily Tribune*, July 9, 1939.

219 *Malachy McCourt himself knew*: Malachy McCourt, interview with the author, New York City, April 15, 2016.

219 *Gloria Barnes Harper, with lagoon-blue eyes*: Gloria Barnes Harper, interview with the author, New York City, April 16, 2015.

219 *It was the hypocrisy*: McCourt, interview.

220 *In those days, on the respectable Upper East Side*: McCourt, interview with the author.

220 *Malachy would later write*: McCourt, *A Monk Swimming*, 33.

221 *The phrase persisted*: Sylvia Plath, *The Bell Jar* (New York: Harper Perennial, 2005), 72.

222 *When the question of Barbara Chase's potential*: Edward M. McGlynn, memo to BTB, May 28, 1956, box 2 correspondence, 1948–1961, BTBC.

222 *There were questions*: WAT, confidential memo to BTB, April 13, 1956, box 3 correspondence, 1951–1964, BTBC.

223 *Yet anticipating this issue*: McGlynn, memo to BTB.

223 *Barbara arrived in New York*: Barbara Chase-Riboud, interview with the author, New York City, November 13, 2018.

223 *In her* Mademoiselle *bio*: Johnnie Johnstone, "Memo from the Guest Editor," *Mademoiselle*, August 1956, College Issue, 254.

224 *Barbara guessed that*: Chase-Riboud, interview.

224 *Fashion editor Edie Locke*: Edie Raymond Locke, interview with the author, Thousand Oaks, CA, October 25–26, 2018.

225 *Another article is about integration*: Virginia Voss, "University of Alabama," *Mademoiselle*, August 1956, College Issue, 310.

225 *One GE was instantly in awe*: Emilie Griffin, "The Lure of Fame: The Yearning, the Drive, the Question Mark," in *Ambition: Essays by Members of the Chrysostom Society*, eds. Luci Shaw and Jeanne Murray Walker (Eugene, OR: Cascade Books, 2016), 37–38.

226 *She never spotted another African American*: Chase-Riboud, interview.

227 *In the annual rite of passage*: Johnnie Johnstone, "Memo from the Guest Editor," 202.

228 *In 1961, Willette Murphy*: Cody Bay, "Willette Murphy Made History as a Black Woman in 1961. But It's No Big Deal: She's Used to That," *On This Day in Fashion*, July 27, 2010.

228 *In the "We Hitch Our Wagons" series*: "We Hitch Our Wagons," *Mademoiselle*, August 1956, College Issue, 257.

229 *Barbara would later write*: From Barbara Chase-Riboud's unpublished manuscript about her travels through Europe told through her letters home: "I Always Knew," 14, generously shared with the author.

CHAPTER EIGHT

233 *At first glance, Sylvia Plath*: Andrew Wilson, *Mad Girl's Love Song: Sylvia Plath and Life Before Ted* (New York: Scribner, 2013), 197.

233 *Mary Cantwell, who would go on*: Neva Nelson, interview with the author, Cape May, NJ, May 21, 2016.

233 *She was "afraid to take the subway"*: Mary Cantwell, "Manhattan, When I Was Young," in *Manhattan Memoir* (New York: Penguin, 2000), 151.

233 *In her view, Abels was basically*: Cantwell, "Manhattan," 155.

234 *Abels proscribed to the rule*: Cantwell, "Manhattan," 156.

234 *During the interview, Mary made it clear*: Cantwell, "Manhattan," 153.

234 *The Street & Smith building on Madison*: Cantwell, "Manhattan," 161.

234 *Lunch, much like hats*: Cantwell, "Manhattan," 161.

235 *Even then, finding "the best"*: Cantwell, "Manhattan," 161.

235 *Clothing, just like hats*: Cantwell, "Manhattan," 158.

235 *Even as she had the fresh, young look*: Cantwell, "Manhattan," 164.

235 *The drugstore "employed"*: Cantwell, "Manhattan," 161–62.

235 *Sylvia Plath and Neva Nelson had often gone*: Elizabeth Winder, *Pain, Parties, Work: Sylvia Plath in New York, Summer 1953* (New York: Harper, 2013), 102.

235 *In* The Bell Jar: Sylvia Plath, *The Bell Jar* (New York: Harper Perennial, 2005), 77–78.

236 *In 1951, a petition*: Petition November 30, 1951, box 4 correspondence, 1945–1965, BTBC.

236 *One of her first tasks*: Cantwell, "Manhattan," 152.

236 *Mary Cantwell asked her boss*: Cantwell, "Manhattan," 153.

236 *Edie Locke, then assistant fashion editor*: Edie Raymond Locke, telephone interview with the author, April 12, 2016.

236 *Many years later, Mary Cantwell*: Cantwell, "Manhattan," 153.

237 *In 1956, Polly Weaver*: Winder, *Pain, Parties, Work*, 169.

237 *In her journal Sylvia Plath*: Winder, *Pain, Parties, Work*, 128.

238 *In memo after memo*: Nancy Lynch, memo to Cyrilly Abels [hereafter cited as CA], June 17, 1953, box 6 correspondence, 1953, BTBC.

238 *"I must say this is far from"*: MW, memo to CA, June 17, 1953, box 6 correspondence, 1953, BTBC.

238 *"should be read with interest"*: JBM, memo to CA, June 17, 1953, box 6 correspondence, 1953, BTBC.

239 *"this certainly should hit our readers"*: Leslie Felker, memo to CA, June 17, 1953, box 6 correspondence, 1953, BTBC.

239 *The debate around the Kinsey Report*: Memo: REPORT ON KINSEY REPORT (confidential), June 19, 1953, box 6 correspondence, 1953, BTBC.

239 *Neva Nelson offered*: Neva Nelson, 1955, San Jose State, memo to CA re: Kinsey Report, June 19, 1953, box 6 correspondence, 1953, BTBC.

239 *Janet Wagner was game*: Janet Wagner, 1954, Knox College, memo to CA re: Kinsey Report, June 19, 1953, box 6 correspondence, 1953, BTBC.

240 *Laurie Glazer was perhaps the most direct*: Laurie Glazer, 1953, University of Michigan, memo to CA re: Kinsey Report, June 19, 1953, box 6 correspondence, 1953, BTBC.

240 *Carol LeVarn, Sylvia's best friend*: Carol LeVarn, 1953, Sweet Briar College, memo to CA re: Kinsey Report, June 19, 1953, box 6 correspondence, 1953, BTBC.

240 *Sylvia Plath wrote the longest report*: Sylvia Plath, 1954, Smith, memo to CA re: Kinsey Report, June 19, 1953, box 6 correspondence, 1953, BTBC.

241 *The kind of frankness Sylvia showed*: Plath, *Bell Jar*, 81.

241 *That very night, when the guest editors*: BTB, memo to Gerald Smith, June 18, 1953, box 6 correspondence, 1953, BTBC.

241 *But by the next day*: Bob Park, memo to BTB, June 19, 1953, box 6 correspondence, 1953, BTBC.

242 *Guest editor Dinny Lain (later Diane Johnson)*: Diane Johnson, "Nostalgia," *Vogue*, September 2003, 208.

242 *As another 1953 GE explained*: Winder, *Pain, Parties, Work*, 154.

242 *Mary Cantwell witnessed*: Winder, *Pain, Parties, Work*, 155.

243 *John Appleton had wanted*: Neva Nelson, interview with the author, Cape May, NJ, May 21, 2016. With follow-up correspondence in June 2020.

243 *Toward the end of the month*: Laurie Levy, "Outside the Bell Jar," in *Sylvia Plath: The Woman & the Work*, ed. Edward Butscher (New York: Dodd, Mead & Company, 1985), 46.

244 *In* The Bell Jar, *Sylvia wrote*: Plath, *Bell Jar*, 85.

244 *Diane Johnson returned home*: Diane Johnson, telephone interview with the author, November 27, 2018.

244 *Earlier in the summer of 1953*: Nelson, interview.

245 *"Sylvia saved me"*: Nelson, interview.

245 *Years earlier, Betsy Talbot Blackwell*: BTB, "Suburbia. The New Challenge," speech given to the Fashion Group, Washington, May 1955, box 20, BTBC.

246 *By the late 1950s*: Betty Friedan, *The Feminine Mystique* (New York: Dell Books, 1974), 20.

246 *The number of women*: Friedan, *Feminine Mystique*, 12–13.

246 *In summer 1960*: Phyllis Lee Levin, "Road from Sophocles to Spock Is Often a Bumpy One," *New York Times*, June 28, 1960.

247 *The writer Janet Burroway*: Janet Burroway, "I Didn't Know Sylvia Plath," in *Embalming Mom: Essays in Life* (Iowa City: University of Iowa Press, 2004), 6.

247 *But it was at a party*: Burroway, "I Didn't Know Sylvia Plath," 15.

247 *Later that year, Sylvia wrote a short story*: Burroway, "I Didn't Know Sylvia Plath," 16.

248 *She wrote to the novelist and poet*: Burroway, "I Didn't Know Sylvia Plath," 7–8.

248 *Looking back, one former bridesmaid*: Patricia Rice, *St. Louis Post-Dispatch*, August 2, 1989, E1.

248 *For Laurie Glazer*: Levy, "Outside the Bell Jar," 46.

249 *Laurie was standing in line*: Levy, "Outside the Bell Jar," 43.

249 *Even in the pages*: Levy, "Outside the Bell Jar," 47.

249 *As for Carol LeVarn*: Carol McCabe, email to Neva Nelson, May 22, 2010, NN.

249 *Each generation has its couple*: Burroway, "I Didn't Know Sylvia Plath," 18.

250 *Laurie Glazer, in 1973*: Laurie Glazer Levy to Neva Nelson, May 8, 1973, NN.

250 *Neva Nelson, in a fit of patriotism*: Neva Nelson, correspondence with the author, 2016.

250 *In 1972, under pressure to bring equality*: Edie Raymond Locke, interview with the author, Thousand Oaks, CA, October 25–26, 2018.

250 *One 1972 GE*: Angela Taylor, "Until Now, These Jobs Were Strictly for Coeds," *New York Times*, June 14, 1972.

251 *The eleven female guest editors*: "GE Journal: Notes on 30 Hectic Days and Nights in New York," *Mademoiselle*, College Issue, August 1977, 101–3.

251 *The 1953 guest editor Laurie Glazer*: Neva Nelson, newsletter to the 1953 GEs, December 1977, NN.

251 *A young woman who was welcoming everyone*: Ann Burnside Love, "The Legend of Plath, the Scent of Roses," *Washington Post*, April 29, 1979. Ann Burnside Love was one of the 1953 GEs.

251   *Already* The Bell Jar *had sullied their memories*: Burnside Love, "The Legend of Plath."

251   *Looking back, Anne blamed*: Winder, *Pain, Parties, Work*, 89. And Nelson, interview.

252   *When Laurie Glazer expressed regret*: Alex Witchel, "After 'The Bell Jar,' Life Went On," *New York Times*, June 22, 2003. Laurie Glazer Levy recently published a novel—*The Stendhal Summer*—and is working on another.

252   *After the reunion*: As quoted in a letter from Neva Nelson to her fellow guest editors, February 4, 2011, NN.

252   *Dinny Lain/Diane Johnson noted*: Diane Johnson, "Novelist Remembers Sylvia Plath," *New York Magazine*, May 26, 1979, 7.

CHAPTER NINE

257   *As a "gesture"*: Eve Auchincloss to Allen Ginsberg, September 23, 1959, box 4 correspondence; 1959–1960, BTBC.

257   *The January 1960 issue created tremendous buzz*: Tracy Daugherty, *The Last Love Song: A Biography of Joan Didion* (New York: St. Martin's Griffin, 2016), 102.

258   *Judith Innes, Radcliffe College graduate and Barbizon resident*: Judith Innes, video interview with Melodie Bryant, October 16, 2012, generously shared with the author.

258   *Tippi Hedren, the dazzling blond star*: Donal Lynch, "Tippi Hedren: Why I Love Being Free as a Bird," *Belfast Telegraph*, June 12, 2012.

259   *Joan Gage, a budding writer*: Joan Gage, "Those Fabulous Magazine Divas—A Memoir," *Rolling Crone*, November 5, 2009, http://arollingcrone.blogspot .com/2009/11/those-fabulous-magazine-divas-memoir.html.

259   *Joan, who was from the Midwest*: Joan Gage, interview with the author, New York City, May 3, 2015.

259   *"I think marriage is insurance"*: Helen Gurley Brown, *Sex and the Single Girl* (Fort Lee, NJ: Barricade Books, 1962; 2003), 4–5.

260   *A woman should do anything*: Judith Thurman, "Helenism: The Birth of the Cosmo Girl," *New Yorker*, May 11, 2009.

260   *The novelist Mary McCarthy*: As quoted in Joan Didion, "Bosses Make Lousy Lovers," *Saturday Evening Post*, January 30, 1965.

261   *Joan Didion followed Brown*: Didion, "Bosses Make Lousy Lovers."

261   *In one of Betsy Talbot Blackwell's*: BTB, "Changing Women—And the Need to Grow with Them," speech draft, 1956?—online, BTBC.

261   *While Helen Gurley Brown made a name*: Friedan, *Feminine Mystique*, 11.

262   *Actress and Charlie's Angel Jaclyn Smith*: Jaclyn Smith, telephone interview with the author, April 8, 2016.

263   *There was the case, for example, of Dana*: Nan Robertson, "Where the Boys Are Not," *Saturday Evening Post*, October 19, 1963, 28.

263   *Betty Buckley, later the stepmother*: Paul Rosenfield, "Betty Buckley Getting Her Acts Together," *Los Angeles Times*, June 30, 1983.

263   *The same year, a seventeen-year-old high-school dropout*: "Lorna Yearns for Her Own Fame," *Atlanta Constitution*, September 27, 1975.

264   *A 1963* Saturday Evening Post *article noted*: Robertson, "Where the Boys Are Not," 28.

264   *Betsey Johnson, the future fashion designer*: Princeton Review, "Exclusive Interview with Betsey Johnson," in *The Internship Bible*, 10th ed. (New York: Princeton Review, 2005).

265   *On that very same day*: Amy Gross, interview with the author, New York City, November 29, 2018.

265   *Days after moving into the Barbizon*: Melodee K. Currier, "Boy Crazy Adventures in New York City," *IdeaGems* 6, no. 1: 13, http://www.melodee currier.com/published-articles.html.

266   *After the secretarial course was over*: Melodee K. Currier, "First Person: 'Mad Men' Sexier than Ad Agencies of Real '60s," *Columbus Dispatch* (Ohio), September 24, 2011.

266   *Phylicia Rashad, the actress*: Phylicia Rashad, telephone interview with the author, April 19, 2016.

267   *On August 26, 1970, Helen Gurley Brown*: Anna Gedal, "Behind the Scenes: The 1970 Women's March for Equality in NYC," *New-York Historical Society*, March 10, 2015.

267   *Men stood on New York's sidewalks*: Linda Charlton, "Women March Down Fifth in Equality Drive," *New York Times*, August 27, 1970.

267   *Editor-in-chief Betsy Talbot Blackwell was stepping down*: Angela Taylor, "At *Mademoiselle*, Changing of the Guard," *New York Times*, April 4, 1971.

268   *In her parting "Editor's Memo"*: BTB, "Memo from the Editor," *Mademoiselle*, June 1971, 88.

268   *As one former resident complained*: Robertson, "Where the Boys Are Not," 30

269   *Free afternoon tea continued*: Robertson, "Where the Boys Are Not," 30.

269   *The Barbizon thus found itself joining forces*: Lacey Fosburgh, "City Rights Unit Ponders Sex Law," *New York Times*, January 15, 1971.

270   *Even the city's police force*: Kevin Baker, "'Welcome to Fear City'—The Inside Story of New York's Civil War, 40 Years On," *Guardian*, May 18, 2015.

270   *When Joan Faier encountered the Barbizon*: Terry Trucco, "Grace Kelly Slept Here: The Barbizon Hotel for Women Flirts with Landmark Status 30 Years After Its Demise," *Overnight New York*, August 11, 2011, https://overnight newyork.com/hotels-in-the-news/in-the-news-the-barbizon-hotel-for -women/.

270   *in 1975, seventy-nine-year-old Ruth Harding*: George Goodman, "Woman, 79, Found Slain in Room at the Barbizon," *New York Times*, August 18, 1975.

271   *Her murder went unsolved*: "Follow-Up News," *New York Times*, August 22, 1976.

271 *The Barbizon's owners*: Didi Moore, "The Developer as Hero," *Metropolitan Home*, October 1982.

271 *Lori Nathanson, just graduated from Vassar College*: Lori Nathanson, email correspondence with the author, December 29, 2015.

271 *The Women had become a serious eyesore*: Vivian Brown, "Refurbishing the Barbizon," *Washington Post*, August 27, 1977.

271 *One Barbizon resident recalled the benches*: Interview with Kitty Yerkes, May 1, 2009, UNCW Archives and Special Collections; Randall Library Oral History Collection, 1990–Present; Series 2: Southeast North Carolina; Subseries 2.3: Notables; Item 108.

272 *With the new manager, Barry Mann*: Connie Lauerman, "Barbizon Hotel: Still Home Away from Home for Women," *Chicago Tribune*, December 28, 1977.

272 *Out too went the pink and lime furniture*: "Home Style: Beautifying the Barbizon," *New York Times*, October 10, 1976.

272 *He wanted to continue to offer*: Lauerman, "Barbizon Hotel."

272 *With that done, he organized*: Judy Klemesrud, "Barbizon Hotel Celebrates Half Century of Service to Women," *New York Times*, October 31, 1977.

273 *The hotel had changed from "a fresh-faced starlet"*: Ellan Cates, "Barbizon Hotel for Women Goes Coed," *Journal-Register* (Medina, NY), February 10, 1981.

273 *The only former-resident-turned-celebrity*: Klemesrud, "Barbizon Hotel Celebrates."

273 *Kim Neblett, once checked into the Barbizon*: Dee Wedemeyer, "Barbizon, at 49: A Tradition Survives," *New York Times*, March 13, 1977.

273 *Her hair fragrant*: Meg Wolitzer, "My *Mademoiselle* Summer," *New York Times*, July 21, 2013.

274 *there were still only 130 rooms*: Alan S. Oser, "Barbizon Hotel, Long an Anachronism, Begins a New Life," *New York Times*, February 27, 1981.

274 *But this was 1979 New York*: Wolitzer, "My *Mademoiselle* Summer."

274 *Two years earlier, New York*: Angela Derouin, email correspondence with author, January 17, 2016.

274 *At a Scent Seminar at Revlon*: Wolitzer, "My *Mademoiselle* Summer."

275 *The city would find salvation*: Frank Bruni, "Why Early '80s New York Matters Today," *New York Times Style Magazine*, April 17, 2018.

276 *When David Teitelbaum was first hired*: Wedemeyer, "Barbizon, at 49."

276 *A "bejeweled" elderly resident*: Ellan Cates, "End of an Era: Barbizon Hotel for Women," UPI Archives, March 1, 1981.

276 *The Women momentarily put aside*: Paul Blustein, "New Owners May Mix Things Up at Women-Only Barbizon Hotel," *Wall Street Journal*, November 13, 1980.

276 *At first, Teitelbaum offered $1 million*: Edward A. Gargan, "For 114 Women at the Barbizon, a Grim Uncertainty," *New York Times*, December 29, 1980.

277 *Under New York rental laws*: Blustein, "New Owners May Mix Things Up."

278 *The male raffle winner*: Luce Press Clippings (Television News Transcripts), February 15, 1981, 7:00 a.m., accessed June 4, 2019, at http://www.starwarmer .org/personalbarbizon.html.

279 *William Nicholas of Long Island*: "Sammy Cahn Sings 'It's Been a Long, Long Time' to First Male Guests at the Barbizon; Ten-Story Heart Unfurled to Mark Occasion," press release, copy accessed June 4, 2019, at http://www .starwarmer.org/personalbarbizon.html.

279 *The splashy event had made an impression*: Luce Press Clippings (Television News Transcripts), February 14, 1981, 10:30 p.m., accessed June 4, 2019, at http://www.starwarmer.org/personalbarbizon.html.

279 *He continued to insist*: Horace Sutton, "New York's Barbizon Hotel Is Finally Going Coed," *Chicago Tribune*, June 20, 1982.

280 *In 1984, the hotel's reincarnation finally complete*: "New York Day by Day: Festival at the Barbizon," *New York Times*, April 20, 1984.

281 *The menu at the Café Barbizon*: 1987 menu for the Café Barbizon, SC.

282 *Police were called to a room*: Marianne Yen and Bill Dedman, "Spence Faces Drug, Weapon Charges After Being Found in New York Hotel," *Washington Post*, August 9, 1989.

282 *Soon after, Georgette Mosbacher*: "Uzi-Toting Thief Robs Georgette Mosbacher," *Los Angeles Times*, June 13, 1990.

283 *This time, to lower costs*: Linda Dyett, "The Medical-Beauty Convergence," *American Spa*, September/October 2000, 50.

284 *Shortly before the Twin Towers came down*: "Barbizon Moves Ahead and Its Great Ladies Remember," *New York Post*, October 28, 1997.

286 *The challenge of the condominium project*: Josh Barbanel, "A New Chapter for the Barbizon," *New York Times*, March 19, 2006.

286 *Among those who first bought*: Josh Barbanel, "The New 30 Is Now 50," *New York Times*, August 19, 2007.

287 *The former chairman of Meow Mix*: Christine Haughney, "$6 Million for the Co-op, Then Start to Renovate," *New York Times*, October 6, 2007.

289 *In 2011, the Friends of the Upper East Side Historic Districts*: Sarah Kershaw, "Still Waiting in the Wings," *New York Times*, July 24, 2011.

Image Credits

ABOUT THE AUTHOR

Paulina Bren is a professor at Vassar College in New York, where she teaches international, gender, and media studies. She is the author of a prize-winning book about soap operas and communism behind the Iron Curtain and co-editor of a collection on consumerism in the Eastern Bloc. Born in the former Czechoslovakia, Paulina spent her childhood in the UK before moving to the United States. She attended Wesleyan University as an undergraduate, later receiving an MA in International Studies from the University of Washington and a PhD in History from New York University. She has held a host of research grants and fellowships, including residencies in Berlin, Budapest, Vienna, and Atlanta. She currently lives in the Bronx with her husband and daughter.